Gold, God, Guns & Goofballs

A Collection of Essays on America

Dwight C. Douglas

ISBN: 9781794175600

DEDICATION

For my mother, Mary Elizabeth, and my father, Charles Edward for bringing me into this world and giving me the love and support that some people never get. I love them evermore.

Table of Contents

Chip on my Shoulder

I love America. I have never thought about making any other country my home, but I must start with a warning. What you are about to read are my opinions, baked into a collection of essays about America. Hopefully you'll enjoy a certain kind of vicarious thrill while I offload my grievances on this great, united land of states and my thoughts on the people who call it home.

Various voices don't represent the sum of all people but seem to speak louder than others. They disparage the concept of political correctness and, I will admit, I'm a political correctness sympathizer. Others' use of language tends to exclude, marginalize or insult groups of people. They have the "ugly American" gene, passed on through generations of malcontents and miscreants who came to America and now dominate our political and societal scenery. We will slay these dragons in due time. Should I offend you, please keep reading. My words might make more sense as you gather more of them. And if you agree, please get off your ass and do something positive to make America better.

There is a vast distance between an indignant putdown of a whole race and telling the truth. The truth is a trick that is being played on us. If we only had a higher force or supreme being to tell us what truth is, maybe we would stop lying so much. Where are those damn deities when we most need them?

We are sourcing more information from more platforms than ever before, yet we don't seem to be getting smarter. We aren't moving any closer to a legitimate reality. What you'll read here are the sparks of a brain that's been overcooking these forceful feelings and logical thoughts for decades. I must let out some steam from the three-pound pressure cooker above my burning sinus cavities. The air and water aren't as clean as they once were, but my sense of humor has been sharpened by the absurd and acidic actions of idiots and egotists.

There are millions of uninformed people in America living their "Archie Bunker" existences. Will these souls wake up one day and see truth? The lack of vision isn't totally their fault, but someone must speak up about our future.

It's painful to see a family walking through their mold infested home after a massive flood. Whether they believe it or not, what destroyed all they owned was "climate change." Even more disconcerting, those suffering the most do not make a connection between the policies, technologies and decisions that brought disaster to their doorstep in the first place. There are too many fools doing nothing to prevent bad things from happening.

The military-industrial complex President Dwight D. Eisenhower warned us about has turned into CORPORATE~GOD syndrome. Thanks to our Supreme Court, a corporation can now have religious feelings and beliefs. We elected a "successful" businessperson to lead our land, even though we can't believe much of anything he says. Corporations lie for as long as they can to get what they want. They alter documents submitted to courts to cover up their bribes and donations to lawmakers. This is clear proof that those who work in these corporations have sold their souls for the demonic dollar.

So, yes, we have a false God in Gold and we'll do anything to get more of it. We even bent our time-honored belief in a "real" God to advance a political agenda. Unlike Jesus, who threw out the money changers from the entryway of the temple, the current pick of professional evangelicals invited the godless Goofballs into the temple.

People like Joel Osteen, who tell their followers his God wants them to be "successful" (in a sense, rich), must be too tall to breathe the common man's air. The power of God and the greed of Gold aren't compatible. The

New Testament socialism is an inconvenient truth for the Goofballs who are seeking re-election in this nation.

That brings us to Guns, tools designed to kill burly beasts and animals. They place the judgement and emotion of one trigger-puller on the line. The law of our land has codified the right to bear arms. This reality always brings out the hardcore people who say we need Guns to protect ourselves against a tyrant or king, but we hardly ever use them against those who illegally or legislatively take our rights away. We use Guns to kill animals and innocent people. There are more than 300 million Guns in America and they truly are weapons of mass destruction. If you are counting, that's almost one Gun for everyone in the land. Wow, such progress.

The fundamental problem with the United States of America is we sometimes follow the ideas and ideals of total Goofballs. Why? How do we get sucked into the schemes and false propositions from unqualified salesmen and cons?

Take the example of getting an email from Dr. Oz, pitching a miracle supplement to help lose weight. You see his name, click the link, order the serum and start to take the supplement, only to find out later that Dr. Oz had nothing to do with the company. Worse yet, you discover that the $12 bottle of liquid is nothing more than colored sugar water. With government, healthcare, communication, religion and business, we've been taken to the woodshed so many times by these ghastly Goofballs we no longer feel the pain they have inflicted on us.

Where were we when people like Larry Nassar, the Women's Olympic gymnastics "doctor," was able to inflict pain on hundreds of young women in the land of the free and the home of the brave? Why didn't someone stop and question what was happening?

We now know we've facilitated a cesspool of business people who carried out or permitted sexual discrimination and misconduct in their corporations and organizations. On-the-job harassment of the highest order has permeated the halls of Hollywood, Congress and the White House. We think social media hashtags will cure the problem and clear the air. Maybe a 6K run will push the bad guys away and cure all the diseases, but most well-meaning activities will do little. What are we doing? Maybe it's time to stop giving Goofballs any power over us.

We know the rich are getting richer, but there's zero proof this is good for the common man. The baseline question might be, "Why do we even have Gold? Why do we have this capitalistic system?" Many of the 1% believe less fortunate people don't deserve more Gold. What would God think?

As we clutch our Bibles and Guns in the closet of unawareness, we have fallen prey to a glowing TV connected to our favorite channel that spews our own personal political view and keeps us sealed comfortably in a cocoon of confirmation bias. Is that feedback loop working well, my friend?

There are customs and expressions which paint a vivid picture of the American psyche and why we say and do the things we do. Our politics, beliefs, theories and technologies have involved us in every world culture, so we've got to get it right. As related to reforms, our country sometimes moves like a melting glacier, while at other times, it shifts so quickly that we can't see the flaws in what we've done. Do we ever learn lessons from the past, or are we just hamsters on the wheel, running until we drop?

To my negative friends who whine "We are doomed," I say we aren't totally lost, but it's going to take a lot of work and a great sense of humor to help get us back on track. This collection of essays is really an anti-conspiracy, conspiracy book. The conspiracy is that America has been hijacked by money, religion, arms, war and power-hungry politicians.

We must take a stand against those people who keep us from achieving more freedom and peace of mind. We will confront the Gold, God,

Guns and Goofballs head-on. Don't sit back and think there's any other way to deal with the deconstruction of our country. This book is not an antidote for the left or right, it's an accelerant to move the middle off their asses to go do something positive for America.

I have always admired the slogan the New York City Police Department uses to solicit citizens' help in crime fighting, "If you see something, say something." That is what this book is all about. It's just me, one citizen, saying things about the country I love and the people who think they are in control. I write with a desire to make sure the USA stays strong and safe for my kids, grandkids and generations to come.

As we go through these essays together, let's look at the way we use Gold, the need for a true God, our lust for Guns and the lack of a valid shit-detector to protect us from the Goofballs who believe they're right about everything. I respectfully submit it's time we do something or forever lose our chance to make a difference.

We the People

A country cannot exist without people, that collection of souls under a banner or flag sharing a common bond, culture, language, customs and food stuffs. The circumstances around the invention of this country made us who we are, although there are some dark clouds over that history.

I know, I know, you ask, "Why so negative?" We should never attempt to delete the memory of a nation, no matter how bad it might be. We must face the fact we stole our land from the natives who lived here. The diseases and murder the European conquerors brought to North America eradicated hundreds of thousands of natives. We built our country on free labor we called slavery. There are many other senseless decisions that sacrificed people and took away their rights and beliefs in the name of nation building, religion or a flimsy excuse of national security.

The United States of America was launched by a bunch of well-to-do land owners who had the audacity to interleave into the law of the land the notion that every man was created equal, but that only rich, white, male landowners had the right to vote. Women did not get a vote because of a belief they did not have the intellectual capacity to decide such weighty matters. Slavery, being codified by the Holy Bible, gave the early settlers cover. Slaves couldn't vote, because they had no status at all. In a sense, they were "non-people."

Through our evolution as human beings and citizens, we came to understand some of our "freedom declarations" and "morally toned" language conflicted with the very laws we put into action. That old maxim "the spirit of the law and the letter of the law" comes to mind.

It took America 144 years to rectify the lack of logic on the female vote, and 89 years to legally end slavery, but discrimination and hate crimes continue today. Have we not learned anything?

When you base a country on the tenets of the Bill of Rights, the first ten amendments of the Constitution, you are going to have some wickedly painful slithers of sinful, salacious and politically dangerous activities slip through the cracks. In this land of laws, you must know which laws to ignore and who's getting away with bullshit.

Our Bill of Rights says there can be no laws against a religion or making any effort to thwart the practicing of a religion. The Branch Davidians believed their leader was the new Messiah, yet the federal government managed to kill him. Rights are not always defined by the people; sometimes the Goofballs step in. More on this later.

Our laws say free speech and the press can't be prohibited, but the legal system has teetered on the brink of stifling that right with little chips and stabs. Our founding guidelines also say we have the privilege to assemble peacefully and petition the government for a redress of grievances. In short, we have a right to challenge our government and gather in groups to do so. That doesn't stop local, state and federal police officers from bashing your head with a wooden stick or blowing a tear gas missile into your face. They have the Guns.

As painful as this might feel, and however bad it might smell, very few police or national guard are ever convicted of wrongful death for taking orders or acting against those expressing their First Amendment rights. Google: Kent State May 4, 1970.

Now we come to the Second Amendment, which gives everyone the right to have a Gun, so they can join a militia to secure the free state. Okay, that seemed like a good idea at the time, but the reality is almost 40,000 people are killed or injured by Guns in the US every year. I'm not sure if those Guns were going to be used by a militia to protect us from some imaginary "deep state," but they did kill people.

According to the BBC, 13,286 people were killed in the US by firearms in 2015, while the Center for Disease Control says that 10,265 people died in alcohol-impaired driving crashes in the same year. Remember, every state highly regulates the use and sale of alcohol.

We must rely on older Gun estimates because the National Rifle Association (NRA) has effectively blocked the collection of statistics on Gun violence. One would think the NRA, the protectors and so-called "safety" group, would like to know the number of people killed by firearms.

In the Affordable Care Act, we find a "Protection of Second Amendment Gun Rights" paragraph which codifies the cover-up on Gun injuries and fatalities statistics, "Wellness and prevention programs may not require the disclosure or collection of information relating to the presence or storage of a lawfully possessed firearm or the use of a firearm." A doctor or medical professional cannot ask you if that bleeding wound was caused by a firearm. REALLY? This is more than a subtle attempt to stifle research related to Gun violence. It is a clause which must be eliminated from our healthcare laws and policies.

Another right relates to our homesteads. Normally, soldiers can't forcibly take over our houses without our permission, but they can in time of war. Man, that sounds okay on the surface, but there are examples of police departments taking control of homes for surveillance of other Americans. When an active shooter is involved, the police don't have time to read the Constitution.

We also have an ironclad rule that we are protected against unreasonable searches and seizures of our property, houses, papers and effects. If you follow the news at all, you know the National Security Agency (NSA), Central Intelligence Agency (CIA) and Federal Bureau of Investigation (FBI) use the United States Foreign Intelligence Surveillance Court (FISA) to legally record American phone calls and intercept our electronic communications. There have been thousands of court cases where the proper procedures were not followed in searches.

The Fifth Amendment is a good one. It says that you can't be tried for the same crime twice or compelled to testify against yourself. If you look a little closer, it also says we have due process and no private property can be taken without proper compensation. Yet in drug arrests, the Drug Enforcement Agency (DEA) often confiscates a house, a boat or a car. I'm not sure how difficult it is to get back such seized possessions.

We have the right to counsel and, if we can't afford a lawyer, one will be provided for us. We have a right to a speedy trial and to be judged by an "impartial" jury, but with mass communication and social media, is it truly possible to find an objective group of people who will judge?

The Fifth Amendment also says neither "excessive bail" should be required nor excessive fines or cruel and unusual punishment be inflicted. We aren't sure what "cruel and unusual" means in today's world, but it's clear our founding fathers were not interested in being drawn and quartered.

The Constitution also includes a line to preserve the notion that we aren't just a country but, in fact, a collection of united states, a group of self-regulating entities with their own rules, provided they don't challenge or violate the federal statutes. Thus, some states have laws legalizing marijuana for medical or recreational use, while other states have laws against lotteries. The court dockets are stacked with suits between States and the Federal government. The laws and ongoing debates about state's rights versus federal control draws the courts into many debates.

It's reasonable to assume the newest laws of a land determine the human profile of its citizenry, but many of the customs, traditions and common understandings of America start with pieces of paper those rebels penned in 1776.

We do hold these truths to be self-evident. Most Americans have bought into the concept that all men (and women) are created equal and are endowed by their "Creator" (you can insert any supreme being, spirit or energy source here) with certain unalienable rights. Clearly, no government can take these away. That group of "modern" thinkers in 1776 listed those rights as **Life, Liberty and the Pursuit of Happiness.**

Surely, we don't want to die. We need to be free, which makes us happy most of the time. The "pursuit of happiness" ideal sometimes pulls us into the weeds. If I'm not hurting anyone, why should the Attorney General or the President himself attempt to control my pursuits? Just because one may not believe in your specific "Creator" doesn't mean they don't have the same rights as you do. You can't make me follow any specific religion, so why do you keep foisting one on me?

Nationalism vs. Patriotism

Family is nature's first and most important force. When families form into one large group, they become tribes. When tribes unite, they become cities. When cities merge, they become city-states. Erecting fences and walls around our lands and territories make us a nation, even if the wall is only metaphorical.

And then, something strange happens to the human brain. We start to develop an inward monolithic culture with belief systems and laws. We imagine that our culture is part of our bloodline. If a nation believed it had to find a virgin every spring girl and throw her off a cliff as a sacrifice for better crops, everyone supported it. You just hoped your daughter wasn't a virgin.

If people had just stayed in one place, like Brits on an island, that would've been fine, but inevitably they invented boats. Every nation has a healthy collection of people with ADD. These souls have a chemical need to know what is on the other side of the fog. When mankind started to explore outside his little nation and found things he didn't have, he either traded for the valuables or took them with force. We justified the most horrible crimes in the name of our nation's honor. From Gold, to chocolate or tobacco, we brought the plunder and rewards back home.

As we expanded, we saw the need for a powerful army and navy, not only to keep our land safe but to venture forth and get what we needed to impress the women-folk back home. We were on a quest to either protect what we owned as a nation or to expand our borders. This progression produced a larger population, and more numbers meant more power. Is this an innate instinct or the product of sexual dominance, ego or machismo?

We believed our laws and customs were a validation of our civilized nature. We carried a deep-seated need to force those beliefs and laws on the people we conquered. We were and still are under "the rapture" of our tribe. We believe that we are more "right" or "righteous" than those we view as inferior. We marched into lands with no regard for its local customs and we wiped out their people. We missed great ideas and advanced innovations that could have helped us, but there was so little time and so much to conquer.

The fervor of nationalism can be one of the most dangerous forces of "civilized" man. History clearly shows this. Just because you can overpower a group of people doesn't justify your central national premise. Like debating who was a smarter leader, Napoleon or Hitler, we can't ignore their actions to spread xenophobia and death inside and outside of their borders. Even Napoleon had a "Napoleonic" complex, which some have explained as his real need for power.

Rather than spend a lot of time on what happened before "God gave us America," let's focus on what America is, what it has become, and why this seems to be the craziest time in our history.

Nationalism is a neat, little word, because you can play with it ever so slightly and get many different meanings. If you put the word "white" in front of it, you get a venomous group of haters who think they are protecting an imaginary DNA strain. Slap the word "patriotic" before it, and you inadvertently give the government the right to take away your privacy. Add the prefix "ethnic," and harken back to the days when men wore hoods and sheets and hanged people from trees because they didn't like them.

When the family morphed from tribe to state to nation, it was for all the right reasons. In fact, human beings are an advanced form of animal who know that protection of their own kind is paramount. The division of labor was needed to guarantee both food production and protection. We have always had a need to protect ourselves from the grifters and Gun lovers on the other side of the hill. The enemy was out to steal our food and women.

Protecting women is sewn into man's biological wiring and this was quite evident when we invented America.

As history has shown, armies protect us from enemies and tyrants. They also protect egomaniacs and tyrants from being overthrown by those tribes in a nation who believe they are being exploited. In either case, Guns were involved. The idea that having a weapon is part of being patriotic is foolish. Nations have armies to protect their people, but in America we honor the document that gives us personal power to protect ourselves.

The driving force of this belief system is nationalism. I contend that, below its shiny veneer, nationalism is a form of religion. We ask God to bless our nation all the time. It's become the mandated signoff of many American politicians. We have "In God We Trust" blazoned on our official seal and on our money. Some in this country truly believe the Christian God literally blessed and ordained America and its government. One of our major churches believes Jesus paid a visit to America and traveled with us. I wonder if he flew coach?

We are a nation of immigrants, so why does that term rankle so many conservatives and right-wing hooeys? This fact of life might annoy some people, but if you study American history you will discover there are few true "natives" who can say North America was their land. We took it from them with the will of our God and in the name of building our nation. When people say they want to take their country back, they should run out and get one of those inexpensive DNA tests. They will probably find out they are more European or Asian than North American.

We must bust the myth of a "true" American, which is pure bullshit. It's funny to me how the Goofballs of America cast a shadow over immigration. I agree we must control the flow of people into our country, but we can do so in a moralistic and orderly manner. I'm always amazed when people who are only second or third generation Americans malign people who are today seeking asylum and protection in our country.

The origin of your genes has little to do with the nationalism you adopted. Therefore, the Western Europeans who first came here were able to give up their loyalty to Kings, Queens or fascists to fight for independence. You can have an ancestral tree and be proud of your origin, but that doesn't nullify your need to cling to nationalism "American style." Everyone loves the country where they live!

People shouldn't live in a country they don't like. There are two choices: either leave town or try to make the country of your birth better. You can complain about what you don't like but, short of taking your Second Amendment right too seriously, you need to deal with the good parts of America. It's actually a great place, once you get to know it.

I have always believed that our wonderful country is somewhat like a relative. You can love your drunk uncle for who he is, but you don't let him drive. If the Goofball in the White House is an idiot, get rid of him. ALERT: when the most powerful person claims that God has mandated his reign, get rid of him or her ASAP.

The money being spent to convince you that rich people know better than all the rest of us is insane. As the 1% get more money and power, it's important that we 99% never forget our powerful voice. We are the majority. If one million citizens circled the White House and announced they wouldn't leave until the President resigned, he would most likely resign. What else could they do, arrest or shoot everyone?

If you truly believe you own nationalism and think you can tell me what is right, I will run from you as fast as possible. Populism is not Nationalism. Just because something is popular doesn't mean that it's healthy for the nation. Nationalism is more than wearing a red, white and blue T-shirt on the 4th of July. It's more than attempting to display your patriotism on a 9-inch bumper sticker. The next person who tells me I'm not being patriotic because I disagree with what I consider a bad idea, can go stuff it. No one has a right to challenge my patriotism.

The definitional difference between patriotism and nationalism doesn't really help us. Patriotism is a vigorous support for one's country, while extreme forms of nationalism include a **feeling of superiority over other countries.** We have used these terms so interchangeably and so often that there is little distinction between the two words in Americanese.

Overpaid experts and Goofballs keep adding qualifiers to help test our patriotism. For instance, if I'm protesting something the current power structure doesn't like, I'm being unpatriotic. If I'm fighting for something with my First Amendment voice, don't make me feel like I have no right to my point of view. We need to figure out why we can't all return to civility. This "I'm right, you're wrong" rhetoric is stupid and tiresome.

There is a fallacy in the populace that speaking up about something seen as wrong or bad for America is a terrible sin. Some people believe disagreeing makes you less patriotic. If I say I love America, it doesn't automatically make me a nationalist or a patriot. If I say I believe in open and free trade, it doesn't make me less patriotic. If I object to torture, it doesn't make me your enemy. When we, as a nation, agree to things like the Geneva Convention, we fulfill our promise not as a political party or administration, but as a people. We can't turn morality on and off like a light bulb. We can't agree with one law one moment and not obey another law the next.

I vividly remember one of my father's friends, a Christian in every sense of the word, explaining to the powers building an army for World War II against Hitler, that he couldn't be a solider. He said killing was against his religion. People couldn't understand how this man could put his religious beliefs before his country. While there are many people in power who would agree with the statement Mike Pence made, "I'm a Christian, a conservative, and a Republican, in that order," I must assume that every decision he makes is based mostly on his faith and not the law of our land. His oath was to the Constitution, not the Holy Bible. What is the difference between filtering everything through the Bible or using Sharia Law as a basis for official government business?

Being a patriot is very difficult because reasonable and secure human beings don't typically declare themselves to be patriotic. One would think someone should have to do something to earn that title. The devaluation of the term "hero" in America has bothered me greatly. We've set the bar too low. On a televised baseball game, I saw a man catch a ball and then hand it to a little boy sitting next to him. The announcer called him a "hero." Really?

The common man doesn't see the slow-moving political climate change in Washington. The deep-rooted values of our forefathers have gradually melted away. Our large glacier of democracy is in danger of extinction. We have had too many "deciders" who did more dividing than uniting. Most people in America don't dwell on the possible ramifications of change. If they are down and out, they want their country to return to a better time. But if they are doing well, they prefer the government to have a sloth-like, lackadaisical attitude. You can hear them saying, "Just leave things the way they are."

I'm not sure why the past looks so bright, but if that floats your boat then prepare to pilot your craft through a very rough sea of bullshit. If you are young, you might believe that the best times are yet to come, and that's good. The middle class of America cares about things they must focus on, like little league schedules or putting food on the table. They look the other way or don't have time to research what is true and what is fake about bigger issues.

We are addicted to technology and don't even remember when we took the first toke. Even though we want to return to the glorious good old days, we won't give up our brand-new AR-15, our cell phones, our special pews at church or our built-in American need to show we have more money and toys than our neighbors. Americans love status.

When the Goofball at the top keeps telling us how bad things are and they can fix everything, including the problems they invented by their own stupid actions, we are in real trouble. We might feel they know what they're doing, but history often proves they don't have a clue. While we argue about the Guns, watch our Gold (stock market) and feed on the "soma" of the mass media machine, do we really care? Are we happy about this?

While God is there for many people as a spiritual enrichment and provider of glowing feelings, the truth is that simply praying and believing will not change your major arc. Try praying for a bundle of money to drop onto your doorstep tomorrow. When it doesn't arrive, should you just keep praying? Sorry to break the news to you, but if it was that easy wouldn't EVERYONE believe? That's why the phrase, "thoughts and prayers" after a mass shooting is an impotent action of self-condolence. I call BS!

In our ever-increasing need for confirmation of our own beliefs, we have lost all objectivity. We have been sucked into the raps of Goofballs and God-huggers who are attempting to take away our inner voices. We want someone else to tell us what we should believe. We have been worn down to the point where we have lost our sharp edges. Just because you profess your love for some leader who peddles xenophobic fears and racism, doesn't mean you've shut down your frontal lobes, or maybe you have? We lack the ability to put things in context. Our collective memories are being shaped by false narratives and cons every day. How do we find truth?

There are people who say the United States of America is a country of law and order. There's something to be said for a uniformity we can all recognize and use to make our lives better. We expect the law to protect us and to be, at all costs, fair and just. With more than 326 million people living here, law and order needs to work for everyone. Being patriotic, like being nationalistic, or religious, can make people feel good inside. I believe the meaning of patriotism is under fire. When the title of a bill is, "The Patriot Act," and we find out later it was a vehicle to take away our freedoms and privacy, that is when we start to lose it. Words matter.

Whether you consider yourself a patriot or a nationalist, you must separate those meanings. You can't gain credibility just claiming to be better than someone else. We are told we shouldn't covet our neighbors' house, wife, servants, animals or anything else. If you believe you are better than another person on a "nationalistic" basis, do you also have a deep desire for them to covet what you have? That doesn't sound like a biblical attitude.

When we let the lawmakers take away our rights, we lose part of our collective essence. The soul of America must be protected. If you truly call yourself a patriot and religious believer, you know it's our soul we pass along to the next generation. If you are a true nationalist, you know we are a country of laws and representation, not titles.

Two Kinds of People

There are people who serve and people who self-serve. There's an empathy gene some people have that makes their norm pure altruism. On the other side, there are those humans who view everything around them as something put there for them. This has been proven by people much smarter than me, and both categories are valid.

In the fantastic book, *Democracy in Chains: The Deep History of the Radical Right's Stealth Plan for America* by Nancy MacLean, she describes this as "collective security versus individual liberty." To simplify, she uses the terms "makers," and "takers" to depict the difference between "makers" who decry the concept of handouts and "takers" who freely accept any help along the way.

I have been asked why people follow certain charismatic actors. Many people seem to be blind to facts put before them or, worse, believe untruths and slickly packaged propaganda. I believe their bigotry and nearsightedness is based on something else, like that growing debt on those plastic credit cards.

Be it religious or cult-like loyalty to a person, any shared myth will not be broken with a logical discussion. The problem with false prophets and famous people is the power of TV. Imprinting from social media gives wickedly divisive people a special glow.

Sometimes, there is a missing reasoning circuit in our brains. We believe famous people must be right. That's how we get programs like *Keeping Up with the Kardashians*. I've never understood what I was keeping up with on that lowbrow show. The Kardashians banal existence and trivial pursuits seem to be nothing but a waste time. Why would anyone want to keep up with them?

There are people in America I call Lowest Complicated Denominators (LCD), who just want to live their lives in peace without drama. Eventually, boredom sets in and some of the LCDs fly into brain washing like a moth to the flame. Some become Christian zealots, hardcore Zionists and conspiracy theorists and eventually shut off their own trusted inner voice.

Once these less complicated souls get the message, they gather around other like-minded souls. Some become slaves of someone else's dogma, and after years of giving most of their savings to sinister manipulators only a family intervention can save their souls.

We have recently seen the outward display of demonstrations by White Nationalists, Neo-Nazis and White Supremacists who want to save the white race. Why do white people need to be saved? Most of these young Neo-Nazis have never read Oliver, Pierce or Rockwell, the founding fathers of their movement. These kids march around in their white shirts and khakis holding K-Mart Tiki torches while chanting "Jews will not replace us," unaware that true white nationalism propagates an anti-Christianity position.

When you're a brain-dead swastika flagsucker, you can't see anything but the fellow white nationalist in front of you. If these blind followers stopped marching and looked deeply into the core beliefs of their group, they would realize many of their most famous leaders believed that both the Christian religion and political conservativism were keeping them from saving the white race from annihilation. There aren't good guys on both sides, Mr. President.

If you have an unselfish regard for the welfare of others, you don't think of yourself as special. You don't need to overthink an instinctual desire to make things better. There are those who want to label this as socialism, but there is a vast valley separating the classic definition of socialism and how we use the word today.

Socialism, that means of production, distribution, and exchange of goods when owned or regulated by the community, might be a true definition but it doesn't work today. If it sounds a bit like communism, you would be semi-right. Without socialism, powerful men in the early 1800's couldn't have dreamed of running a country. If the people had only waited for history to sort it out, they would've known it wouldn't work. In most communistic countries, the leaders took charge of powerful corporations and raked profits into their own hands. This is happening in Russia right now.

Humans have a natural corruptibility factor. There never was a pure communism or reasonable use of socialism. Most of those attempts were false promises of totalitarian regimes who were more fascist than utopian. Ask North Korea about the food distribution in a country being sanctioned by most of the world. Communism doesn't produce food by itself, farmers do. North Korea is a great example of a country that invests more money and people on military than agriculture. When a country is being run by a boy king, he will always be more important than all his people.

In America today, people from the Republican party, the National Rifle Association (NRA) and even the president himself, attempt to paint "socialism" as an evil boogeyman. I'm fairly sure that the young generation does not see socialism as a dirty word. Research on young people who followed Bernie Sanders during the 2016 US election found that supporters thought "socialism" had something to do with "social media." I guess they missed the point that free college education for everyone would have to be a political belief, not a phone app.

Goofballs running around America don't even realize that the slogan "America First" is not new. It was first used by Charles Lindbergh in the late 1930s and early 40s to convince America to stay out of the conflict with Hitler. Lindbergh was openly sure of his position, saying, "A war with

Germany would be bad for the United States and it would be bad for 'the white races.'" A real patriot?

Lindbergh was recruited by **America First**, an antiwar group founded by several Yale students, including the future President Gerald Ford and Potter Stewart, a future Supreme Court Justice who believed Lindbergh was the perfect man for their propaganda.

The flying hero Lindbergh claimed "agitators" were pushing the US to get into the war against Germany. Lindbergh said the groups promoting war were the British, the US government, and "the Jewish race." He added this warning about the influence of the Jews when he spoke in Des Moines, Iowa on September 11, 1941, "Their greatest danger to this country lies in their large ownership and influence in our motion pictures, our press, our radio, and our government." The fact that it happened on September 11th is rather strange, don't you think? And what a perplexing thing, saying that people who worked in the US government were "agitators." That would be like a president saying bad things about the FBI.

In today's climate, Lindbergh's remarks would be immediately denounced, as they were back then by President Franklin D. Roosevelt. As the article in The New Yorker magazine, *America First, for Charles Lindbergh and Donald Trump* written by Louisa Thomas published July 24, 2016 points out, "It's tempting to substitute "Muslims" or "Latinos" for "the Jewish race" and hear echoes of Lindbergh's speech in Trump's fear-mongering about so-called foreign threats in American society." Even though Ms. Thomas decided not to push the comparisons, I will. Lindbergh was a racist and anti-Semite.

If your political fiber is based on the reasoning that "OTHERS" inside of this country are an evil force out to harm us, how can you truly lead all the people once you've divided them? How can you be successful when dealing with other nations when your core belief is based on prejudices and misinformation driven by hate? If you disparage all forces other than your own kind, you push the whole country into *protectionism.*

Today, we have globalists and nationalists. Any citizen of a country should have a certain amount of nationalism, but if that ideology is your justification for not helping people and letting poverty and despair overthrow a whole group of Americans, then you probably are a soulless human being.

Few people fully comprehend the reason we established the Marshall Plan. It's the notion that aid, in the form of goods and money to troubled spots in the world, might avoid wars. Wars drain money, men and women from our nation and, unless our sovereignty is challenged, these intervention conflicts are generally bad bets. We think we are helping the good guys until we find out the new boss is same as the old boss, then the new guys throw us out. Study history and try to understand the political reasoning for giving money to other nations. President Harry Truman knew war was bad and his administration gave us the Marshall Plan.

When the talking heads on TV create an "US" and "THEM" attitude, we must face the mirror and ask the question, "Who are we?" At this point, many people in America are locked into their positions and less open to seeing any other opinion or goal. That's not America.

It would be inaccurate to link all non-altruistic persons to extreme groups, like white nationalism or Neo-Nazis. Just because someone has an isolationist viewpoint, or even uses phrases like "America First," doesn't necessarily mean they think all the other nations in the world are out to get them.

In understanding the need to trade our money for food, our desire to worship a supreme being and our instinct to protect ourselves and our families, we have a social predisposition to allow one voice to lead our tribe. Without structure, nothing can be accomplished. Besides that, when you are busy raising a family, growing food or hunting animals, you don't have a lot of time to decide where to throw your shit and garbage.

The early development of the two kinds of people was a successful way to balance those views in the community. We needed one group of people helping others, and another group protecting us from wild animals and aggressive tribes gathering just over the ridge. As we became more civilized, we spent less time helping people and more time focused on fun, food and stupid TV shows. There have always been poor and rich people in America. For some, their wealth came from hard work, while others had luck or wealthy parents to help them gain financial independence. Let's admit it, we Americans are lucky!

The current trends in American politics make it very easy to say the Republicans seem to be more self-serving than altruistic. On the other hand, we would be jumping the gun to imply all Democrats are here to serve others. I believe the mechanisms of American politics have little to do with helping people or promoting a "more perfect union." People in power usually believe in their own viewpoints, while some open-minded souls do see the world through more altruistic eyes.

Raw politics in the good old USA means lying about your opponent and getting wealthy people or mega corporations to bankroll your campaigns for reelection. We even have people who have claimed to be lifelong party loyalists who then changed parties just to get reelected. So much for loyalty to one party. The concept of being a statesperson has been lost on those ego-driven Goofballs.

As we stroll through these pages, let's think about how these two kinds of people shape our world and, thus, our country. We might not be able to change the other guy, but we will certainly have to maneuver through these two forces in our pursuit of happiness.

We can't just build a big wall or fence around those who have a different viewpoint and believe we never have to deal with our neighbors and fellow citizens. The other side isn't going anywhere. They live here, too. It might be best to trim the radical edges of both sides, rather than attempt to teach the world to sing the same song. Different opinions surely create more drama, but to move forward we will need agreeable people to talk to those other "assholes." Compromise is a very important American skill.

I Speak Americanese

So, there I was, in a restaurant perusing the menu to decide what I wanted to eat. I stated my choice and the wait person said, "Oh, good choice." I then said, "If I change to something else on the menu, will it still be a good choice?" Wearing a patronizing smile, the waiter responded, "Everything is good here." Why did we even have this conversation?

Much of our everyday interactions contains format-speak, like a waitress's pronouncement, "Good evening, I'm Claire and I'm going to be your waitress." And I say, "Hi there Claire. My name is Dwight and I'm going to be your customer." This is a great test of a wait person's sense of humor and capacity for improv.

All languages and cultures have polite idioms and phrases to fill in the blanks as their speakers travel through their days, but in America bullshit is Number 1! Another example of format speak happens right after we've explained something amazing to someone. They say, "Tell me about it!" Excuse me, but I have already told you about it. Are you asking me to tell you again?

We have a unique form of English in America that's been polished over the years. Around 1776 we separated from our keepers back in Britain, and we have been creating our own language since the first foot landed on our sandy shores.

A British friend of mine, Mike Powell, has compiled a wonderful book that covers the difference between the UK and US versions of English words. From trunk vs. boot to cornflour vs. cornstarch, you'll find them all in Mike's, *Amglish: Two Nations Divided by a Common Language.*

We constantly add words to the American language that we find more descriptive or more fun to use. Like the word "humongous," which is a mash-up of the words, huge, monstrous and stupendous. By the way, the hyphenated word, "mash-up," made its way into our language in 1859.

We give things weird names that are morphs of meanings and perversions of words or things from the past, like Lollapalooza, an alternative music concert in America. The word "lollapalootza" originated in 1901 when people described a "remarkable or wonderful person or something exceptional" or "the heart of a goof." When we get attached to a word in America, we use it as a suffix and put it together with other words, like *"Homerpalooza"* from *The Simpsons* TV cartoon or *"Bacon-palooza,"* which I suppose is a joyous celebration of pig meat.

The American writer Neil Postman made a great point in his fabulous book, *Amusing Ourselves to Death: Public Discourse in the Age of Show Business,* "The clearest way to see through a culture is to attend to its tools for conversation." Postman says we talk differently on a phone than face-to-face, and I agree. Let's also remember what the Canadian media visionary Marshall McLuhan said about the "global village" we live in, "The medium is the message." Later in this collection of essays we will get into the devices we use to communicate, but for now let's focus on our words and what we are trying to say.

Americans have a peculiar habit of using food metaphors to describe things. For instance, when someone is accused of something bad the denial is laced with the expression, "Oh, that's a nothing burger." What is that? Burgers have toppings and beef and cheese. Once you say "burger," you have a something, not a nothing. If it was a nothing, an America would scream, "Where's the beef?"

And let's not stop there. Something easy is a "piece of cake" and a "lemon" is a bad thing. Our jobs become our "bread and butter" which, where I come from, isn't much of a meal. We must work hard, earn some money and "bring home the bacon!" We are told to never "cry over spilled milk." No wonder most of the people in this country are overweight. All we think about is food.

We generally have a unique patois, depending on where we live. Our local accents and words enrich our country, even though it makes it quite difficult to learn our language. In New York you hear "yous guys," while in Western Pennsylvania they say "yinz guys," while in the Southern states it's "Y'all."

If a person in Cincinnati, Ohio, doesn't hear what you said, they will ask, "Please?" In most other places, a person would say, "Excuse me?" If you are from my hometown of Pittsburgh, you would say, "Huh?"

Americans who live in New York and north to New England use the word "Bring" as in "Bring this to the car" when they are standing next to you, while most other people when that close to you would use the term, "Take." Americans typically say "Bring" when they are further away, as in the plea, "Please bring me the keys!" I would be remiss if I didn't bring up that old George Carlin saw at this point, "America is the only place where we drive on the parkway and park on the driveway." That's America, buddy!

We fall prey to "portmanteau" all the time. It's the blending of two words to make a new word. We took "smoke" and "fog" and created the word "smog." We also do that with celebrity couples; Brad Pitt and Angelina Jolie becomes "Brangelina." I'm not sure who got the name in the divorce. We are a bit silly in this country.

We also excel with acronyms, an abbreviation formed by the initial letters of the words in a name or phrase to create a new word. We are famous for our presidential acronyms, like FDR, JFK, and LBJ, but they don't always stick. For example, George Washington didn't have a middle name, so no one ever called him GW; that's a bridge in New York City.

Acronyms often become more famous than the original words. We hear LSD, but rarely do people know that the letters mean lysergic acid diethylamide. Then there's AWOL (Away without Leave) or DUD (Device Un-Detonated) or, the word SEAL as in Navy SEALs (SEa, Air, and Land), the places where they fight. There are even times when one acronym gets knocked off by another. Consider this story of WJFK, a radio station in Washington, DC. When an account executive there was making a presentation to a young advertising media buyer in New York, that person asked, "Why would you name your radio station after an airport?" Oops!

In my home town of Pittsburgh, we created the word, "jagoff" which is a stupid or irritating person. "Jag" as in prick or poke and "off" as in "jerk off." Indeed, most jagoffs are pricks.

As Neil Postman described in his 1985 book, we moved from a more literary form of speech in the 1700s and 1800s to a shorter, blunter usage of language because radio and TV shaped the way we talk. Portman points out that books and newspapers were read more often when we didn't have movies, TV or radio. He reminded us that the Lincoln – Douglas debates lasted three to four hours. Nowadays, you couldn't get Americans to sit outside in the heat for hours to hear men speaking in full paragraphs and eloquent sentences. Our attention span is usually no greater whether reading or listening.

We have become a nation of headline readers and Twitter consumers. TV's graphic panel on the lower portion of the screen scrolls, captions and messages, constantly begging for our attention. It's there to hold our attention even when the volume is down. They have trained our eyes and brains to constantly consume information in small bites. We've become lazy and superficial with spoon-fed messaging.

Media outlets in this country play a big part in pushing phrases into our brains. Coupled with one of those BREAKING NEWS graphics, a TV reported might say, "Boy, there's a lot to unpack here," as if the information has arrived in a box and the commentator must now unpack and lay out the contents. If the story had been written properly, there would be no need to unpack the meaning. It's just more hamburger helper in the newspeak of TV to lead us into the commenting part of their program.

A wonderful critique on CNN and all cable news networks' obsessive use of the term BREAKING NEWS came from Michelle Wolf's line at the 2018 White House Correspondent's Dinner in Washington when she said, "You guys love breaking news, and you did it, you broke the news." They have killed the meaning of those words.

Another phrase bubble-headed blondes and man-tanned announcers use on TV is "Needless to say…" If you say it's needless, then why the hell say it? Why should I listen if it's needless?

We are a nation that adjusts to current events and unilaterally bans certain terms. After moving to Florida, I had 80 zillion cardboard boxes (zillion, another made up word). I went to The Home Depot and asked for a box cutter. They said, "We don't sell those, any more." Then, they took me to a counter where they showed me tools that are now called "retractable blade knives" or "utility knives." If you are wondering why, it's because box cutters were used in the hijacking of the airliners during the 9-11 attacks on America. So, we collectively changed the name. Some states have even enacted laws that make it a crime to sell them to people under 21-years of age. I guess terrorists aren't older than 21? I hate to break the news to you, but a retractable blade knife is the same damn tool that we called a box cutter before 2001.

TV has also shaped our ways of speaking. It's a shortened, less polite way of talking. Many Americans use command language, leaving out the words "please" and "thank you." We also refer to a group of people as "guys" regardless of their gender. We obsessively use fad-gimmick words, then throw them away at the drop of a hat. Why are so many people dropping their hats? Lack of grip?

Many people use the phrase, "At the end of the day" as a way to describe a false conclusion, "At the end of the day, we didn't know what we were doing." I would suggest you probably didn't know what you were doing at the beginning of the day, but we seem to be interested only in the state of things when a day ends. The wired generation can hashtag a group of words into everyday usage in minutes.

Broadcast TV and radio have always been afraid of the long-arm of the law in the form of the Federal Communications Commission (FCC). They have the power to fine broadcasters or strip their licenses. Newspapers have generally taken a conservative view of what they print, using asterisks to replace certain letters of a nasty word or euphemisms. TV censorship is rather humorous to me. We can say "ass" or "hole," but we must beep-out the word, "asshole." After our top Goofball used the term "shithole" to describe some African nations, we now regularly hear the word "shit" on TV. The FCC bans any slang term that refers to a bodily function, but they seem to be ignoring this one. Maybe they need to get their shit together?

One of the most bothersome aspects of Americanese happens when people add what I call "hamburger helper," phrases such as, "you know" or "you know what I mean" peppered throughout their conversation. These add nothing and drive me crazy. I am either forced to constantly shake my head while listening or simply delete those qualifications in my mind. Of course, if you are telling me something for the first time, how could I know? You know what I mean?

The other one that gets my goat is the preamble, "Let me be honest with you." There are only two things I can possibly think, either you usually lie, or you must declare your honesty in an attempt to cover lying. I'm not sure what I mean by "gets my goat," because my poor goat has been rendered speechless by all this talk of words.

We often repeat the mindless mush of novice newscasters and faux journalists. I was in Atlanta when a rush hour fire under an overpass caused a section of the downtown freeway to collapse. The TV newsreader said, "This couldn't have happened at a worse time." Oh really, why is that? Traffic is bad in Atlanta all the time, so that couldn't have been the reason it was the "worst time." No one was killed; indeed, it could have been worse. We tend to say stupid things when trying to sensationalize or emphasize the importance of our speech. We believe drama is more important than sentence construction.

I was watching a small-town, local TV news report about an attempted rape of a woman. The reporter read, "The woman was able to beat off her assailant." My jaw dropped, and I stared at the screen thinking, "Oh, you didn't just say that, did you?"

I love it when a TV station or show tells me the number of the studio, they are working in. I really don't care if you are in 1A, 2B or Studio 54; it means nothing to the viewer. Unless I need to find you in the building where you work, I have no reason to know your studio name. It's pure excess.

Speaking of Goofballs, they invented oxymoronic terms like "partial birth abortions" (pro-life people) or "clean coal" (Donald Trump) or "partial zero emissions" (Subaru). None of these things are real. You can't use the adjective "partial" and then imply "zero." This is one of the many reasons why I miss George Carlin, our American language cop.

There's another stupid expression we use when describing something big on Earth, like a forest fire. The announcer says, "It covers such a large area of land you can see it from outer space." I hate to burst your hot air balloon, but with the right camera you can see anything from outer space. Just look at Google Earth and you will see the flaw in the slaw of that expression. Or ask a soldier who runs a drone over a target site. They can read a name on a jersey, even if it's not a new jersey.

And here is another one. A man was recently shot, and the newscaster was quite impressed with the fact it happened "in broad daylight." They think they are using the expression to point out the brazenness of the killer but, really, the victim is dead. I'm sure he could care less if it was "pitch black" or "broad daylight."

About thirty years ago I wrote a magazine article in defense of Howard Stern when the FCC was fining him and his radio stations millions of dollars for being obscene and indecent. After listening to some of the audio clips, I noticed most of the alleged infractions were merely innuendo or double entendre. I pointed out that if the presenter was going out of their way to use fewer offensive words to make their point, they have already engaged in self-censorship. The double meaning of a certain phrase or dialog is just as much the responsibility of the listener as it is the speaker. Recall the old saying, "Hey, your mind is in the gutter." I'm not sure why the FCC has the authority to govern anything already covered by the First Amendment. Really, why would anyone call another human being a "douche bag" on the radio?

The FCC uses three primary factors when analyzing unsuitable broadcast material: (1) Whether the description or depiction is explicit or graphic, (2) Whether the material dwells on or repeats at length descriptions or depictions of sexual or excretory organs and (3) Whether the material appears to pander or is used to **titillate** or shock.

I find that using the word "titillate" to describe what is indecent is quite humorous. That word sounds like it's attempting to titillate me, or is my mind in the gutter? Funny, I don't see gutters; I see breasts.

A young woman from India once asked me, "Douglas, I heard someone say this guy is a real brownnoser. What does that mean?" I stopped for a second, wondering how I could decipher this commonly used American expression. I simply explained the origin of the phrase. She opened her mouth and said, "Oh!" and quickly walked away.

As she left, I wanted to yell out, "That's America, sister!" But I kept quiet. Sometimes you must simply go with the flow, instead of trying to describe what is normal and what is crazy in this country.

One of the wonderful aspects of American life before radio and TV was the invention of games we became driven to watch. We did these "pastimes" when not working. You don't have to participate in a pastime, but it certainly is easy to pass time when doing nothing but watching.

The first two sports in America were boxing and horse racing. There have been loads of time passed and money lost betting on these equines and fighters, and the influences of these sports on our language is undeniable. Even the baseball uniform was loosely based on the jockey's outfit, thus the small rounded brimmed hats and knickers worn by "the boys of summer."

The term "jock" now means anyone who plays sports in America. And here's a few other bits from horse racing. We say "out of the gate" to mean the beginning of something, and we urge people to "take off their blinkers or blinders" to figuratively request they see the whole picture. When we make a reference to a "dark horse," we are saying such a person does not have the best chance of winning a contest.

Boxing gave us some incredibly rich phrases like "the knockout punch," meaning the ending of a long struggle. We added "below the belt," to denote an action that wasn't quite right or playing a dirty trick on someone. We talk in terms of "counterpunching" after someone has been aggressive to us. When we say, "down for the count," it means that one of the competitors is nearly done. We talk about people "going the distance," which is what a boxer or a jockey does when they make it through an entire fight or race.

There are times when an American might "pull his punch," meaning he didn't hit someone as hard as he could. Finally, when we want to quit, we "throw in the towel," a white-flag of sorts and a metaphor for the end of a boxing match.

We have bizarre sports rules. Players aren't allowed to fight in hockey, but they do it all the time and those in the sport politely refer to those incidents as "altercations." NOTE: Referees tolerate two hockey players letting off steam by dropping their gloves and punching the crap out of each other, because those players hold wooden sticks which could otherwise be used as weapons. Some say sports is a metaphor for war. In hockey, polite Canadians get to show they are tough guys, too.

In our land of liberty, sports are not only baked into who we are, but have inspired our vocabulary for centuries. Even some inventions were inspired by sports. For example, we invented the straw for our drinks so taking a swig wouldn't block our view of the action on the field. Hot dogs were easy to serve at baseball games in the 19th century and are still sold at ballgames today.

In professional football, the tackling of a quarterback behind his own line of scrimmage is known as "sacking." It's the same term Brits use for being fired. Near the end of the first and second half of a football game, we have a "two-minute warning," to make sure both benches know the period is winding down. Americans use that term to denote a short period of time in real life. When a quarterback throws a long-distance ball, it's "a bomb" and his arm is referred to as a "Gun." When the quarterback wants to alter the play before the ball is hiked, he calls an "audible," which alerts his team mates of the change. Not so strangely, all these terms are used by business people in the USA.

Some of our most cherished Americanese language comes from professional baseball, where there are different rules for different fields. National League stadiums have no "designated hitter," American League parks do. Oh yeah, a designated hitter is someone who bats for a pitcher but doesn't play the field. This arcane rule still exists today, and the debate continues about whether it's a good idea. Yes, where they play determines the rule.

We use an archaic, four-digit percentage system to quantify batting averages leading to the expression "batting a thousand," which in other contexts means a person is perfect at what they do. Successful people in business are known as "big hitters" and really great achievements are referred to as "homeruns." Now for those who don't know the sport, a major batting accomplishment in baseball is getting a hit one third of the times at bat, which is a 70% failure rate. Hey, it's hard to hit a baseball travelling at 90 miles per hour.

Standing on the pitcher's mound, located 60 feet and 6 inches from the batter, a talented baseball player can throw a masterful pitch that causes the ball to move and dip after it's been released from his hand. It's called a "curve ball" and, when used by Americans outside of baseball, it means someone has done something different from what was expected. There are two circles located near the home plate where the next batter waits before he enters the batter's box. That position is called "on deck" and is probably derived from naval terminology, but we all know it means that "you're next." Interestingly, the field manager in baseball is sometimes called "a skipper" obvious seafaring lingo as well.

When we are ready to start again, we say, "It's a brand-new ball game." We also use baseball terms in our physical relationships, as in, "Well, you didn't let him get to second base, did you?" Each base refers to increased touching and groping. And by the way, the term "playing the field" means that a person is dating more than one person.

When someone is crazy, we say they are "really out in left field" or if an idea is not well received it is said to be "off base." When something is less than professional, it's "bush league," which is the term applied to small town American baseball teams below the professional level. In plain talk, "bush league" means an amateur effort.

Most baseball fields face northeast. The visitor's "dugout" is located in the hot afternoon sun and the throwing arm of a left-handed pitcher faces the south, thus the nickname, "southpaw." Quaint, but that's the origin.

Then there's the baseball term "Charlie horse," supposedly derived from Charley Radbourne who had the nickname Old Hoss. During a game in the 1880s, Radbourne's leg cramped with painful spasms, so they named that leg lock-up after him, Charlie Hoss, which evolved into Charlie Horse.

Lou Gehring's disease is another infamous name from baseball that lives on today. This progressive ailment is technically known as Amyotrophic Lateral Sclerosis (ALS). It's incurable and usually becomes a death sentence. Lou Gehring, one of the New York Yankee greats, was cut down at an early age because of ALS.

A more positive medical naming convention derived from baseball is Tommy John surgery, a procedure in which a healthy tendon is extracted from an arm or leg and used to replace an arm's torn ligament. Thomas Edward John Jr. was a major league pitcher who played on many teams from 1963 to 1989. He was the first to undergo this surgery, and it brought his damaged arm back to life and extended his career, thus the appellation. A pitcher lasting 26 years is a medical miracle.

There are some very colorful baseball examples in Americanese sports terms. We use the term "rain check" to reschedule a personal event or appointment. It's derived from the ticket you get when a game is postponed. With terms like, "double-header," two games on the same day, and "ducks on the pond," multiple runners in possible scoring positions, we clearly see baseball's contributions to our American language. Even the onomatopoeia "whiff," comes from baseball. It happens when the bat barely misses the ball and causes the sound "whiff."

When you don't do well with someone, you "strike out," and the judicial system uses a "three strike" metaphor for those who should be punished more harshly or incarcerated. I will not attempt to explain all the 13 possible ways a baseball pitcher can "balk," an illegal motion to deceive a base runner. Google the term if you are interested. When the pitcher balks, all the runners get to move ahead one base.

In baseball, the home team score is in the lower position on the scoreboard because the home team bats last. Eventually, all sporting contests in the world adopted the convention of placing the home team score either below or to the right of the away team score.

Our nation is all about baseball, a game played without a clock on a field of grass and dirt. I won't go into "extra innings" on this subject. We have "our bases covered" and it's time to move on. I mean, there is "always next year" – the bargain every fan makes to focus on the future after a painful season. Our American sports terms continue to be morphed, changed, modified and embellished, so keep up with the changes or look silly asking, "What does that mean?"

Americanese is a proudly extended middle-finger to our once oppressors in Great Britain. We step over the UKs spelling and grammar rules to invent unusual words and phrases that we store in our little brains. Of course, if you want to fully understand Americans, you must learn Americanese. We may be reading less, but we have never stopped looking for and finding ways to screw up the King's English.

Naked Truth

If she were a person, America would be highly conflicted. She would be trapped between her alleged freedoms and puritanical roots. She is so philosophically, morally and ethnically challenged that even three hundred years of therapy hasn't cured her. As a matter of fact, she is still fretting over her melting pot. One would think the tensions would have cooled by now, but when we stick our fingers into that pot we still get burned.

But I digress. Let's get serious about some funny things involving Americans. First, we are really hung up on the human body and its functions and these taboos are reflected in our humor. If you want to make a kid or a grandmother laugh, tell a fart joke. Why do they love them?

The humor trigger of a joke begins by releasing some tension into the air, which is then cut with the sharp knife of a well-designed punchline. That release causes us to laugh. Like cutting the cheese, we feel good about getting through that opening tension. We are so fussy about who we offend, but still laugh when we break out of our goody-two-shoes mentality. I find some of our customs quite amusing, while others are totally confusing.

Some Americans follow an inane routine known as "the five-second rule;" anything that falls on the floor can be picked up and eaten or used, if it's done within five seconds. I walked into a restaurant the other day and the hostess dropped a menu on the floor, picked it up and put it on the table right where I would be eating food a few moments later. Europeans and Asians think we are crazy when we don't take our shoes off when we enter a home. We think they are crazy because they take their clothes off so quickly. We automatically consider nudity as something that must be controlled.

We have a system to judge indecency, profanity and obscenity in movies shown here in the US of A. Back in the mid-sixties, the Motion Picture Association of America (MPAA) film rating system replaced the more onerous Hays Code. Look that one up. Now we have movie ratings that remind me of the Homeland Security risk levels. There's **G** for general audiences, and these films do not include sex and nudity, substance abuse, or realistic violence. Then we jump to **PG** movies, which can include some material that may not be suitable for children. Let's not confuse that with **PG-13** motion pictures, which might contain stuff not suitable for children under 13 years of age. Any nudity must be nonsexual and swear words must be used sparingly. Violence must be bloodless. That would also mean all coups would have to be bloodless. I'm not sure that all 13-year-olds are the same, but, hey, I didn't invent this system.

The big **R** stands for restricted, and no one under 17 is admitted without an accompanying parent or guardian. If you are an unlucky producer and your movie gets an **NC-17** rating, no one under the age of 17 will be admitted, which basically means no theater in America will show your film. If you want to know how all this plays out in the real world, I highly recommend the documentary *This Film Is Not Yet Rated*.

The television industry has its own rating system, with a code displayed in the upper left corner of the screen at the start of each show. The TV rating codes are: TV-Y, TV-Y7, TV-G, TV-PG, TV-14 and TV-MA, but content descriptors are added based on the kind of objectionable content in the individual program or episode and to make sense of those cryptic letters.

Over the years we have abandoned many media rules and restrictions. In the 1960s, a male TV actor always had to keep one foot on the ground when in a bed with a woman. Our current rules are much better, and certainly help parents decide which shows their kids shouldn't watch, but it's all part of our national obsession with "smut." Sometimes a harsher rating will help the success of art, like the old "Banned in Boston" creating curiosity. I have never seen a TV show description that says, Gratuitous Nudity,

Stimulating and Titillating Sexual Encounters with Multiple Happy Endings. Now there's a show I would watch!

Back to nudity. Why is it appropriate that a handful of people with a rule book determine what we see? The overriding driver should be the culture itself. We do move to more liberal positions at times, but eventually the prudes push us back to an arrangement that makes them comfortable. I don't want Father Mike Pence or Lucky Larry Flynt to determine what America watches. Community standards should be considered, and sometime those are local, not national. San Francisco and New York are different from Omaha and Kansas City.

I find it quite bizarre that pubic hair disgusts people, but male chest hair does not. We can show a man full frontal with his glistening nipples, which have no nutritional value, but show a woman's breast and BANG! the rating changes and, of course, the actress gets more money. It was rumored Halle Berry was paid $500,000 for showing both her breasts in the movie *Swordfish*. That's $250,000 per tit and, tit for tat here, a man hardly, or softly, ever shows his penis unless it's an art film or an episode in an HBO original series. Not that I need to see more penis, but more cowbell would be nice.

If film makers follow the FCC rules and the MPAA codes, they will never show sexual penetration of any kind. That would make it porn. When you work in porn, you generally make less than a feature film or top-rated TV show actor. Why is it that the more you show the less you get?

Not everyone is into a nude body. People who work in the motion picture industry have no problem stepping aside for a more attractive extra, known as a double, to participate in certain scenes. In the HBO series *Game of Thrones,* there was a scene called the walk of atonement, in which the confessed sinner, stripped of all clothing, walked through the streets with the town locals looking on. Actress Lena Headey was pregnant when she shot the scene. The GOT fans got their knickers in a knot because a body double was used. So, you want nudity but only if the actor's actual body is seen? Perplexing.

Our censorship is designed to not only protect our children, but also to please the Sisters of Perpetual Guilt. You can put my name on the list of someone who doesn't enjoy seeing bodily functions on display. I'm not interested in seeing a man taking a dump or a woman throwing up, even if it moves the plot forward. Remember, this is a country that brings its Chinese food home in bait containers!

We know people like Howard Stern have moved the invisible "line" and reshaped community standards. More recently, the Goofball in the White House has taken a perfectly inappropriate expression like "shithole" and blasted it out for all to hear. Even nighttime cable TV is starting to use the word "shit." It won't be long before the word makes its way to broadcast TV, should it still exist. Ironically, we try to censor content to protect our kids, but our kids know more than we do. I've always thought most censorship was done for those adults in the room who get nervous when someone else talks about sex.

The real world has become flashes of Anthony Weiner's "bonerized" underpants, porn stars having sex with presidents, doctors sexually assaulting gymnasts, coaches and priests being convicted as serial rapists or child molesters. This pushes the people in the middle to act. These emotional generalizations bring about more rules based on a few deviants and perverts, which doesn't make America a better country. What we really need are better people.

The human body isn't a temple that needs to be protected by the thought police. Don't get me wrong, the human body is beautiful, and in the right context can stimulate us into doing what we are supposed to do, make more humans. We should admit, however, that we want to see only good-looking nudity. We American males are nudity snobs, thanks to Playboy magazine and Hugh "Airbrush" Hefner.

Our thoughts on nudity are based on our own self-imposed embarrassment cemented into our religious codes, and these paint Americans as silly puritans, not moral leaders of the world. Think about a person who railed against homosexuality in Congress, only to be arrested in a restroom for soliciting sex. We need to remember those who screamed bloody murder about sexual depravity, who then bought the silence of interns they sexually assaulted.

In the end, are our children more stable because we protected them from raunchy sex and nudity? They can find that stuff on the internet on their own. When we take them to the museum and see great works of art, they notice one statue with an uncircumcised penis or another with a leaf covering his private parts. Does this give our kids, leaf envy? I'm pressed to ask, why did the artist use a leaf to cover a bush?

Marketing & Media

There is a myth in our country that all marketing is truth. We have been trained to believe the stuff we see on TV are things we must have, but the sad reality is they don't always do what the commercials say. I'm not stupid, but I have bought some of those things under the category of ONLY SEEN ON TV, and many of those pieces of shit didn't work anywhere near what was claimed. But that's a small price to pay for freedom, right?

Whatever happened to truth in advertising? Do politicians ever tell us the truth? We have a system of government that permits and supports lies. In fact, the government's radio and TV watchdog, the Federal Communications Commission (FCC), has a law that no one can edit, alter or change a blatant lie in a political commercial. Another law states that once a radio or TV outlet sells and broadcasts one political spot, they must accept and air all other political spots, as they exist. The candidates paying for the ads are legally allowed to lie.

In the introductory chapter of Matt Taibbi's 2008 book, *The Great Derangement: A Terrifying True Story of War, Politics & Religion at the Twilight of the American Empire,* this sentence appears, "Trained for decades to be little more than good consumers, we had become a nation of reality shoppers, mixing and matching news items to fit our own self-created identities, rejoicing in the idea that reality was not an absolute but a choice, something we select to fit our own conception not of the world but of ourselves." He was describing the electorate in the lead up to the second Obama election. Matt's opinion was formed by going to super religious and conservative areas in America and talking to real voters.

I love the term "Reality Shoppers," as if we get to pick out our own personal reality at the truth store. Contrary to the way we act, we are reading more, but only snippets, bullets and headlines. We see a meme online and we digest the major point. If we agree with it, we keep it; if we think it's wrong, we simply move on. We want instant gratification and to be "rubbed the right way" by other people. We believe only those polls that prove what we want to believe and disregard or build an argument against anything contrary.

Here's another great quote from the book, *Democracy in Chains: The Deep History of the Radical Right's Stealth Plan for America*. Nancy MacLean presented thoughts about the American voter from Gordon Tullock, an economist and professor of law and economics at the George Mason University School of Law, "Rational ignorance: the individual voter had scant effect on outcomes, so why bother to follow politics closely? Busy with other matters, 'they devote relatively little time and effort in acquiring information about social policy alternatives'; rather, 'they accept what they are told' by news sources they trust." Our greatest challenge right now is no one seems to be trustworthy. The president lies, Congress lies, maybe even the Judiciary lies to us. With the advent of the recent attacks on the press, the Goofballs in Washington are aiming to get the free press approval rating down to as low as their own. Why would that be good?

I remember attending a local street fair where the guy at the booth selling subscriptions to the local newspaper offered his opinion, "That whole Black Lives Matter thing is a false narrative." I thought that was a strange way to sell a newspaper subscription. Maybe it was my University of Alabama baseball cap that made him think, "Oh, he's one of us." I very quickly asked, "Is it?" and then he stopped talking. I was more than happy to continue the interaction with the gentleman, but he clammed up. I was going to probe, "What makes a slogan by a group asking for respect constitute a 'false narrative?'" But instead, I took it to the next level. I said, "You know if you were a young black man, this conversation would be different." He replied by telling me why I needed the newspaper delivered to my front door every morning.

You see, the phrase "false narrative" can be used as a deception tactic to "chop-block" a speaker, and both sides use it. Realize that once a person uses the term "false," there is an implied need for them to prove it. Without taking the time to mount a defense and deliver some facts, our truth-blocker is just as right as a broken clock, which is correct two times a day, unless it's an international clock which is right only once a day. A sundial is never right at night. Hey, I didn't write the rules.

Here's a point from the Neil Postman book, *Amusing Ourselves to Death*. He writes that TV news has moved from serious journalism to the province of pure entertainment. He is right. When people like Wolf Blitzer, Anderson Cooper or Dan Rather appear in a movie as themselves, their credibility as journalists is lost. Once you imprint the audience with visuals of a news authority as a character rather than a person wearing their stoic news face, how can you ever see them as anything but an entertainer? We never saw Walter Cronkite do that.

When I was a kid growing up in Pittsburgh, I would hear the old lore that the media was "controlled by the Jews." I never could figure out what that meant, but those speaking the words were surely convinced. This narrative came from our fathers, uncles and neighbors who fought against Adolf Hitler, who said the same thing. These truck drivers, steel workers and hardworking blue-collar guys felt the need to hold onto something they heard as being true, but they made no effort to dig deeper to see if the statement held any water. Sure, many people of the Jewish faith work in TV, radio and show business in America, but most of those large media firms are public companies that sell stock to anyone. Furthermore, why would "too many" Jews working in media be a problem any greater than too many Catholics on the Supreme Court?

According to the Holocaust Encyclopedia, the well-known German daily *Vossische Zeitung* employed 10,000 people and was the largest publishing house company in Europe. In 1933, German officials forced the Ullstein family, who ran the company, to resign from its board of directors and a year later made them sell all company assets. To those people who continually shovel the concept that the Jews own the media, they should remember what occurred shortly after Hitler took over all media in Germany. It's not only a "false narrative" that people of the Jewish faith control the media, but those who believe it are dangerous sources of hate. Ask the Pittsburghers in the Squirrel Hill temple. Now there's a "true narrative."

I grew up in a Protestant home and many of the non-Catholics in my neighborhood believed that if John Kennedy was elected President, he would be taking orders from the Pope. Kennedy made a speech to straighten out this misconception. One of the things I dislike about Americans is they are prone to jump on the darkest viewpoint and amplify it.

In the sixties, many hard core "patriots" believed anti-Vietnam war protesters were controlled by communists. They also opined that any woman who protested the war was a whore. How did sex come into that equation? Why is a woman who has strong opinions a "whore," while a man with an attitude is just an "asshole?" After all, it was the sixties, and we had birth control pills, free love and no AIDS… yet.

One almost must laugh out loud seeing these things in print. People exposed to the marriage of marketing and media tend to get overwhelmed by certain accounts that make them feel good, or that lock their recalcitrant brains into certain beliefs. We no longer see truth and news as the same thing. It's impossible to resist the repetition and the crafty expressions that attempt to convince us that a given thing is either good or bad. The more the media use their marketing magic, the more we absolutely believe everything they say, even when they are dead wrong.

After a few well-placed but poorly researched stories backed by a celebrity's support, we believe the lie and block our kids from getting vaccinations. Why would any loving parent want their offspring to contract a disease society has already conquered? How can years of science be disregarded just because Jenny McCarthy tells us those shots will make our kids autistic? Diseases like measles and mumps are making a comeback, after they were once totally defeated.

The religious right has decided that treating teenagers for the Human Papilloma Virus (HPV) is immoral. The shot protects them from a virus that is spread during unprotected sex. Who told those parents this treatment is bad? Ostrich-like behavior like this might make an adult feel good, but if their kid is impacted by the virus later in life an attempt to pray it away might not work. Do these parents think this shot will encourage unprotected sex? What bird brains! Even birds would know better. Science is your friend people; quit screwing her!

Imagine a Goofball with the power to control medical research funding not knowing the difference between HIV and HPV. That would be like a private prison company picking the jurors for every trial to keep the incoming prisoner count on schedule.

Andy Warhola, shortened to Andy Warhol, was raised in my home town of Pittsburgh. He was a unique artist and thinker. Some of his quotes are fabulous, like this one, "Art is what you can get away with." Then there's this burner, "They always say time changes things, but you actually have to change them yourself." But the one he will be most remembered for is this, **"Everyone will be famous for 15 minutes."** And during their fifteen minutes of fame, some people get a platform more powerful than others.

When the internet became famous enough to demand a capital "I," we all raced to make our YouTube videos, Facebook pages and Twitter feeds. Some young performers became millionaires by selling clickable ads to go along with their "comedy." Others simply banged out their thoughts with no vetting, screening, researching or verifying, and then dumped their vituperative vomit onto the world wide web. In effect, media and marketing have married, while their offspring slowly consumes the frontal cortex of the addicted souls who have turned away from newsprint and scholarly attempts to discern the truth. Just because the First Amendment says, in part, Congress shall make no law... prohibiting the free exercise thereof; or abridging the freedom of speech, or of the press..." doesn't mean that opinionated bloggers and internet provocateurs should be allowed to write whatever they want. Russian campaigns against America are indeed also protected in this context, or are they? We will see how the Goofballs with the Guns handle it when they become the target.

The me-marketing that has taken over the thoughts of some of us cannot be put back in the box. People lie all the time, as do politicians. Those Goofballs we elected tell us what the press says about them is not true. Many of those bastard politicians who get caught doing something questionable use the dismissive line, "I denied it!" as if muttering a denial is the final word on what truly happened. They can say they are the victims when they must resign, but without public pressure these Goofballs would continue to do whatever they wanted.

Let's be clear. Not all stories written, printed or posted are immune to an untruthful, or bad source. If a source lies and the writer publishes it, next day corrections usually lead to a pink slip. Whatever happened to the rule of checking facts with three independent sources? Journalists should go out of their way to prove their first source wrong. It's a mindset that not only saves face and delivers truth but keeps a publication's lawyers off the books.

People in high places will eventually learn that it's impossible to quench the fire in the fingers of people who have the power of the keyboard. In today's world, that's the internet. It has been said that free and open internet access to all can create a revolution and tear down a dictator. The truth will find its way to the young revolutionaries. The only question for those of us in the USA is this, would we even recognize a dictator in the making?

Misconceptions & Generalizations

I laugh at America when we make up things and then take them to a level of absurdity. Think about how many hours of cable TV news have been dedicated to debating the merits of something that was a lie. Our creativity should be focused on more useful pursuits. We need inventions that are tremendously useful for our citizens and people around the world. When we are creative and productive like this, our people get rich and we spread our culture worldwide in bits and bytes.

In the United States, there is always the possibility of someone having a better idea or method, which makes us a powerful and successful country. Unfortunately, we have too many Goofballs getting in the way. Would someone please explain to the head Goofball that all industries and technologies in the world are connected? What is this ongoing need for authority figures to put forth misconceptions and generalizations? It steals time from our national dialogue and problem-solving nature. We could use a little less pontification and much more leadership.

Let's start with the big guys, like Washington, Jefferson, Madison and all those other white landowners and slaveowners. They were never going to give up the African slaves they owned, going as far as waging a war to keep them. They also generalized that women were ill-equipped to vote, and half the population followed right along. Over time we became somewhat more reasonable, but we continued to fall prey to a vocal minority who wielded an unexplainable power over many decision-makers in our government. There are even some billionaires in this country who think "majority rule" is a bad idea and would like to change it.

Let's look at America in the 1920s. A group of church people began organizing against something they thought was ruining our country. They were able to apply pressure to Congress to win their fight against alcohol.

The 1920 to 1933 ban against manufacturing, selling and consumption of the stuff became a giant win for a very vocal minority, but it was a terrible idea for America. For those thirteen years, our country was under the control of a small segment of Bible thumping theocrats who manipulated Congress. It took the leadership and awareness of President Franklin Roosevelt to end this stupid rule. How did it ever get that far? Was it the fact women were becoming a major voting block and they were tired of seeing their husbands crawling home from the bar? Those were tough times for America, but it serves as a lesson that we must always be vigilant about regressive policies and agendas of the far right or the far left.

Although we eliminated Prohibition, local communities and states are constantly passing foolish "blue laws." In some places, you can't buy alcohol on Sunday until after 12:30 PM because, the good Lord knows, we would never want anyone in church who deployed the "hair of the dog" for breakfast. In some states, a restaurant cannot be built within 500-feet of a church. Now if my memory serves me right, some of those very churches serve little glasses of alcohol as part of their services, you know, the blood of Christ. By the way, isn't it a sin to mix spirits with holy spirits?

Our legal system has a notion of "precedents," where we start with a statute or law that becomes locked in over time. Today's judges and juries then use these old laws to guide and shape their rulings. Some ignore the past and cast secondary decisions to either reinforce or reshape the original law. Not all of that is bad; legal reforms can be good. Think about the many who were caught with a couple of marijuana joints years ago. Are they still sitting in prison? Most states have many "archaic" laws on the books which their legislatures don't reform. The people must ask for it.

In the recent past, several boondock judges decided to ban students from wearing blue jeans to school. Judges in the 1950s didn't think they were violating the rights of students, so they upheld the rulings. Our society keeps carting out similar rulings to prevent people doing what they want, even though the "infraction" does no harm to anyone. Back in my school days, we couldn't wear blue jeans and we couldn't eat meat on Friday. Maybe that's why I love wearing jeans, especially on a Friday when eating meat.

It's bizarre to me that an enforceable agreement must be in writing and signed. Our binding legal process is all about written language verified with signatures. Yet, when things are really on the line, we get sworn in to the tell the truth, the whole truth and nothing but the truth, but that's not done in writing. We must orally take our stand. I imagine the roots of this trace back to a time when a large percentage of people in America couldn't read or write, but it highlights a profound truth. We trust written laws and mistrust a written testimony, but we hold up a written confession without challenge. Damn confusing, isn't it? I guess we are still working out the kinks.

Another strange generalization comes into play is when the court determines that someone is unfit to be tried. We move the most notorious killers and schemers into this category of insanity. The defense argues the defendant is not responsible for his or her actions due to an episodic or persistent psychiatric disease at the time of their criminal act. Even if they are perceived to be able and willing to stand trial, they can still use the insanity defense. Some are held in hospitals, but some get released. I have to say a crazy man with a Gun is highly dangerous. If someone has a persistent psychiatric condition, why would they be allowed to go free? After all, any murderer must be a little bit crazy to kill someone, right? It's all part of our ongoing debate between compassion and treacherous tribal excess, like the death penalty.

We have a deep misconception about law. Ever since lawyers and attorneys have been given the right to advertise, Americans see the legal system as a means of retribution. If your employer's unhealthy physical plant poisoned you over a period of years, you should be able to get justice in the matter. However, the courts are overloaded with frivolous lawsuits which can prevent important cases from being heard. Recently, the Supreme Court made it harder for workers to bring class-action law suits. We still need the long arm of the law to gain leverage over large multi-national corporations. This is where state law may prevail.

One of the great quotes in the Nancy MacLean book *Democracy in Chains: The Deep History of the Radical Right's Stealth Plan for America*, concerned a Reagan-era appointed judge who said, "Ominously, business has a good chance of opting out of the legal system altogether and misbehaving without reproach." Ms. MacLean suggests a headline for what might happen if the Supreme Court swings further from protection of the individual and closer to the rights of corporations. That headline is this, "Privatization of the Justice System."

Words blathered from the talking head mouths of so-called legal experts on TV are not necessarily qualified legal opinions. We often get pulled into believing hype and marketing, such as credit card security. I was amazed when all the credit card companies put chips in their cards, claiming this would make consumerism safer. They were being optimistic. Rampant breaches and the theft of personal information has not eased. The chip is a visual marketing idea, certainly not a fail-safe system.

The developers of security devices and gimmicks appear to be doing things, but with each incremental step someone out there will crack their "invincible" idea. Any data moved from one server to another is prone to a hack. Your ATM is connected to a server. All the encryption in the world will not keep that data safe for long; just look at what happened to Facebook.

The grandest misconception comes from the fat ass Goofballs who tell us we need to extract more coal and drill for more oil to keep America safer. What will actually keep this country on a sound path to the future is solar, natural gas and wind power. I included natural gas because it's used by many Americans for cooking. One highly negative aspect of natural gas is the use of fracking, the devil's method to get the stuff out of the ground. Hey, anything that makes your drinking water brown and combustible must be bad, right?

We could see through slapdash generalizations and alarming misconceptions if we only took the time to examine and question what people say. This is why the CBS-TV show *60 Minutes* has been so important to truth in America for more than 50-years.

When a Senator asks a nominee for the directorship of the Central Intelligence Agency (CIA) if torture is immoral, I just shake my head. Everyone knows torture is immoral and ILLEGAL, but the answer isn't important. We all know the CIA kills people who get in the way of their mission. They will do anything in the pursuit of the agency's directives. If so ordered, they will kill, eavesdrop, spy, torture, follow and investigate you, ruining your life. We don't need an answer to a question on morality, we just need to know where they would stop or the severity of the misdeed they would find acceptable.

When the Goofballs in power try to make you believe they have oversight or control of these agencies, they are fooling themselves. They may ask for guarantees in a Senate nomination hearing, but where the rubber meets the road, they have no power over the actions of agency personnel once in office. It's all part of their fantasy about their self-worth. They use generalizations to win arguments. When they say, "Everybody knows that!" we should be asking them, how do they know what others know? It's like saying every snowflake is unique, when no human has seen every snowflake to verify the claim. Stop saying "everybody" unless you have the time and balls to ask everyone what they think.

Religion & Politics

When I was growing up, my parents always offered a bit of wisdom to us right before we had company over for dinner, "Don't talk politics or religion." I always thought that was odd, because to me those were the most compelling topics, and that didn't stop my mother from putting the Bible on the mantle, depending on who was coming over.

Even when younger, I loved to debate about how things worked in Washington. I also had this burning question. If we all believe in and worship the same God, why are there so many different churches? Our church was the United Presbyterian Church, as opposed the plain old Presbyterian Church or now Presbyterian (USA) with more branches than a city library. My small mind couldn't comprehend the notion of factions within factions within institutions. I had questions.

We are a severely divided nation and will be forever. It's not completely the fault of one Goofball. It's the perfect storm of misinformation, propaganda, lies and mind fucking. Yes, in this essay on religion and politics, I suggest that America is being MIND FUCKED, by Gold, God, Guns and Goofballs. Permit me to paint a perfectly pure picture.

One of the lessons I have learned is that politics and religion are intertwined, and because the Goofballs keep using the phrase, "We are a Judeo-Christian nation," the deal is signed. The far-right attacks science and thinks they are protecting God when, in fact, the only thing that religion and science agree on is **circumcision**. Yes, the medical profession, Christians, Jews and Muslims all believe that man's God-given body must be altered because "cleanliness is next to Godliness." It's painfully funny that we men never get a chance to make our circumcision decisions.

Maybe the fissure between God and Science starts with the Holy Bible's book of *Genesis*. You see, we are slaves to our myths and once we are indoctrinated, we tend to stay on beam with those early teachings seared into our brains. After all, we're only human.

The good book first introduces the Garden of Eden, which experts believe was located somewhere in Persia, today known as Iraq. The first book of the Old Testament is Genesis, and we can loosely refer to it as our "origin" story. The Garden of Eden was perfect in every way. Our leading man and lady didn't even have to wear any clothing. Oh yeah, they were the only people there and they were without sin, so it's assumed they could be naked all the time.

God placed two trees in this mythical garden. One was the Tree of Life and the other was the Tree of Good and Evil, more commonly known as the Tree of Knowledge. Now you can debate this issue, but the Tree of Life was said to bear a fruit that imparts eternal life. Not bad if you can get it, but I can't find it at Whole Foods. The other tree's fruit supposedly imparted knowledge. God told Adam and Eve not to eat the fruit from the Tree of Knowledge. You know, stay dumb, happy and live forever. Why then, would Eve think about convincing Adam to eat that damn fruit?

This is the part of the show where the announcer says, "Could it be, that Ancient Aliens who came from another dimension in the form of a snake …" You know the rest. Seriously, the serpent was the devil and that chap Lucifer wanted man to know the difference between good and evil. Once Adam ate the fruit, Earth's first humans lost mankind's right to live forever, unless they followed certain rules. Oh, one more thing. Suddenly, nakedness was bad, and we became ashamed to be seen without clothes.

God's bargain, and it can't be called anything short of a negotiated deal, was to simply trust in him and you would feel no need to know anything else. So, in our opening story, religion pitted God and blind faith against awareness of good, evil and, eventually, science. Because our ancestors believed in God, they had the courage to travel across the turbulent sea to arrive in a new country. In short, science and knowledge could have convinced them to stay in Europe and eat from the King's "Tree of Strife," until they could fly "Upper Class" on Virgin Atlantic.

When you migrate to escape persecution because of religious beliefs and customs, you tend to make sure your destination has some protections in that regard. I truly believe in the First Amendment and genuflect to its elegant language. I surely don't want a government pushing any religion on its people. Every time this has been tried, something terrible happened.

Within our capacity to fixate on a single God is a blind obedience to rules, written by men who claimed they have talked directly to him. Embedded in this relationship between man and God is the power and mandate to control women. Matthew, Mark, Luke and John were all men. Most scholars will admit that not one of the books of the Bible was written by a woman. Would the status of women be better if a female was involved in the communication with God? Doesn't it seem suspicious that God picked only men to receive his word? Was God afraid to talk to a woman? Do you think he was intimidated, believing she was still miffed by his infamous snake and apple trick?

Wait a minute! You mean to tell me that all I must do is claim that God gave me some tablets, golden plates or a PDF file and I can construct a tax-free organization where people give me money? Yes, I can hear you saying that I am cynical, and you are right, but please open your mind to understand this essay.

There was a time when men and women worshipped many gods. It made sense to them. They assigned the sun to this one and the moon to that one; this was the god of war and that was the god of making babies. Later, a few wise guys decided there is only one God. Okay, that certainly simplified things but I'm sure their declaration really pissed off the other gods. Could this be why mankind suffers so to this very day?

We humans have confirmation bias, which causes us to seek only those opinions we already agree with. This keeps us from logically analyzing many things such as biology, human behavior and God. We challenge the notion of evolution with a sketchy idea of creationism. We now know the age of the Earth and the science of human evolution. The evangelicals have a theory as worthy as the one those Ancient Aliens guys have, but Christians generally look down on extraterrestrials and scientologists, believing they aren't legit. I mean, even Pastafarians, who celebrate every Friday as a holy day and worship a Flying Spaghetti Monster, have a place at the table, and why not? They serve pasta for dinner.

Some would have you believe the world restarted after Noah's big boat expedition. Noah's good, old ark and many other stories are myths that circulated long before there was a Moses, Jesus, Allah, Mohammed, Bible or Quran.

We simply take on board so many things we were taught without questioning the timetable, logic or facts. Many believe the Holy Bible is just a retelling of older myths and ancient fables. All ageless legends feature a messiah coming to help conquer evil. There is always a flood. There is always a baby found in the weeds who grows up with the royal family where he discovers his destiny and finds his roots to help his people escape persecution. He leads his people to freedom and becomes a forever prophet.

If God is a solidly proven deity, why are there so many miscreants, malcontents and perverts in the very churches where we worship? The Catholic Church has been a bastion of corruption, sexual deviance and political ill deeds. Protestant churches were just as bad during the reformation. We know the ancient Islamic ways demanded they conquer and convert or kill their captives. To this day, we still see fierce actions by small radical bunches of zealots in that faith, but it's hardly all Muslims. Organized religion has a bad reputation.

We also find some strange, historical "facts" about the Jewish tribes, like this from Deuteronomy, Chapter 20 "…in the cities of these peoples that the LORD your God gives you for an inheritance, you shall save alive nothing that breathes, you shall utterly destroy them, the Hittites and the Amorites, the Canaanites and the Per'izzites, the Hivites and the Jeb'usites, as the LORD your God has commanded." So, the God of the Old Testament told the Jews to take land and kill everyone there. What is the basis of morality if the word of God says killing is okay?

These kinds of hand-picked quotes from the Bible may have given people like Adolf Hitler the idea that wiping out a whole clan of people would be permissible under the watchful eye of God. Some historians say Hitler thought of Jesus as an "Aryan fighter" against the corrupt "Pharisees" and what he called "Jewish materialism." Some say Hitler thought that Christianity was a harmful superstition. If you judge a man by his actions, we hope this man is burning in hell. Even atheists think there is a special place for Hitler there. You don't need to believe in God to hope there is a hell.

There are times when a wild hair like David Koresh will crop up. He believed himself to be the messiah and claimed God had instructed him to father children with all the women in his congregation, no matter what their age. Clearly, he was a prophet with benefits.

That story didn't have a happy ending. The FBI and ATF attacked the Branch Davidian's complex in Waco, Texas. For 51 days, the authorities engaged in a stand-off with Koresh and his "family." After all talks broke down, the FBI and ATF advanced on the main building. Between the gunfire, the tear gas and perhaps followers inside starting fires, the complex burned to the ground. 79 perished in the blaze and 22 of those poor victims were children. It wasn't long thereafter that Timothy McVeigh came along. He decided to blow up the Federal Building in Oklahoma City as retribution for what he believed were the government's misdeeds at the Branch Davidian compound in Waco. The attack on the Alfred P. Murrah Federal Building took the lives of 168 people, including nineteen children in a day care center on the second floor. Six-hundred eighty-four others were injured in the blast.

The Waco tragedy was caused by people wanting to worship their concept of God, while the United States government declared their "messiah" a pure nut case. Our law enforcement organizations decided to take matters into their own hands.

Please don't be defensive when I suggest that the ATF and the FBI were, in a sense, following the same role Pontius Pilate played in the case against Jesus. Remember the Romans had less of a beef with Jesus than the high priests in the temple. After all, Jesus said one didn't need a rabbi or high priest to talk directly with God. He told his followers they could cut out the middle man. His death sentence was based on the "fake news" that he had declared himself to be the "King of Man," which might have simply been an informal title from the populace.

McVeigh was put to death by the US Government in the ultimate eye for an eye situation, but the lingering reality is a story that unusual religions are always challenged by the majority faith. Some of those in power will have us believe that people who believe differently than mainstream folk pose a threat to our freedom. Politicians sometimes hide under the cloak of their own Messiah to justify their actions against people of different religions.

We would be irresponsible if we didn't disclose the following. Information the state received from followers who had left the Waco compound became the ATF's and FBI's prime justification for entering the Branch Davidian complex. They told law enforcement that Koresh had forced underage girls into sexual relationships. The age of consent in Texas is 17-years, but a girl under that age can legally have sex with any man who is not more than three years older than her. However, that was not the application of law in this case.

If Koresh claimed each one of the girls was his wife, then he was in violation of the bigamy law of the state which makes having multiple wives or husbands a criminal offense. This inside information gave the feds probable cause to demand examination of the premises, permit interviews with the kids and launch an intervention. The authorities were not permitted to enter the premises by Koresh.

It's also important to point out a significant, controversial player who stirred up negative publicity in what has been called the "Waco Siege." If you are aware of the website site InfoWars, then you know Alex Jones. He not only confronted FBI agents on live TV but continues to foment resentment toward the government agencies today. This far-right use of the First Amendment may have motivated people like Timothy McVeigh, and his accomplice Terry Nichols, to bomb the Federal Building in Oklahoma City.

There is evidence that conspiracy-minded TV shock talkers like Alex Jones, Rush Limbaugh and Glenn Beck inspired McVeigh. Perhaps they should share some of the blame for those who McVeigh called "collateral damage." If you scream "Fire!" in a crowded theater where there isn't a fire, then you are the problem. It's like going on the radio and saying the massacre at Sandy Hook Elementary School was a hoax and twenty children and six adults weren't killed on that December day in 2012. Who does he think he is, God?

The Waco case has been studied by law enforcement professionals for years, and experts can point out many of the FBI's flaws and fallacies during the siege. The violent overkill and military actions taken against this religious group fueled the debate about separation of Church and State but didn't resolve this most important question. How should we deal with zealous religious orders whose beliefs are contra to our values and rules?

The far right in America pushes a narrative against Muslims, whose fantasy dictates that Sharia Law can be enacted in the land of the free should its population become too powerful. Those same people protested outside of the Alabama courthouse when the government ordered the removal of a two-ton piece of granite etched with the Ten Commandments. Those Christians believed their religious dogma should take precedence over all others, with no comprehension that they were pushing other people into a religion they didn't want. One of the things that deep-seated loyalty to a religion eliminates is tolerance. To people like Alex Jones, I say W.W.J.D. (What Would Jesus Do?).

The author Paul Krassner considered religion "organized superstition." Of course, this is the same guy who wrote the book *Confessions of a Raving, Unconfined Nut*. There is some truth to the notion that if we removed from religion all controlling, power-hungry people, we'd be a lot better off. I, for one, want God or some other messiah figure to return to Earth and give us the word directly. In my viewpoint, the deity doesn't have to destroy the Earth, just set a few people straight. It would be wasteful to destroy a whole planet because of a few assholes. Can't we just get rid of the useless humans?

A person who spends many hours of each day hyperventilating and perpetuating an on-going conversation with God doesn't have to think. The person who doesn't need God as the master of their own inner voice, is questioning and trying to learn why, who, when or what. There is no proof that either of those people will be happier, have a better life or become more morally fit.

Religious belief is a never-ending debate. I have no gripe with people who take comfort in religion and see it as their guiding light. We all have superstitions, curses, delusions and fantasies that we use to prop ourselves up and push through another day. Why is it when someone doesn't totally agree with your special doctrine, they're seen as less American?

Some research suggests that devout followers of the Lord, God or other deities are a bit happier and can frequently summon contentment. Does praying produce more serotonin? Other research and personal observation suggest uptight zealots are miserable. It could simply depend on the temperament every person caries within themselves.

As an American, I would like to see all references to God or religion taken out of government. There is nothing about the Constitution, Civil Code or US law in the Bible. We can be moral without having God brought into the discussion. The United States of America didn't exist when the Holy Bible was written. English as a language didn't exist when Jesus walked the Earth. Even if you believe the Bible is a recorded history of a part of the world, there was a whole other world out there and the Mormons later created their own history of the world. Which do you believe, or was Joseph Smith, founder of the Church of Latter-Day Saints, just inventing "alternative facts?"

Any attempt to label the United States as anything but a political domicile or domain, even with its acknowledged status as a sovereign establishment, would be wrong. We are not, and have never been, a religious state. Thank God. Yes, I said it. Why do our politicians patronize the far-right evangelicals? Because they want their vote in the spirit of "the end justifies the means." Some of these Goofballs are so reborn during their campaigns they think they have an ordained right to rule, and that's their con.

If you are puckering your God hole, let me add one more thought for you. Who the hell, and I borrow this concept from several good books, decided to tell their followers that God was the "intelligent creator?" REALLY? What parts of the human body and existence do you find so gloriously intelligent? Our eyes are bad, we grow our teeth back only once, we use the same areas of our bodies to dispel waste and reproduce, our joints eventually wear out and some of us lose all our hair. Yes, our prostates are positioned above our bladders and some of us bleed from our vaginas every 28 days. To keep me clean, you cut off part of my penis shortly after I am born. So, was my penis designed intelligently? It's more like a bad fifth grade science project!

Maybe between here and the end of the book I will be reborn. I don't have to be labeled a Christian, a Jew or a Buddhist to be a good, moral person. I learned to be compassionate, fair and honest because these are good ideas, and not being a bad person makes me feel even better. Do we truly need a deity and rules to know right from wrong?

As we are thinking about our fellow men and women with our warm and fuzzy God-glow, let's take another look at humans. Watch someone eat an ice cream cone. Think about it; we eat it like a cat would, lick-lick-licking away. So, they got nine lives and we got God.

Three-Legged Stool

I've often contemplated the invention of the three-legged stool. These backless chairs have been around since, well, forever. Some experts believe they came from the Norse and were spread by the Normans. I wonder how many people were named Norman back then?

The design of the three-legged stool is such that it falls if one of its legs is removed. That's become a metaphor for many aspects of life, from battle strategies to business structure, and that's exactly how I want to proceed. Imagine America, our great, wonderful country, is being supported by three legs. You might be thinking about the Executive, Legislative and Judiciary branches of government, but those aren't the legs I envision. Bear with me for a paragraph.

People believe America is controlled by two parties, two vastly polar factions, but it's a bit more complex than that. I have come to the same conclusion Matt Taibbi did when he said, "It is possible in America to govern entirely on the appearance of principle—while changing absolutely nothing." He's 100% correct regardless if a Republican or a Democrat is in office. Some members of both parties are criminals who should be locked up in the same cell. They became corrupt the day they decided to run for office and were then manipulated after being sworn in. The place we find ourselves will never be changed or conquered through voting alone. The underpinning of power is a seat with three legs, each having a separate agenda that needs no input from us.

The three legs are these classes: Evangelical, Neo-Con, and the Rich Owner. When these three forces join together, they form a tour-de-force that controls everything happening in America. We are forced to sit on the structure they have created. "Grin and bear it."

First, we have a legal system that bans the taxing of churches and religion based on the First Amendment. The government has no power over a church or its land. By rights, a church should be able to shelter a person in its confines without attack. By setting up a tax-free, non-profit status for churches, we have opened ourselves to any belief system that qualifies. The ability to qualify isn't always easy, but if you have enough money you can get it done, just like the Scientologists did.

The group that controls this classification is the Internal Revenue Service. They were legally worn to the bone by L. Ron Hubbard's team of space alien followers. The IRS simply gave up and awarded the Scientologists the status of a church. After all, if you claim that a power you call God is only provable in your own mind, then who can say aliens aren't just another form of God?

The Johnson Amendment is one of the rules governing religion and taxes. It is not a real "amendment," but it does regulate activities of tax-exempt organizations such as churches. Under terms of this 1954 legislation, named for then Senator Lyndon Johnson, churches and other nonprofit organizations are exempt from taxation. They're also prohibited from directly or indirectly participating or intervening in any political campaign on behalf of, or in opposition to, any candidate for elective public office.

According to National Public Radio, "Organizations claiming tax-exempt status cannot collect contributions on behalf of political campaigns or make any statement for or against a particular candidate. Clergy are not allowed to endorse candidates from the pulpit." It's right there in the US Tax Code, but some Goofballs want to eliminate it. It would take Congress to nullify what has been done, but they don't do or undo much of anything.

Pastors, preachers, priests, and possible future messiahs don't follow the rule at all. It's no secret that leaders of non-profit churches regularly endorse or discredit candidates from the pulpit.

In 2018, the Catholic Church was challenged in court by the Pennsylvania State Attorney General. The Grand Jury found that thousands of boys and girls were raped and suffered other forms of sexual abuse from 1947 to present in dioceses throughout the state. The unsealed indictment named 300 priests who attacked children. If the state was more vindictive, they would take the church's tax-free status away until they proved they solved this problem. These "holy" men would have had to sell the Gold from their coffers to pay taxes. That probably would have gotten their attention.

United States churches and religious leaders are always involved with politics. Once politicians like George W. Bush realized this powerful group of Americans could help him get elected, he did a reverse Johnson amendment and endorsed the church leaders.

Evangelicals don't see the similarity between their preachers attempting to control their flocks politically with the happenings of an Islamic state. The idea that a Christian or Jewish leader would decide how their followers should think politically is exactly like Sharia Law, except for hands being chopped off. Once you allow the church and state to merge, even philosophically, you have launched Mike Pence's priority list, Christian before American. I can't believe that a Goofball in high office here in the USA would ever say his church was more important than protecting the Constitution.

The new conservatives, loosely known as Neo-Cons, are a very formidable leg on the seat of power. What started as a reaction to pacifist movements, anti-war peace protests, left wing organizers and counterculture concepts rolling over the country, became a major force. You may be a Neo-Con and not even know it.

These "hawks" have always wanted to blow up enemies abroad rather than co-exist with communism, socialism and other non-democratic world regimes. Their Guns and Gold helped prop up some incredibly nasty dudes who ignored human rights, while they saw no problem wasting our tax dollars on "nation building" thousands of miles away.

The "neoconservative" label was used by Irving Kristol in his 1979 article *Confessions of a True, Self-Confessed Neoconservative.* Irving is the father of conservative writer and pundit Bill Kristol. Many of the early leaders of the movement were Jewish New Yorkers with never-wavering support for Israel. Find someone with devout or loud support for Israel in America, and you have probably bagged yourself a Neo-Con. And to be clear here, dear, I have no problem defending Israel, but we all must realize that Israel is another country. In the year 2018, we gave more money to Israel than to Puerto Rico, which is part of our country. There you see the power of the Neo-Cons. Among other things, they surely don't give a shit about Puerto Rico.

In 1991, the Neo-Cons supported the first Iraq War promoted by George H.W. Bush. Then some turned against Bush for not overthrowing Saddam Hussein or for not supporting the Kurds and Shiites, who could have overthrown the dictator. Those hawkish Neo-Cons just love war. I guess they believe anyone against Israel is a Canaanite who must be eradicated. Hey, don't blame me, it's in the Bible.

Neo-Cons played a major role in the 2003 invasion of Iraq and have continued to push and pay Republicans in Congress, so they will deploy the aggressive actions they endorse. A good example of a contemporary vintage Neo-Con is John Bolton. He uses the phrase "pre-emptive strike" like it's a marketing slogan for whitening toothpaste. Use it every day and keep the commies away, or Islamists, or [insert bad guy name here].

These Neo-Cons don't necessarily apply science or logic to their positions. In the late 1990s, Irving Kristol and other writers in neoconservative magazines began touting anti-Darwinist views and endorsed the concept of intelligent design. Some thought this was a way to attract Christian souls to their political group. This was folly because many of the pro-Israeli Americans are doctors, professors and lawyers. The idea that we were somehow going to kill Darwin because his theories weren't fit enough to survive the wrath of Neo-Con bullshit was ill-advised. These far-flung ideas held no water with thinking conservative Americans, so they were abandoned.

In 2008, the Neo-Cons backed John McCain for President with the assurance he would continue the Iraq War and not pull out of the fight. Most of the hard-wired reasons for their position in world affairs rotate around helping Israel. This fact brought criticism from some who thought the Neo-Cons overplayed their support of Israel at the risk of diluting their position on domestic issues. Neo-Cons never liked President Obama because of his moderate positions on Israel and his attempts to neutralize Iran.

While neoconservatism seems to be primarily focused on foreign policy, there is a domestic economic agenda. Neoconservatives like free markets and capitalism and they favor supply-side economics, but they have some disagreements with classical liberalism and fiscal conservatism. The Tea Party movement had a bunch of Neo-Cons camouflaged as reformers. Polish-born Israeli historian and political scientist Zeev Sternhell said, "Neoconservatism has succeeded in convincing the great majority of Americans that the main questions that concern a society are not economic, and that social questions are really moral questions."

I love reading the words of people who are supposed to be smart and have all the answers. It reminds me of that great philosopher Jimmy Webb, who asked us to consider the plight of someone who left the cake out in the rain. Even though it took so long to make it, we must ask this question, "Can the common non-Neo-Con man or woman be satisfied by simply eating cake?" That makes about as much sense as the lyrics of "McArthur Park."

If all social and domestic questions are somehow rooted in morality, then why do Neo-Cons offer little support for programs that would stabilize the middle-class and the unemployed? Does being a NEW CONSERVATIVE really mean you don't care about people?

If you're confused, don't feel you are alone. Much of the foolish Neo-Con positions on economics seem isolated from US citizen's needs and priorities. Hey, we need soldiers to win the war in Iraq; find some and send them. This may be unfair, but they seem unable to comprehend the connection between their political desires and the eternal pain a family feels when their sons or daughters are sacrificed to help the Neo-Con's "fix the world" crusades. We didn't fix Vietnam, we didn't fix Afghanistan and we totally screwed up Iraq. Why do we still have the permission of other world powers to resolve anything? It must be our Gold. Now they're floating the idea of privatizing the army. What?

Why do Neo-Cons command such an important role in my metaphor of the three-legged stool? Because they not only claim their ideology should have a major influence on American domestic and foreign policy, but they pull it off all the time. Can anyone stop them?

People like Sheldon Adelson, Dick and Liz Cheney, Newt Gingrich, Pastor John Hagee, Representatives Peter King and Devin Nunes, Senator Marco Rubio and Paul Wolfowitz are the "smart people" who give opinions to our leaders, which then turn into actions by our country. You can blame Paul Wolfowitz and Dick Cheney for the $2.5 trillion dollars we wasted in the Middle East. That's the fine legacy of over-zealous Neo-Cons.

Vegas tycoon Sheldon Adelson's endorsements and political contributions are a must for any conservative candidate. The Neo-Cons pledge allegiance to Israel to get money from Sheldon. I thought we pledged allegiance to the flag of America and to the country for which it stands? When you spend money in Las Vegas, you are lining the pockets of Adelson to further his political agenda. This "gutmensch" Adelson is happy only when he is buying people and controlling their actions.

Power preacher John Hagee leads the evangelical group Christians United for Israel, and he fronts draconian encouragement for aid to Israel. It is said he rejects any "land for peace" formula in dealing with the Palestinians, and he has had the ears of every Republican and conservative politician. Now why should a Christian preacher have that much power over people running for office? This preacher is clinging to two legs of the stool, making him doubly important, in his own mind.

I believe the Neo-Cons are destined to become nothing but an isolated cold-war culture that occasionally heats up in a socio-geo-political petri-dish filled with the spores of their rhetoric. They may claim those spores were collected from the unrest of our society, but they've been fermenting this stew in their own likeness for years. Someone like Dick Cheney will never admit it was wrong to torture enemy combatants. He will never admit that invading Iraq was a huge mistake. He simply believes he is right. If you want to learn about this heartless man, with someone else's heart, see the movie *Vice* written and directed by Adam McKay.

And this brings us to the third-leg of the stool, the Rich Owner class, that 1% of truly rich Americans who are generally connected to a large company or enterprise that wields power over people who run for office. They give money to an auxiliary industry in the nation's capital called LOBBYISTS. Even Hobby Lobby has a lobbyist, sitting in the lobby!

Nothing happens in America without cost consideration and the flow of Gold. Money moves mountains and gets bridges or walls built, even when we don't need them. Follow the Gold and you will find corruption in every state. Let me be perfectly clear. The very wealthy are both Democrats and Republicans. Some just pay to play, like Donald Trump, the builder who openly gave money to candidates without a regard of the politician's party or positions. His philosophy has always been, I'll grease your palm if you grease mine. He was bribing the candidates and politicians to push through the items on his agenda.

When there is a case against your phony "university," be sure to contribute to the local state Attorney General (as in Florida) so your problem will go away. And guess what? In states where this was done, the problem went away.

We know rich people and their egos keep industries running, but today's brand of billionaire seems to be a bit heartless. For every three Martin Shkreli's (the "Pharma-Bro" guy who increased the price of medication for children by a factor of 56), there is only one Bill Gates. In the old days, people like Andrew Carnegie financed libraries and museums, but maybe that was his Scottish guilt driving him to contribute to the common man after paying puny worker wages at his mills.

Today's unseemly use of wealth to influence the outcome of an election is the mark of a hard-core moral deficiency. Maybe we need to redefine the word "bribe" and make laws to guarantee that long-term quid pro quo is just as bad as immediate pay to play. The scumbag rich people bought a President and Congress, and then eliminated the inheritance tax so that more of their Gold could be passed on to their kids. Were they doing that for you? Not really.

The only cure for this problem would be the elimination of all political contributions from corporations, Super PACS, influence groups and "churches." If we mandated that those running for office could get a maximum of $100 from each contributor, things would change.

While I'm dreaming here, let's have everyone running for office, Executive, Legislative or Judicial branches, submit the last four years of their income tax returns. We need to know if there is any funny business in their business. This is more important than term limits, because should their taxes prove they've been sucking the hard-earned dollars from all of us, we will vote them out.

The idea of America has nothing to do with kings, queens and families inheriting power. Citizens have a voice that should determine who represents us. We are now living in an age that's not so much capitalism versus socialism, or Republican against Democrat, but a time where little is being done to help people. We have a structurally unbalanced society and we must find our way back to real people making the decisions. Religious folk, neoconservatives and the wealthy shouldn't be writing the script for America. Certainly, they are part of this country, but they shouldn't have an ordained or mandated power of more than one vote. Our government and laws should be derived from all the people's voices and needs.

Back to our stool, if you remove one of the legs from power, the whole seat collapses. Why can't America get back to honest, hard-working rewards? Why do the middle class, lower-income people and undocumented workers have to bust their asses to protect the lifestyles of the rich and famous? Who determined this plot?

I hate to break the news to you, but the Neo-Cons, the Evangelicals and the Rich, without us even knowing it, have conspired to make things worse. There are people like Charles Koch, whose missions involve only the implementation of their goals, their dogma and their perverted views of American values.

The objectives of these small groups are out in plain sight. They want to make abortions illegal, return prayer to our schools, rework the text books to present the Bible's limited historical viewpoint and send billions of dollars to Israel.

Rich people want the corporation to Win, Win, Win! What a way to treat your customers. Some people just ignore the fact that rich people are taxed a smaller percentage of their annual take home pay because of loopholes. Warren Buffet brought it to light during the last tax reform go around. Why do we let this happen? Why do we believe the "trickle down" myth?

We need to remove these three legs from our stool of power before they make America less, well, less American.

Mind Control Menace

We have lots of smart people living in America, but some also have an unhealthy love affair with conspiracies fueled by our overactive imaginations. The fibs and fabrications are given credibility by some of our bored writers, fringe cable news presenters and lunatic lug nuts in the land of the First Amendment.

Although the *Ancient Aliens* program on cable doesn't rate as highly as shows about Adolf Hitler, it has a loyal, consistent audience who believe aliens came here to create mankind. Some say this uptick in believing unbelievable myths is due to the slowly dissolving love of Christianity. Others think the use of scientific data makes the alien theorists' pitch more credible to a conspiracy-oriented brain. These things may or may not be drivers for a desire to cling to falsehoods or conspiracy theories, but who can blame a gullible brain from hearing, "If A and B are true, shouldn't C be true, as well?"

In the 1930's, people thought the government was poisoning alcohol to slow illicit drinking during prohibition. The fact so many people were getting sick on bad booze lent some credibility to that myth and gave us the term, "Bathtub Gin." It wasn't the Goofballs in government making the bad booze, it was the crazies who thought they had the talent to distill spirits on their own. For years, some people have believed the "deep state" government has been putting chemicals in our drinking water to control our brains. Ask the kids in Flint, Michigan; they would believe that one. Our water supply has always been thought to be safe, until now. And that fosters a belief in conspiracies as well.

Another myth contends that jet streams in the sky are filled with mind altering drugs. I must ask, if that's true, where's the high?

In the late 1980s, a myth was perpetrated that the CIA invented HIV/AIDS as a weapon against Africa. The source of that untruth is believed to be Russia and many Africans still believe this to be true. It's just another example of Russian interference in world views.

We have been regularly trafficking in myths, tales and theories in America. It's like the ancient concept of "Old Wives' Tales," superstitions or traditional beliefs regarded as unscientific or incorrect. Here are a few examples, "swimming right after lunch will give the swimmer cramps," "it's bad luck to open an umbrella indoors," "if you swallow gum it will stay in your stomach for seven years" and my favorite, "masturbation will make you blind." Hey, I'm over here.

I have argued with close friends about some of the most stupid things they say are true, when science, experience and logic scream otherwise. Another wave of insanity happens when conspiracies matriculate into "movements."

The fires are stoked by all the bores, bullies and bigots given too much press and TV time. The right attacks the left or the left assaults the right, depending on the speaker. Donald J. Trump, a New York developer and builder at the time, claimed Barack Obama wasn't born in the United States and therefore wasn't eligible to be President. Trump kept at the myth until Obama produced his birth certificate from Hawaii. Trump even delayed admitting it was a farce until he ran for President. He was pressured by moderate Republicans, and he eventually made a half-hearted statement saying he was sure about the legitimacy of the 44th President, but the damage was already done.

This backlash against Obama drew out the true racism of several online and on-air personalities like Rush Limbaugh, Glenn Beck, Alex Jones, Sean Hannity, Tucker Carlson and Bill O'Reilly. I'm sure they don't think they are racists and I'll bet they say some of their best friends are black. They must face the music and admit they have inner demons. It's a short walk from their words to contemptible actions.

We also have the local copycats, who pumped up the conspiracies of not just the birther myth, but the "black-guy president" coming to confiscate all our Guns theory, and FEMA camps, where law abiding Gun owners would be taken and incarcerated.

With groups like the 9-12 Project and Oath Keepers, the bright white underbelly of disgruntled American paranoia at work is slowly revealed. The more Alex Jones and Glenn Beck filled the airwaves with their lies, hate, xenophobia and racism, the more dangerous some off-center people became in real life. Remember the earlier mention of Alex Jones and his link to domestic terrorism? When you keep stoking a fire, innocent people get burned, or worse, killed. These assholes have weaponized paranoia.

Richard Andrew Poplawski was at the center of an extremely disturbing story that took place in my hometown of Pittsburgh, Pennsylvania. I have no problem linking his behavior to some of these brainwashing shows and websites that make tons of money for their owners and presenters. These enablers can push regular Joes to the edge, even to the point of committing murder. All the ratings and page views you guys are racking up for your sponsors is absolutely a misuse of the media. You aren't part of any solution. You are, indeed, the problem.

According to the Pittsburgh Post-Gazette, Poplawski joined the Marines in 2004 and attended boot camp, but he was discharged three weeks later. There is a theme here of people who served in the military, or felt they were mistreated by the military, and are now in the throes of post-traumatic stress disorder (PTSD). They are striking back at what they feel is wrong with America, or maybe they are just listening to evil voices in their heads.

For Poplawski, it started with an emergency 911 call by his mother, who said she and her son were having an argument about dogs urinating on a rug. During the call she told the 911 operator that Poplawksi had Guns and needed to be taken away. The Guns part of the call wasn't conveyed to the first two officers who came to the home, and this may have led to the ambush that took place there. Both policemen were shot and killed. An off-duty officer who came to the house when he heard shots in the neighborhood was also gunned down while approaching.

According to the Post-Gazette, Eddie Perkovic, a man who claimed he was Poplawski's best friend, said his friend feared "the Obama Gun ban that's on the way" and "didn't like our rights being infringed upon." And he allegedly said he "didn't like the Zionists controlling the media." This surely sounds like someone who has bought into things heard on some of that good old right-winged radio.

The tragedy in Pittsburgh is just one story. There's also the Dylann Roof saga in Charleston, South Carolina, in which a self-described white supremacist was convicted of killing nine people at a prayer meeting in the Emanuel African Methodist Episcopal Church. He later confessed to committing the shootings in hopes of igniting a race war.

This is all part of the bubbling stew of resentment and conspiratorial rhetoric from groups like the Oath Keepers, an anti-government, far-right organization associated with the patriot and militia movements. You can also add Glenn Beck's anti-government 9-12 Project to the list of organizations that were created to put forth a viewpoint of US versus THEM. For years, Beck used his platform of an afternoon show on Fox News to promote a "Don't Tread on Me" philosophy. It included such positions like, "I work hard for what I have, and I will share it with who I want to. Government cannot force me to be charitable. It is not un-American for me to disagree with authority or to share my opinion. The government works for me. I do not answer to them, they answer to me." On paper, the words sound as if they might have come from Jefferson and Washington but embedded in those words were the seeds that would be germinated by Neo-Nazi, White Nationalists and modern-day closet KKK members. They all believed that

America was in trouble because it elected an African-American president. It was their time to take their country back, and people like Beck played with fire.

The same government these people think they need to confront with arms is now giving Poplawski every opportunity to stay alive in prison. The judicial system is letting him appeal, much to the chagrin of the families of the three slain officers. As of this writing, Dylann Roof is on death row, and he will probably live longer than he deserves. Remember that I'm a liberal, but I fail to see any of these sick minds reforming or regretting what they have done. My grievance with these half-baked preachers and big mouth radio manipulators is they have the nerve to use fear and hate to make lots of money. Where does the Bible say that is okay? It's not mentioned in the Book of Mormon, either.

In his book, *The Backlash: Right-Wing Radicals, High-Def Hucksters, and Paranoid Politics in the Age of Obama*, Will Bunch reported that Glenn Beck made more than $30 million a year with his various enterprises, including speeches and rallies. He also hinted that while Beck was decrying global warming on TV as a hoax, he affixed solar panels to the roof of his $4 million home in Connecticut. I guess if you can't beat them, you join them.

Unfortunately, we have bigots, racists and xenophobes walking the Earth believing they are suffering discrimination. If these "patriots," "minutemen" and "militia" types won the lottery tomorrow, would they feel liberated from their views or just head out to buy more ammo and camo?

I'm sure Glenn Beck and Alex Jones don't go to bed hungry at night. They keep up the agitation by saying stupid things. After dedicating three shows to the FEMA concentration camp theory, Beck first said he couldn't debunk it and later he discredited his own conspiracy. Who is this guy? He should go back to alcohol and drugs. At least then he was hurting only himself.

What Beck may have thought was a funny theatrical trick was a harmful deception played on millions of Americans. Glenn helped create distrust and anguish in his followers. Even after Beck admitted the FEMA camp story was a lie, people still believed it. Glenn Beck is nothing but an exploitation crackpot dealing in the mass distribution of hate. Hey Glenn, "White Lives Matter!"

It's not just men on cable TV and radio who are creating the polarity slowly making America a less understanding place. There are two female broadcasters who are fomenters of the most wretched, vile kind of deceit. One is Ann Coulter and the other is Laura Ingraham. I put them in the same basket but permit me to focus on the Fox News host who is part of their opinion programming, Laura Ingraham.

I don't usually start off with a discussion of someone's pedigree, a line of questioning that would be more appropriate for a dog owner. That said, I'm curious what breed of mutt Ingraham could possibly be. Her maternal grandparents were Polish immigrants and her father was of Irish and English descent. We don't need the results of a 23andMe DNA test to know her mouth is directly wired to the white side of her Anglo brain. Had she been alive in the 1930s and living with her grandmother, she would have been a one-woman, flag-waving, welcome wagon for Adolf and the boys as they marched into her homeland of Poland.

In August of 2018, she said these things on the air, "In some parts of the country, it does seem like the America that we know, and love doesn't exist anymore." Now I don't know where she has been visiting, but I believe that America never stays the same and change is a built-in benefit. She continued, "Massive demographic changes have been foisted upon the American people. And they're changes that none of us ever voted for, and most of us don't like."

Laura dear, demographic changes just happen, and they aren't "foisted" on anyone; they occur for millions of reasons — 325.7 million reasons as a matter of fact. Americans do what they want, and that's why we call America "the land of the free."

People get to "vote" in America in various ways, like the babies they make and the U-Hauls they rent. When you say, "most of us don't like," are you saying you have the right to vote on where I live, what I do or who I love? No one asked you what you thought, but you keep telling us. When you say "most of us" who the hell are you talking about? Did you take a poll? If it was up to me, you would be heard ONLY on a 1,000-watt daytime AM station in Flint, Michigan with bad coffee, poor ventilation and gnats in the bathrooms. And you would be forced to drink the tap water. Then you could feel the pure pleasure of an unregulated, old-fashioned America that sets your hair on fire.

Ms. Ingraham, you need to go back to the Libertarian hypnotists at the University of Virginia, where you got your law degree, and check on the true meaning of freedom. You know, like your First Amendment right to say stupid things on cable TV and the basic human privilege to live where you want and carry out your pursuing of happiness. Don't think, however, that you have the power or privilege to infringe on common sense. America has always been changed by immigrants, and that's a good thing. Wake up and smell the cappuccino!

Ingraham continued, "From Virginia to California, we see stark examples of how radically in some ways the country has changed. Now, much of this is related to both illegal, and in some cases, legal immigration."

Okay, I get it. You must occasionally take out and blow that big dog whistle of yours. The sound that comes out screams, ***"I am a racist."*** We all understand we don't get a vote on the vitriol, hate and poison you spew, but we do have the right to call you out.

You may like the organic tomatoes you pluck at Whole Paycheck, and you probably never take the time to think that a human hand had to pick that fruit, vegetable, or whatever the hell it is, but you should know that a brown hand pulled that plump morsel from the vine and placed it in a box. The hands of legal or illegal immigrants lift and push food along the path to your mouth. Eat it and smile!

Laura Ingraham doesn't give a shit about anyone outside of her little circle of whiteness, rightness, self- important friends. She may think America is just for Caucasians, but we are all Americans, even white racists with large megaphones. When your sponsors pull some of their commercials, you will get the message that not all us think like you. If you are asking why "love doesn't exist anymore" perhaps you should look in the mirror and ask yourself why you hate so much.

Laura, you are just a silly little lawyer whose thin lips are drenched with xenophobic and racist spittle. Your clenched jaw holds that dog whistle so tightly we can see your intense insensitivity. Your whistle plays only a one note song of hatred. And by the way, that spit is really annoying to everyone who holds the true meaning of America in their heart.

So, this is where we are in America. We have people on large stages and big pulpits who have decided that there is no need to research any fact or theory, just say it's true. That is exactly what Hitler did in Germany. He convinced millions of people that everything bad that ever happened in his country was perpetrated by those of the Jewish religion and culture.

It's sad that some people right here in America believe the same thing but, in this case, they have added brown immigrants to their personal enemies list. The founder of the Oath Keepers organization openly admits he was inspired by Hitler's thoughts. I don't want to stir up their base, but most Nazis are pig fuckers. There, I said it. Makes me feel better.

We will talk more about "Fake News" and all the backlash that's created by self-serving political whores like Ingraham, Beck and Jones. For now, I would simply like to quote that great American martyr, Rodney King, "Why can't we all just get along?"

Age of Conspiracies

Many of us carry the burden of believing in one or more half-baked conspiracy theories. Sometimes I laugh at my friends' crazy ideas or argue a bit to disprove their latest fantasy myth. If one becomes too annoying and continues dwelling, I cancel their friend ticket. When some wacko says the Holocaust didn't happen, I recoil and refute their lie. My father was there and saw the aftermath of that tragedy and sin. I have seen the pictures. The holocaust is not a hoax.

One of the writers and thinkers I admire greatly is Michael Shermer. On his Website, MichaelShermer.com, you can find a wonderful article he wrote almost two decades ago titled *The Conspiracy Theory Detector*. It covers some of the conspiracies people believe. They range from "the fluoridation of water, who really killed JFK, RFK, MLK, Jr., Jimmy Hoffa and Princess Diana, along with the nefarious goings on of the Federal Reserve, the New World Order, the Trilateral Commission, the Council on Foreign Relations, Yale University's secret society Skull and Bones, the Knights Templar, the Freemasons, the Illuminati, the Bilderberg Group, the Rothschilds, the Rockefellers and the Learned Elders of Zion."

Most of the time, the mere game of connecting the dots and seeing larger than life truth in these myths isn't much different than believing in God. After all, you have a collection of concepts carried through the years without any firm confirmation or validation. Conspiracies can intrigue even the most educated and reasoned thinkers. Anyone can delve into these theories and seek confirmation from others who speculate about what "really" happened.

In the summer of 2018, the face of Mark Zuckerberg, the founder and head of Facebook, became tinged with red when he was caught in the middle of the Holocaust denial issue. Zuckerberg, who is Jewish, said he found Holocaust denial "deeply offensive," but added, "I don't believe our platform should take that down. I don't think they're intentionally getting it wrong." Mark focused on the difficulty of impugning or understanding intent. He later apologized to people he may have offended and said he wasn't trying to defend the people who hold that belief. We get it, Mark, you just think they're stupid and not intentionally using Facebook to promote "fake news." Huh? When did stupid people get the right to lie while you make money on their friends? What are your intentions?

So, here's the challenge. We have conspiracies and lies that flow through much of the content of America. If Facebook and Twitter don't believe denying the Holocaust is "fake news," then what is? **Does the Federal Government think one of its roles is to protect the American public from themselves?** We've seen coverups occur in every institution, even in places of worship.

The long history of Catholic Church priests sexually abusing young church members isn't a writer's vision or fantasy mythology. These accusations were and are real, as well-documented by court cases and victim payouts. According to the Guardian newspaper, Pope Francis once said the victims of abuse in Chile at the hands of Bishop Juan Barros were guilty of "slander" for pressing their case against him. The pontiff demanded "proof" of the claims. The Pope twice rejected Barros's resignation and believed he was innocent. I'm not sure why. I guess it's just his way. What if someone posted on Facebook that the Catholic Church scandal was a myth? Would that be an attempt of interfering with ongoing investigations?

In Michael Shermer's article on conspiracy theories and how to detect them, he wrote, "Similarly, the conspiracy involves large numbers of people who would all need to keep silent about their secrets. The more people involved, the less realistic it becomes." As much as I agree with his premise and observations, that area of detection doesn't apply to the conspiracy of silence in the Catholic Church. There were thousands of people involved in covering up the facts and it took more than one hundred years for them to surface.

Theories and myths get embellished by writers like Dan Brown. His stories suggest the existence of a deep religious state. We can swallow the notion of bad deeds by the Illuminati because Dan is such a fabulous writer. His books seem real because his fictitious accounts are based on facts. The previous sentence shows the challenge of sorting out truths when dealing with complex conspiracy theories and well-written fiction. The basis of most widely held myths is a mix of just enough facts with intriguing fantasy to complete a compelling conspiratorial concept.

According to Vox.com, "In a historical sense, the term 'Illuminati' refers to the Bavarian Illuminati, a secret society that operated for only a decade, from 1776 to 1785. This organization was founded by Adam Weishaupt, a German law professor who believed strongly in Enlightenment ideals, and his lluminatenorden sought to promote those ideals among elites. Weishaupt wanted to educate Illuminati members in reason, philanthropy, and other secular values so that they could influence political decisions when they came to power."

I always found the entanglement between the Freemasons and the Illuminati weird, but there are experts who believe the Illuminati infiltrated the Freemasons to observe what they were up to, or maybe it's just an old conspiracy theory. The earliest documentation of the group dates to the minutes from the Lodge of Edinburgh (Mary's Chapel) No. 1 in Scotland and proves a continuously operating Freemason Lodge since 1598. Freemasons regulated the qualifications of stone workers and their interaction with authorities and customers. Operating from their Grand Lodges, this tight-knit group of men had a bond beyond business. They thought of themselves as a "beautiful system of morality, veiled in allegory and illustrated by symbols." Members had to believe in a supreme being and scripture as a condition of membership. They were entrusted with passwords, signs and secret handshakes.

Today, there are Freemasons in every walk of life. Some claim their judicial members, will find in favor of a fellow member without regard to justice and law. The connection between the Knights Templar, who were a military force ordained by the Catholic Church to engage in several Crusades to take back the Holy Land, and other secret societies seems to be based more on symbolism as opposed to a wired correlation. It's interesting how the term "Grand Master" was used by both the Knights Templar and Freemasons. Even our first President, George Washington, was a Grand Master of his Virginia Freemason lodge. There are also more modern attempts at Freemason organizations like DeMolay International, which recruits young men and is named for Jacques de Molay, who was the final Grand Master of the Knights Templar. Most of the Knights were killed on Friday the 13th, October 1307, and since then that day is believed to bring "bad luck."

America liked the idea of secret society gatherings and male bonding, which may have led to modern-day "man caves" seen in many American homes. Universities have always been a breeding ground for non-inclusive groups and one of the most famous societies began on the campus of Yale University in 1832. It is called Skull & Bones.

If Yale's Bonesmen have carried out any negative exploits, they will never be fully known. After all, they are a secret society. What we do know is that the group's trust owns their building in New Haven and Deer Island in the Saint Lawrence Seaway, the latter is used for member retreats.

Some of Yale's most famous students are members of Skull & Bones: William Taft, George H.W. Bush, George W. Bush, McGeorge

Bundy, John Kerry, William F. Buckley, Jr., Fred Smith (FedEx) as well as White House financial advisors, Austan Goolsbee and Steve Mnuchin.

Much has been written about the puzzling customs and deeds of Skull & Bones, but I'm not going to talk about naked men laying in coffins or a tomb holding the stolen skull of Geronimo, the famous native American. There are many Goofballs who believe Skull & Bones members are the "deep state" which supposedly controls everything in the American government. In their IRS filing for tax exempt status, Skull & Bones claim recent topics have included homeland security, corporate governance and US international relations. Sure sounds like a camp for those deeply involved in our government.

Americans have a need to believe. We walk through our daily routines wanting to know the truth. There have been many terrible things done to people throughout the ages and one of the first things the news media asks is, "Why?" Why did another mass shooting take place? What was the perpetrator's motivation to execute innocent human beings? Sometimes we get an answer and go on from there. If we don't get the answer we want, we keep digging and trying to "connect the dots."

What I am sure of is this. Our thirst for conspiracy theories is not a new phenonium. It was born in the early days of European enlightenment. Churches have always held secrets and, perhaps, some people in government think the citizens of America are too naïve and ill-equipped to deal with the real answers. If we are still believing unproven conspiracy theories, then perhaps we are not ready to be given the truth. Our need to know secrets is most likely, part of our human DNA.

Aliens & Assassinations

It didn't take long for a major cult to form after the John F. Kennedy assassination in Dallas. That event has been plagued by the hard-wired conspiratorial question, WHO KILLED KENNEDY? Remember, once you have a slogan, you have a movement. As the great writer and philosopher Eric Hoffer said, "Every great cause begins as a movement, becomes a business, and eventually degenerates into a racket." The racket creates so much noise that it's hard to hear the truth.

Kennedy wackos first believed Cuba did it and then they changed it to Russians. The whodunit later became the FBI, led by the cross-dressing J. Edgar Hoover. Not to be upstaged, some said the CIA should get the blame. Others focused on the Mafia, because Bobby Kennedy investigated the mob as Attorney General. I wonder why there are so many possibilities on this one.

Much smoke has blown around this national tragedy and we still don't believe what the government told us. According to a Gallup poll in 1975, 81% of Americans believed there were more people involved in the plot than Lee Harvey Oswald. Only 11% believe he acted alone. The latest figures show that 61% think there was a conspiracy of some kind, while only 30% concur with the government findings.

A commission, headed by Supreme Court Chief Justice Earl Warren, investigated the JFK assassination. When something unbelievable happens in America, we create a commission to study it or we have hearings to "get to the bottom" of things. Either usually makes matters worse. Sometimes we learn what really happened, but when people don't get the answer they want, they may look elsewhere for a "better conclusion." When amateur theorists and weekend detectives dig through the available facts, weird things often happen. When those investigating don't get the cooperation they want, they scream "coverup!"

A commission or special prosecutor not only investigate the facts, but the very nature of our citizens often compels them to disprove a conspiracy theory before it's imagined. The only sure truth here is that Hoover, the Director of the FBI, indeed dressed up like a woman in his private moments. If only he had taken a selfie.

The Warren Report on the JFK assassination told us that Lee Harvey Oswald acted alone. This document was picked apart by everyone from Joe Lunchbox to Oliver Stone. Everyone presented their theories about what really happened. For years, people have asked that all government records pertaining to the assassination be released. In 1994, the testimony of Richard Helms was declassified and, according to the New York Times, he said, "And my recollection is that I informed Mr. McCone [Director of the CIA, 1961-1965] that we could find no evidence that Oswald had any connection with the CIA." There is a recently released CIA document that proves that Lee Harvey Oswald did meet with the KGB (Soviet intelligence) in Mexico City a few months before the assassination. But then, can we believe the CIA? Boy if we can't then we are really in trouble.

One of the books I forced myself to read was *Oswald and the CIA: The Documented Truth About the Unknown Relationship Between the U.S. Government and the Alleged Killer of JFK* researched and written by John Newman. I would recommend this work to anyone not sure of where they stand on the issue of the Kennedy assassination. After reading John Newman's book, I learned of the amazing wealth of documentation about Lee Harvey Oswald that the FBI and CIA had filed before November 22, 1963. They certainly knew where he was on the day of the assassination, but never connected their own dots. The other aspect was how much effort our government and our politicians expended to cover up information related to the murder of the president. Almost makes me think like the conspiracy types.

John Newman squarely hit the nail on its head with these great questions, "What legal term should we use to describe the action of a government agency when it lies to a presidentially appointed investigation? Obstruction of justice? Can institutions be held accountable if the people who work for them lie to a formal congressional investigation? Is this 'perjury' or 'misleading Congress?'"

I contend the infighting and lack of organization within our structures continues to haunt our agencies. It's similar how we failed to comprehend the threat Hitler posed to the entire world in the 1930s. We couldn't protect a president from an assassination in the 1960s because we didn't pull all the data together. The same thing happened when Saudi nationals were on our soil planning to attack us on 9-11, and then the questions about "weapons of mass destruction" in Iraq. We cannot trust a reasonable conclusion that a Crown Prince murdered a journalist because of the rather provable lack of intelligence of the head Goofball. All documents pertaining to these subjects should be released.

A bad aspect of a national tragedy arises when we are forced to reinterpret words, names and meanings that have been changed by an event. Different emotions are etched into our different brains with different meanings. When I hear someone talk about a beautiful tree on a grassy knoll, I think of the Kennedy Assassination in Dallas. My friend Les Izmor said, "Yeah, I have the same thing when someone talks about school book suppositories." I pointed out that it's "depository" not "suppositories." Both things sound uncomfortable.

The *Ancient Alien* people have a holy spot called Area 51, which is where they claim the US government has been covering up possible evidence of Unidentified Flying Objects (UFOs). According to the CIA, Area 51 is the

Homey Airport and Groom Lake in southern Nevada. The name Area 51 comes from a grid numbering system defined by the Atomic Energy Commission, but that isn't the important thing. Some believe this top-secret place holds the answers to many conspiracy questions such as the existence of UFOs.

The Groom Lake test facility became top secret in 1955 when the CIA used its long runways for the development of the Lockheed U-2 strategic reconnaissance aircraft. If you remember, one of those U-2 planes was shot down over the Soviet Union in 1960 and the pilot, Francis Gary Powers, was captured. Powers was part of a prisoner swap in 1962, but that didn't end the conspiracy talk about Area 51. And by the way, Lee Harvey Oswald was trained on the U-2 radar system before his attempted defection to Russia. Hmmmm.

Let's go back to 1947, when the government claims an Air Force weather balloon fell to the ground in Roswell, New Mexico. The local newspaper, the *Roswell Daily Record*, ran a headline on the front page that announced a flying saucer was **"captured."** I'm sure that caught the attention of many people in the country. Some believe parts of the UFO were taken to Area 51 for study. Others believe the 1969 moon landing was staged and filmed in one of the hangers at the Groom Lake Air Force base. All of this dramatically demonstrates how conspiracy theorists connect the dots and nurture belief in a "deep-government-state." May I continue, with the icing on the cake known as the Majestic 12?

This one begins in 1984 with the discovery of aged "documents" detailing a secret committee of scientists, military leaders, and government officials. The document says this group was brought together in 1947 by an executive order from President Harry S. Truman. The document that appears on the Internet uses the term "Operation Majestic Twelve," but doesn't say what the order is about. According to Alien enthusiasts, the gang of 12 was to recover and investigate alien spacecraft and attempt to verify sightings. All the real documents should be released.

Many experts claim these documents are bogus, especially the one that looks like it was pulled from a fire. Call me crazy, but who half burns something they are trying to destroy? It's just too "made-for-TV" for me to believe.

Conspiracy buffs think the Majestic group was involved in a giant coverup of the alleged 1947 UFO landing in Roswell, New Mexico, but they don't stop there. They claim the first Secretary of Defense, James Forrestal, was assassinated because he was about to reveal to the world the existence of the MJ-12, the shortened name of the Majestic team. Forrestal's death occurred while he was under the care of doctors who had diagnosed him with "reactive depression" and his death was eventually ruled a suicide. Forrestal allegedly jumped to his death from the 16th floor of the National Medical Center in Bethesda, Maryland on May 22, 1949, the day after I was born. Only a coincidence, I'm certain.

Now that would be enough to spin your head around like the little girl in the *Exorcist*, but it gets richer. The Goofballs, who probably created these fake documents, think President John F. Kennedy was about to release all the information about the Majestic 12 and was therefore killed by the CIA.

The entanglement of Area 51, the UFO sighting in Roswell and the Forrestal and Kennedy deaths certainly would make the MJ-12 a good premise for a movie, but until they prove that the big Goofball in the White House is an alien sent here to facilitate the merger of Russia and the United States, I would prefer these rusty metal lunch boxes stay off the grid. You know who you are.

Oh, and the moon landing was fake? Of course, who would ever be able to go to the moon? I mean, it's only 238,900 miles from here. That's only 9.6 trips around the world. People spend hours looking at the moonwalk video and still pictures shot on the orb seeking evidence that it was all faked. Maybe the moon isn't real either. It could be just a large projected visual graphic on a reflective black hole. Then, what did the Chinese space program just land on?

And finally, we come to the most disturbing sect of flag-sucking Americans who have decided, based on, not sure what, that Skull & Bones member George W. Bush blew up the World Trade buildings and launched a rocket into the Pentagon on September 11, 2001 so that our government could return to the Middle East and execute regime change in Iraq. They call themselves the 9/11 Truth Movement and they believe the first attack in history on US soil was an inside job. That is tantamount to taking a piss on the graves of everyone who died because of those incidents that day. All the documents should be released.

Once a conspiracy theory becomes big enough it morphs into a movement and inherits a catchy title or slogan. Then things get weirdly odd. You know, like the "Birther Movement" or, in the case of the JFK assassination, "the mother of all conspiracies."

I was captivated by a story that appeared in the *Washington Post* the day after the 50th anniversary of the assassination of Martin Luther King, Jr. in Memphis. The article was titled *Who killed Martin Luther King Jr.? His Family Believes James Earl Ray was Framed*. I was shocked to learn that many family members believe that the FBI killed MLK and cite J. Edgar Hoover's hatred of King as motivation for the crime. Wow!

The best line in the article comes from Dave Garrow, a Pulitzer Prize-winning biographer of Dr. King, who said, "The King children are part of a larger population of American people who need to believe that the assassination of a King or a Kennedy must be the work of mightier forces rather than victims of small-fry, lifetime losers."

To cap this, I must tell you that I always shake my head when I hear the Ancient Aliens guys claim there is no way the pyramids could have been built by humans. Their laughable claim is the Egyptian slaves would have needed the help of gray aliens from afar. If you tell thousands of men to move a three-ton piece of stone or they will be killed, believe me, those human beings will find a way to get the job done. Don't look down on those "lifetime losers." They were just making sure they weren't beheaded.

Selling Science

The name applied to a thing should clearly match its purpose or meaning. For example, most of the bills that Congress writes have a meaning opposite to their title. The Clean Air Act gives some factories that pollute the air a greater latitude to do so. The poorly named Affordable Care Act (ACA) had no provisions to keep prices of pharmaceuticals under control and affordable. In fifteen years, the cost of a Viagra pill increased from $8 to $50. If that doesn't arouse you in some negative way, you obviously have no sex life!

Scientists' branding of global warming demonstrated their lack of advertising and marketing skill. The name "Global Warming" was poorly chosen. Warming is not necessarily negative to someone who lives in a cold climate. Once the science community figured out the error, they quickly changed the handle to "Climate Change," another poor choice because of its vagueness. Not all change is terrible, but pollution is unhealthy and understandable to a larger audience. Maybe they should have named it "Global Pollution." Doesn't that seem to be a better fit?

When an ocean or lake is polluted, the beaches fill up with crap and dead fish. Everyone gets it. The climate change deniers ignore current data or quote a small number of unqualified scientists who align with their own myopic viewpoint. The Goofballs create rules and regulations that are the exact opposite of how the Environment Protection Agency should remedy the problem. The deniers think they can continue to pollute today and get someone else to clean it up tomorrow. These moldy cheese heads question whether climate change is even caused by people. HUH?

I was in Wellington, New Zealand in their winter of 1996. It was a brisk, biting day with a stiff wind and low temperatures. I was getting cabin fever and wanted to escape my hotel room, so I decided to take a short walk down to the dock at the bottom of the hill. When I got back to my hotel room, the bathroom mirror disclosed my big fat bright red face. I had been gone no more than half an hour and thought, "Wow, that wind must have been worse than it felt."

It wasn't until later that night when a co-worker commented, "Boy, you really got some sun today." Then I realized I was seeing evidence of how we've been slowly destroying the ozone layer with our cars and factories. We humans have created an atmospheric hole over Australia and New Zealand. This was an eye-opening environmental lesson. If we continue, we will not only melt the ice caps, we will also burn the skin cells off our faces. China, with their massive pollution problem, will create an equally damaging hole over America. You should hope you aren't going bald. And, as of this writing, the head Goofball pulled the USA out of the Paris Climate Accord, so I hope you are still around to read this book.

I live on the west coast of Florida and we have a nastiness in the Gulf of Mexico water called "Red Tide." Don't be fooled by the colorful name, it's a discoloration of seawater caused by the Karenia brevis bloom of toxic red dinoflagellates, and it can burn the eyes and irritate the respiratory system of certain humans. Oh yeah, it also kills sea life.

The Mote Marine Laboratory of Sarasota, Florida and two universities researched and explained that Red Tide is caused by leaking sewage, runoff of mining waste and agriculture fertilizers and pesticides. All these MAN-MADE THINGS are creating lethal conditions for the corals. The Goofballs in Washington who claim the whole climate change thing is a hoax and not man made should remove their heads from their anuses. Their brains are polluted!

If we knew that living in a home for many years with tons of asbestos in the walls would hurt us, would we have stayed? Let's make a promise to every person dying of lung cancer, mesothelioma or asbestosis poisoning that we will do everything we can to eliminate any further human exposure to poisons and pollutants. That is the least a moral nation could do, right? Many structures built before 1980 contain asbestos. We didn't ban the use of asbestos until 1989. Personal medical crises wake up the living and get people's attention, but there are still many other polluting chemicals out there.

Someone should have known that a new source of water (a polluted river) sent through decaying pipes in Flint, Michigan would contaminate the water. How could someone make a decision based on budget rather than the health of the populace? They took a path any expert could have told them would become an environmental tragedy to simply achieve cheaper water.

The result of the contaminated water in Flint is children who will have lower IQs. Those public Goofballs sentenced many families to a less productive life. The people in power and Michigan's cover-up-governor ignored the science and data at the expense of their citizens.

If you think a vaccine will do harm to your children and you purposely avoid a medically safe way to protect them, you aren't being a good parent. Saying it that way might make you feel a little uptight because no parent wants to be told they are doing a bad job raising their kids, but you are just another victim of "fake news." I remind you that vaccines wiped out Smallpox, Rinderpest, Poliomyelitis (polio). Dracunculiasis, Yaws, Malaria, Hookworm, Lymphatic filariasis, Hookworm, Measles, Rubella, Onchocerciasis, Bovine spongiform encephalopathy, Syphilis and Rabies in this country. Why would we want to go backwards?

A bunch of scientists wearing white lab coats helped us conquer these scourges, but there are total dingbats on TV saying you should merely let God do his work. Ask Steve Jobs how that worked out for him. Spiritual treatments and cosmic cures are great fodder for self-help books, but don't work all that well in the real world.

Americans should embrace science, not Washington politicians. The Goofballs are not qualified to comment on medicine and healthcare. There are too many times when credentialed doctors in Congress follow the voting plan proposed by their big pharm donors, not their constituents. When you hear someone in Congress open a statement with, "Well, I'm a doctor," that's your warning to get a second opinion. I wouldn't let someone like Dr. Rand Paul near my eyes, my wallet or my children.

There is an anti-science scheme being cooked up by some folks who cling closely to a belief system based on the final redemption rather than caring for those living on this planet right now. This anti-intellectual conspiracy has been promoted by generations buttressed by generalizations from self-ordained holy ones and frothing at the mouth nincompoops. The use of social media megaphones to dissuade people from medicine is disheartening.

These overly certain zealots cast doubt on what it all means because science wasn't covered in the holy books from thousands of years ago. Technology wasn't yet invented when those books were written, but we look to the text contained there for all answers. Why? Good journalistic reporters and editors ask an important question, "Do you have three sources?" They require three sources. What would Jesus think if you stood by and didn't use a man-made miracle medication to keep another human being alive? Which three sources guide you on the drugs you give your kids?

These are the same convoluted half-wits who did their thing with cigarettes, especially when their local economy was driven by tobacco harvests. Using marketing and lawyers, tobacco corporations conned millions of Americans into believing that smoking cigarettes was good for them. Thankfully, science ultimately won. Negative medical reality crept into enough people's lives and doctors finally stood up to big tobacco and explained, "Yes, Uncle Louie died of lung cancer caused by his lifetime of smoking cigarettes."

I had nothing to do with killing these marketing messengers, but it's a fact that at least four "Marlboro Men" died of smoking-related diseases. A guy named Philip Morris (whose namesake cigarette company is now called Altria Group, Inc.) named his new brand of cigarette, the "Miracle of Marlboro." Those who used the product needed a miracle to survive. We always thought "miracles" were the province of the Lord, not Madison Avenue, and we still let these companies make money by killing Americans. By the way, fun fact here, Philip Morris died of cancer in 1873.

According to CBS News, "More than two of every five Americans reside in counties with unhealthy levels of smog and air pollution, thanks largely to the effect of global warming." And they added, "Of the 25 cities with the highest ozone levels, 16 experienced an increase in high-ozone days in 2016." Many were in smog-plagued California. I have no respect for any of those catheter bags who claim climate change is a hoax. What fucking planet are you living on?

If you have experience scuba diving, you know what is seen at the bottom of oceans, bays and rivers, alarming garbage heaps. We use 500 million plastic drinking straws every day. They get in the gills and nostrils of sea life, killing them. Between the beer cans and wine bottles, I wonder why the Earth hasn't exploded in defiance of mankind. Maybe that's what volcanos are all about. What you can't see will hurt you and what is on the surface will disgust you. There are floating masses of debris slowing making their way to our shores. If only we could find out who put all that trash in the ocean and make them clean it up.

Our science has taken us far and we need to heed the warnings of our brilliant scientists about **"Global Pollution."** God didn't give us cell phones, science did. God didn't give us Guns, man created weapons and perfected them. The Goofballs don't have a vision about the future, because they cannot apply what they do not understand.

Humans & Technology

I was moved when viewing a nature film that showed how monkeys use sharp rocks to break open nuts. Some experts say we share over 90% of our DNA with our primate cousins. Just like those distant relatives, we always find unique ways to put food into our mouths, protect our women and offspring and take terrible risks for sex. Animals and insects love to get laid as much as we humans do.

There is no way you are going to train a monkey to use a spreadsheet to determine risk factors on Wall Street, but if you could combine all the smart habits and actions of all the monkeys, birds and reptiles in the world into one animal, you would have the basic human prototype. We are the mistake that happened when some negative traits were eliminated, while other more useful ones, like language, were developed. We change because of evolution. We lost the things we didn't need or use, like tons of body hair and a long tail. We no longer sleep in trees and hardly ever play with our poop.

We don't have time to trace all the inventions and advancements that have taken place in our history, but we will attempt to make some sense of how people have changed because of our technology. One might say we have suffered significant "permanent damage" because we've lost much of the animal in us. While some dedicate their lives to inventing things to make life safer and easier for mankind, others exploit our remaining animal instincts. Screw the brain damage and hand me my cell phone so I can win an argument by using Google.

I stand in my kitchen staring at the toaster and insert a couple pieces of bread. Being an impatient person, I complain to myself that it's 2019 and question why I must wait so long to get a slice of toast. Yes, inventions create an expectation of faster and better but, for now, we wait for our toast.

Things radically changed with the printing press. Later, the disruptive technology of digital data took us into a land far removed from Johannes Gutenberg's ink on paper. We breathe the ether of a connected world every day.

I worked at an international software company for more than fifteen years and this affords me a unique vantage point. I was an electronics hobbyist when I was young, so my viewpoint is also grounded with the simple premise that **we can't stop technology.** Artificial intelligence will become at least as smart and powerful as humans in the next twenty years. Okay, do you feel better now?

Hey, the toaster just announced that I am an idiot. Wait, the toaster can talk? One of things humans find so frustrating revolves around what I call the "toaster complex." We know how to make toast in milliseconds, but we don't want to employ that kind of a super technology in the home. It's too dangerous and expensive to produce, so we do things the older way. We didn't invent fire, we discovered it.

Now let me ask you this. Have you ever wondered why music-on-hold always sounds so bad? Yes, the musical selections are horrible, but I'm talking about the audio quality. Telephones use an 8-bit technology and we will have to live with distorted audio until all the phones in the world evolve into fully digital devices. The audio of most our TV shows and movies is 24-bit or 32-bit, providing high quality and enhancements such as surround sound.

After we moved forward with digital televisions, the government decided to end the use of regular analog transmission and commanded all TV channels to move to digital. That's why you had to throw out all those old TV sets. The telephone industry will be slower, if it ever moves at all. Cell phones have pretty much taken over and most likely, landlines will eventually disappear. As long as the 911 emergency system works, people don't really care about clarity on a phone call. Cell phone dropout and audio distortion are horrible, but we can hope for a day when those problems will be solved. Patience is the only medicine for "toaster syndrome."

We've moved to greater video resolution, bringing us closer to the way the human eye processes light and images, however even with 4K and Ultra-HD our brains remain susceptible to tricks such as optical illusions. We sometimes question what we have captured with our eyes or ears and processed with our brains. Is the dress blue or yellow? Did he say Yanni or Laurel? We not only disagree with others, we disagree with ourselves. So much for the eyewitness.

Technology now converts content to a digital data stream of 1s and 0s which can be moved rapidly over copper wires or high-bandwidth fiber optics. Copper moves electrical pulses, while fiber carries light waves faster than electricity. Any private communication or intellectual property stored on a device or server connected to the internet or to an intranet is traceable at best and hackable at worst. Don't trust any fool who tries to sell you an "impenetrable" security product to keep your data safe. They are lying when they guarantee their product or service. Any data present on a connected device is simply not safe. There is no technology that cannot be compromised by someone having enough smarts and time.

I am impressed when my new car sends me an email stating that my windshield wiper fluid is low. Oh wait, how do they know that? One aspect is your car's Global Positioning System (GPS) spying on you. This was made possible by orbiting satellites, and we can all thank science fiction writer Arthur C. Clarke for the geostationary orbits of satellites used to relay radio signals. Never stop the imagination of a writer. But wait, what else are those satellites tracking? Could my GPS be used against me in the future? Of course. This data is already being applied in cases to prove someone was where they said they weren't.

The insurance company asked me to put a chip in the car to transmit my driving habits to them, so they could lower my insurance premium. They monitored my quick stops, heavy accelerations and other meaningless data points to evaluate my driving. The fact that I stopped quickly to avoid an accident gave me a lower grade and, thus, a smaller discount. Does that make sense? It's all a ruse, a marketing gimmick. Without a camera looking over my shoulder to see what actually happened, those stats are meaningless. Since you are wondering, yes, the car has four cameras, two in the front for lane and collision driving alerts and two in the back for accident prevention. How long will it be until they position that camera to watch my every move? Do you really think manufacturers of products are giving you services for free? Somewhere along the line they will use that data to design new products or to sell you more things.

The notion that we're going to be able to stop drunk driving is foolhardy. The fact is, people drink and will figure out a way to beat the system, just like some people thwart the seatbelt buzzer by plugging in the belt behind their back. As stupid as that is, it's how some people think, and when they are drunk, they don't think at all.

This would be a good time to mention the effects of driving high on pot. We can't detect a driver who is "high." I'm not worried about the long-term pothead who can function baked, blazed or blitzed. I worry more about the first-time marijuana smoker who can't handle the high and loses it behind the wheel. What, me worry?

Say, here's another idea that really doesn't do much, the Emergency Notification System. Is it supposed to give us a sense of security? As we learned recently with the Presidential Alert test, not everyone received it. If you are wondering why your favorite TV show is interrupted by testing of the system, so am I. It serves more to desensitize us rather than make us ready. And can we please get a new audio sounder for that warning? The current one sounds like an old computer modem!

Then there are those weather flashes on TV when a tornado is coming. They make a lot of sense and can save lives, but who watches TV when asleep? The citizen-driven initiative of "Amber Alerts" and "Silver Alerts" can help you find little Amber or Uncle Silver, but those are low-tech solutions. An embedded chip in another human would be high tech. Are we ready for that? Are we ready to inject our babies with tracking microchips?

We learned a serious lesson recently when a false alert was transmitted in Hawaii. It was proof that the human error factor will always be with us. Only months later, the volcano Kilauea erupted on the Big Island of Hawaii and people still didn't leave until the last possible moment. So much for warnings. They didn't leave even when people banged on their front door pleading them to find shelter. Hot lava bombs would get my attention.

As more mistakes and misinformation are fed into the human mind, we sometimes disbelieve even when real danger is present. Remember that jet airliner accident where an engine exploded and killed one of the passengers? Well some Goofballs on that flight were shooting selfies rather than making sure their oxygen masks were properly placed on their birdbrain heads.

We watch so much TV that people who get caught up in a bad event say they feel like they are in a slow-motion scene in a movie. We have slowly orientated ourselves to blend in with technology, and our brains have started to process data the way a camera, or computer would.

Have we become less human and more gullible because we spend so much time watching stupid videos on our phones? Have our brains been damaged by technology?

In the 2016 US Presidential Election, we learned that vast numbers of Americans will believe just about anything. Yes, both sides of the political spectrum allowed an enterprise to convince us that by creating a detailed profile of our thoughts, friends, locations and actions our lives would be better. After they sold all that data to third-parties, the doors and windows were wide open, and a foreign power poked and tweaked our inner minds. We became emotionally driven to hate both candidates. Wow, and we Americans think we are smart.

You clicked OK and gave someone you don't even know permission to make money with your thoughts and prayers. It's the same as letting someone into your house to download all the data on your computers and devices, take pictures of your habitat and your kids and give you a radioactive tattoo that can track your every move. Had you read the End User License Agreement (EULA) you would have known what the bastards were up to and maybe wouldn't have clicked the aptly titled "Submit" button.

One giant step toward our "brave new world" came when the founders of Google, Larry Page and Sergey Brin, sat down with Eric Schmidt, their marketing executive, who suggested the company's knowledge of peoples' internet searches could allow Google to be monetized by selling targeted advertising to their users. Game over. They got rich, America got fucked.

And might I say something here for the dearly departed? If you don't give your Facebook password to someone before you die, your page will go on forever. I have friends who have been dead for years and people still send them Happy Birthday notices. I even saw a post the other day that said, "LARRY, CALL ME! WHY ARE YOU IGNORING ME?" It's sad that they never noticed that good old Larry left the planet five years ago. So, Facebook, Twitter and Google won't delete your data even when you're dead. Hey, at least you won't be forgotten.

Once social media connected you to your behavior, they were able to control you. Facebook, Twitter and all similar platforms are the ultimate narcissistic tools of self-importance, but their most important commodity for sale is YOU. Every day, "showrunners" at social media are peddling you to advertisers who make products or promote political candidates. This isn't their fault, it's yours. Grin and bear it, buddy. Awareness matters. Pay attention next time.

In God We Trust

This phrase is everywhere in America, from famous Washington, D.C. buildings to our one-dollar bill. Why do we use it so much? Well, it goes back to 1782 when it was applied to the official seal of the land and has been our motto ever since.

On July 30, 1956, President Dwight Eisenhower declared "In God We Trust" must appear on all American currency. This set up the tireless joke, "In God We Trust, but all others must pay cash." The expression appears in the Holy Bible and the Quran, and most other religions have no problem with the suggestion that God is always watching over us and will take care of us. However, it really smacks the First Amendment upside the head. The first line of the First Amendment states, "Congress shall make no law respecting an establishment of religion…" Part of what makes America such a mystery to many people around the world is we state our case in crystal clear language, then totally ignore it.

There is an ongoing assumption with the deeply devout in America that God woke up in the late 17th Century and decided to create the best goddamn country in the world, not necessarily in his image, but certainly with a strong endorsement. He looked around and said, "Okay, where can we establish this new, perfect union?" We must have been the "chosen" land mass.

Our founding fathers attempted to validate everything they did by finding the right part of the Bible to bring consequence to their cause. They justified slavery and they gave only white, male land owners the right to vote, while spouting those wonderful words about all men being created equal. By the way, they really meant "men." No matter what might happen in their new world, they knew they trusted God. As they threw off the yoke of a British

King, they surely felt their new country was ordained by a higher power, God himself.

By having God on our side, we knew he would be more powerful than any elected official in our country. God takes an equal seat in any country ruled by a king or queen. Royalty usually defends their actions with the premise they have been ordained to rule by God. A core American belief is that no man is above God or the law. We should always remember this.

It's said that moderation is a wonderful idea and, in this case, it's good that the US government doesn't push this "In God We Trust" thing too far. There are those who misuse the slogan for their own political gain and propaganda. For example, all the paper money and coinage in America can clearly state that we trust in our God but should someone attempt to raise a plaque carved with the Ten Commandments on a public building get ready for a big federal case. You don't have to look any further than the case of Glassroth vs. Moore in Alabama. Yes, that is the same Roy Moore who tried to get into Congress.

While he was the Chief Justice of the Alabama Supreme Court, Moore ordered a mammoth piece of granite engraved with the Ten Commandments and had it installed in the courthouse without anyone's knowledge. I'm not sure how long the dogmatic lunatic and accused hebephile thought he was going to keep that big piece of rock secret, but his methods and decisions were questioned by many. Judge Moore refused to remove the stone, claiming that the Ten Commandments were the basis of the establishment of law in this country. Several courts ordered Moore to get rid of the large edifice, and he was later removed from his office and charged with judicial misconduct for failing to comply with a federal court order to do away with it. The monument was eventually taken out of the public building. It's funny how one man's effort to bring his belief in God into his job site could make people crazy when we have "In God We Trust" plastered everywhere. Isn't this the ultimate example of a double standard?

In case you think I'm defending Roy Moore, I'm not. I'm just looking at this thing from both sides. Let's play a little game. Imagine that in the town of Pleasantville USA we have a judge named Abdul Khavari, a devoted Muslim man. He decides it would be a great idea to erect a huge stone on the courthouse containing the ten most important Islamic Sharia Laws. You know what would happen. And now, let's go to Slippery Junction USA where a judge on the local court is one of the most undevout atheists in the land. This man is so totally over the top with his anti-God rhetoric it's hard to imagine how he got to be a judge. His name is Russell Bertrand. One day he decides to get a three-ton block of granite engraved with quotes from Christopher Hitchens, Richard Dawkins and Stephen Hawking stating that God doesn't exist. Judge Bertrand would be taken out back and shot, or at least removed from his courtroom.

It's clear to me that anyone in government, no matter how large or small, must get over this concept of being right about God and religion. Stop ignoring the First Amendment. There is a reason why James Madison originally wrote 17 amendments that were whittled down to 12 and eventually became the final ten amendments, not Ten Commandments. That is the kind of compromise that makes America work, even if it takes a bit longer to get things done. We do this to avoid mistakes.

God isn't wearing a USA T-shirt and looking over us; he's there only for the people who want or need him. And why do we make him a male? We were told by the men who wrote all our foundational documents that God is a guy. Of course, these early scribes couldn't possibly imagine a female supreme deity. If they did, American women wouldn't have had to wait so long to cast their votes. Equal pay is still being thwarted by our "In God We Trust" mantra. A female God would have certainly written maternity leave into the laws of our land. Oh my God, I'm blaming him for wage inequality. That's a ballsy move. Oops, male reference, again.

There are those who argue that without a belief in God all morality will melt away. That is total malarkey. Just because someone doesn't believe in God doesn't mean their soul has no moral fiber. If a person doesn't believe they have a soul, it doesn't mean they can't have human respect with a humane grounding. I don't need God to have love for my fellow man or woman. What does God have to do with love?

I have always been disturbed that the Ten Commandments never clearly declared that general LYING IS WRONG! There are some scholars who say bearing false witness is far more than perjury, but the commandments originated in Jewish tradition and they say "perjury" isn't the same as "lying."

The ancient Jewish scholars who wrote the Bible and curated the Moses myth never wrote, **"Thou shall not lie."** Some believe they left out a direct commandment on lying because a lie might be needed to keep someone in the tribe from being murdered. They wanted to be able to say, "No, Mr. Roman soldier, we don't have any male children in this house." The person of faith didn't have to commit a sin to save his brethren by lying to the soldier.

There are those, especially Catholics, who will claim that lying is a sin, no matter when it happens. But clearly, the priority of the scriptures was to guard against perjury. Moses wanted to establish more than a moral code with the Ten Commandments, he was also giving legalistic guidance to his flock. The Bible mentions those who were unjustly charged and sentenced to death. If you follow the ancient writings, you know that general lying is forgivable if it doesn't involve perjury. If you want to emulate God you would never lie, because God in unable to lie. If you do lie, according to the Holy

Bible, you should get the same punishment as the person who you perjured got unjustly.

Our US law is based on the agreement that we must tell the truth, so help us God! Whether your hand is on a bible or not, you are compelled to tell the truth in a court of law.

The other rules like, no graven images, only one God, don't use the Lord's name when swearing and keep the Sabbath holy all seem reasonable, but as Bill Maher pointed out the first commandments seem to be focused on the deity. The political comedian also said that nowhere in the commandments are there bans on "torture, rape, child abuse, incest or slavery." That's true.

We want to honor our parents, not kill anyone, not steal, and not bear false witness against our neighbors. We do not want to covet our friend's house, animals, servants or his wife., But nowhere does the Bible say that general LYING IS A SIN.

It's a myth that Moses wrote the commandments more than three thousand years ago. The story goes that God dictated them to Moses and he inscribed them on two tablets. Then Moses came down from Mount Sinai, not the hospital but the real mountain, and laid down the laws.

Even though America trusts in God, we haven't figured out how to rid our society of its greatest problems. The Goofballs are still frothing at the mouth, telling us what we should learn, who we should believe and exactly how we should live. Who died and made them boss?

No one has ever convinced me that placing my trust in God is somehow going to make things better for everyone in America. It seems to work only for the believers, who then disregard everyone else's feelings or thoughts about belief systems and deities.

If it makes them happier, great for them, but there are some questions that need to be answered right now. Why do we send prayers and thoughts when people are suffering after a mass shooting? I'm not being disrespectful. I do subscribe to the old maxim, avoid saying anything bad about the dead, but Hitler deserves no respect, just as dead mass shooters deserve what they got. And, if they are taken alive, they shouldn't receive notoriety from mass media. The shooter may be the story for 72 hours, but their victims are dead forever.

When we say we are praying for those who have died, we are hoping they get into heaven. I guess that makes sense. We pray for the survivors and hope they can cope with the tragedy and that seems righteous. The pain and suffering of losing a loved one sometimes produces guilt. Those people will need empathy and sympathy for the rest of their lives. We get that, but goddamn it, how do we stop the next killing spree?

Trusting in God doesn't eliminate an evil person's free will. When their twisted mind drives them to massacre people with automatic weapons, sending thoughts and prayers is a shallow effort. What we should be doing is making the Goofballs in Washington do something, **anything**, to make this country safer. Obviously, trusting in God has not worked. Sorry, but that's a fact.

Believing in Money

I feel good when I have money in my pocket. The opinions of those half-baked philosophers and bible-thumping idealists who espouse money can't buy happiness are idiots. Those are loopy propositions put forth by people who either have little wealth or have lots of money but still aren't happy. Money, if properly managed, can make a person feel secure, warm and important.

I remember a conversation I had with my father in the early 1970s when we were discussing the salaries of professional athletes at that time. I brought up Alvin Hayes, who had been given a contract to play for the then Washington Bullets basketball team for $250,000. At the time, he was the highest paid player in basketball. Later in this essay, we will reveal who the highest paid player is today.

Much to my surprise, my father went crazy, "No man is worth that much money!" I quickly pointed out Johnny Carson, the host of NBC's *The Tonight Show*, made one million dollars a year. Then he went off the reservation saying the "dirty, foul-mouthed comedian" shouldn't be paid that much. Of course, my father was from another generation so I internally chuckled and let him rant. Then I asked, "If someone asks for a certain amount of money and their employer agrees, wouldn't that mean that the company thought their employee was worth it?"

I understood my father's frustration. He delivered milk for a living and never made more than $15,000 a year, but I also saw the dichotomy of being a good Christian while seeming to covet his neighbor's money. Maybe my father's emotional response was rooted in his lack of upward mobility. After all, he had to leave his wife and first daughter to go overseas to fight the Nazis. He never went back to Europe and hated all he experienced in the World War. This farm boy from Knox, Pennsylvania had a reasonable expectation that his national sacrifice would be rewarded properly. After leaving the farm, he traveled to the big city and became a truck driver and salesman. He was a teamster. He was a union guy. Over the years he saw some of his contemporaries do much better than he did, but he was always supported by his religious faith. He never publicly disrespected those who had more than he did, and he always worked hard for everything he received. He was a proud American and feared debt, which led to the same deep-seated vexation then that many middle-class people feel today.

The distribution of wealth has always been an intellectual discussion with the haves and have nots on either side of the issue. In this country you will quickly be labeled a "communist," or the lesser term "socialist," if you talk about taxing the 1% of the richest to help the other 99%. Even the "good-old" New Testament logic of helping the poor is pooh-poohed. Why? Where is the disconnect between what Jesus taught and how we deal with poverty and the distribution of wealth?

We have no problem passing laws to protect the tax-free status of churches and non-profit groups, which I guess provides a hint of community good, but we have not solved the problem of wealth inequality in the United States. Some suggest that a giant tax-cut for the rich will eventually "trickle down" to the middle and lower-class communities. This is one of the great myths in America. Better stated, it's bullshit.

Some people consider any donation of "their" money to poor people as a socialistic gift from the government, and they would rather not give the money to less successful people. They don't realize that poor people without food could eventually revolt and justify their criminal actions based on a need to get money for food or drugs to dull the pain.

Few conservative people can link lower crime rates, better home values and fewer disruptions in schools to our citizens' more creative use of aid. They have no problem with the US Treasury dishing out funds to build schools on the west bank in Israel, but they fight back hard when social programs are proposed to help people here at home.

America justifies moving money from education to the military every year. The priorities are concocted by the military-industrial-corporate-lobbyist complex, and they steer tax payers' money to things that don't necessarily help the country but fulfill the fear initiative used to rule our nation.

In the richest and most powerful country in the world, why are we always being asked for handouts? Recently, I was asked to contribute to a goodie bag for soldiers fighting on one of the many fronts we inhabit around the world. The sponsoring organization was buying beef jerky and toothpaste for their heroes. Really? Why would any soldier fighting for America need such a supply line? I remember people collecting money for troops' body armor during the Iraq War. What? Why wouldn't the US government provide for all their soldiers' needs?

Here's where I will insert a comment by Donald Rumsfeld, the feckless Secretary of Defense under George W. Bush. He said, "You fight a war with the army you have, not the army you want." Really? Where did all the money go?

How many times have you been asked if you want to give a dollar for this or that charity at the checkout counter? You might want to get your name on one of those paper stickers behind the cash register, but what is at the bottom of it all? Why do we need to prop up these goodie-two-shoed organizations who use a commercial establishment such as a grocery store to suck more money out of us? Once we open our wallet, we are asked again and again to give more money. Why is only the middle class requested to donate? Where are the rich people?

Well, you see, there's a trend here. Rich people become so rich the only way they can protect more of their money is to create non-profit foundations that give away money. On the surface this looks like a great way to spread the wealth, and most well-to-do folks convince themselves that they are doing something good. While their accountants earn big bucks keeping their clients' money, the little guy is pressured to comply. We need to keep a cautionary eye on each campaign to make sure we aren't being scammed. Foundations look good on paper, but without total transparency it's impossible to know where the dough goes.

Some of our Goofballs, and you know who they are, attempt to discolor all foundations and make them seem like evil influence peddlers, or worse, a political criminal enterprise. That is not what I am suggesting here, but if one sets up a foundation to influence people into doing good things, then no charge can be brought. If a foundation is set up to pay personal bills however, the founders should be jailed. That's an IRS violation.

A foundation will either donate funds to support other organizations or provide the source of funding for its own charitable purposes. Now here's where things get dicey. They can give money to themselves. Yes, the cost of FUND RAISING is an expense that can be written off, but when the president of a non-profit foundation is making more money than the President of the United States, something is wrong.

Rich people protect their money, but they also give to good causes. The government tends to protect businesses and corporations more than the middle-class people. Look at train safety, for example. The government has the power to mandate safety railway devices to protect passengers, but they constantly delay the deadlines for installations because the transit companies complain that it's too expensive. People are continually killed or harmed by similar kinds of corporate neglect. Nine times out of ten, the inaction is blamed on cost. Risk assessment teams balance the worth of a human life against the reduced profits should they do something positive, like Positive Train Control, pun intended.

The airline industry and the Federal Aviation Administration (FAA) have cooked up an idea of "cooperative compliance" on rules and regulations. It's a thinly disguised delay tactic. When an airplane's jet engine bursts apart, the FAA seems to look the other way. Are they complicit in the myth that increased prices will hurt the industry? Safety costs shouldn't be part of the equation. Why must money trump human life?

All of this is a common theme in the history of the United States. We didn't want to end slavery because of the economic burden of losing free labor in the south. We waited forever to break up the monopolies because the money was flowing to all the right people. It took a zealot like Teddy Roosevelt to end monopolies and create a level playing field where competition drove service and price. Still, the balance of corporate profits against what's good for the people remains extremely uneven.

Here's another dark side of money that many people don't want to confront. War makes money. In his April 7, 1954 press conference, President Dwight Eisenhower used the term, "domino theory" as it pertained to Southeast Asia. It probably led to 58,220 US military deaths in Vietnam and more than two million Vietnamese fatalities in the almost 20-year war. There's always a concrete reason for entering a war, but the justifications to stay in a war can be complicated beyond logic. We waited forever to take on Hitler, but in Iraq we acted on one person's word. At least we now know what WMD means (Weapons of Mass Destruction).

There are two powerful forces at work here. One is we must HONOR the dead with more fighting. We can't seem to walk away from any war because life has already been lost, even though continuation causes more death without peace. Study the Vietnam War and the lies that kept it going for years beyond the realization that staying in Vietnam was NOT going to work out well. The Generals reported accurate body counts of the Viet Cong army but kept the US death toll secret.

In 1951, New York Times Vietnam reporter Seymour Topping told the new Senator John F. Kennedy that he shouldn't rely on reports that the French were winning the war. Others gave Kennedy advice that war in Vietnam would be a deep black hole for our government. Back then, the great America war machine hadn't yet made it to Vietnam. We had "advisors" there. Now any time you hear the word advisors, understand that it usually leads to war with fewer advisors, more soldiers and much killing.

The other prevailing force is MONEY. States where governmental contracts flourish may be deeply invested in the manufacturing of war armaments. Rigid support of a war effort is promoted by those Senators and Representatives with financial skin in the game. It's really a deal with the devil when they say, "I'll make my local economy better and they will reelect me," while these same Goofballs vote to send more young men and women from their districts to their deaths on foreign soil. It's a "Gordian Knot" with the enemy death count driving the justification for more war. It's a dangerous folly when we claim we must honor those fallen heroes with more war. Politicians even use the phrase, "So, they didn't die in vain" to justify more troops, more surges and, ultimately, more death. Remember the slogan of the GIs in southeast Asia, "I don't want to be the last man sent home in a body bag from Vietnam." Were they thinking about winning or just getting the hell out of there?

In 2001, George W. Bush's Vice President, Dick Cheney, was awarded more than $34 million as his exit package from Halliburton, his former employer (according to papers he filed with the proper agencies). Halliburton then became the go-to contractor for the Iraq War, and the company reportedly earned around $39 billion dollars "helping out" in Iraq. You might dismiss this as simple case of "crony capitalism" but, more accurately, it was a quid pro quo that Cheney pushed through the fog of war.

It's the old gambit, "They paid me so now I must help them make some money too. No harm in that." **Really?**

According to a Congressional Budget Office (CBO) report published in October 2007, the US wars in Iraq and Afghanistan cost taxpayers a total of $2.4 trillion after including the huge interest costs needed by the financing of combat with borrowed money. And one of the missing parts of most of these "little wars" is the lack of planning on what happens after the fight is done. Max Boot, in his new book *The Corrosion of Conservatism: Why I Left the Right* said it best, "Without a political solution, no amount of military action can achieve decisive results." You, think?

Yes, War equals Money. There are those who get rich on the death and destruction while America taxpayers foot the bill. That old maxim, "We have to fight them over there, so we don't have to fight them here!" is pure Neo-Con bullshit. We always pay for war with Gold and human life. Realize that we financed and trained Bin Laden's Al Qaeda army to fight against the Russians in Afghanistan. Once Al Qaeda won that war, they plotted and carried off the 9-11 attacks. We are nonsensical.

The current host of *The Tonight Show* makes around $14 million annually and the top basketball player in the NBA scores $38.5 million per year. We have elevated these people far, far beyond the salaries I discussed with my father 40 years ago. Is LeBron James worth $38.5 million per year? The Los Angeles Lakers think so.

Funny how we know how much those famous people make, but we haven't seen the tax returns of the Goofballs in Congress or the White House. It's time for Congress to draft a transparency bill that would make it a law for anyone running for President, Senate or the House to disclose their tax returns. Hell, even the Supreme Court justices should disclose. I'll keep saying that until I die.

Curious Customs

I find it challenging trying to explain how America works when talking with people from other countries. By traveling throughout the world, I have learned that how we see ourselves much differently than the way we are seen by others.

I use the term, "the ugly American" to label a person presenting the very worst behavior to the world. We have a bizarrely abnormal habit when speaking to someone who we think doesn't speak our language. We talk slowly but in an extremely LOUD and boisterous manner. It gives the listener an impression that we think they're stupid. When we run into a problem in another country, we tend to make an unquestionably embarrassing fuss. Do we have a built in expectation that the world revolves around us?

Just imagine the thoughts of a foreigner visiting America and dealing with our crazy attitudes, methods and customs. If they visited a few years ago and watched ads on TV, they would have thought that every man in this country was suffering from erectile dysfunction. In 2018, they could easily believe that most Americans suffer from psoriasis and mesothelioma. Our media serves up streaks of TV overdose and hype on the latest wonder drugs. It's how we roll. Big pharm wants to drain our bank accounts before we die.

Yes, other countries are guilty of encouraging thoughtless and outrageous behavior, but America has lots of egg on our collective faces. Fraternities and sororities at our universities and colleges often haze their pledges. These unlawful initiations have caused great harm to many college students. There is at least one hazing death every year on our college campuses. Until recently, these dangerous non-inclusion groups have gotten away with murder. The Greek society tradition should be ended. We aren't fucking Greeks, we are Americans. And don't get me started on "date rape."

Then there's this troubling statistic. According to the Washington Post, "More than 26,000 children and teens have been killed in gun violence since 1999." Why are we unable to protect our precious children at school? When asked by outsiders why we have so many Guns, we brag about our Second Amendment rights. Just like ancient man justified throwing a virgin off the cliff, we say we can't change our tradition, our history, our heritage. Many Americans feel that our Constitution is an unbreakable, unchangeable, sacred document. Well, that's not logical. Between 1789 and 1992 there have been 17 modifications. But we must be careful who proposes changes. There are a couple of guys in Wichita, Kansas who would like to end many of your rights. Google: Koch Brothers.

We are proud of our quirky traditions, like asking for a doggie bag to take home uneaten food from a restaurant. Most of us asking don't even have a dog. We are a land of confused souls and distracted humans. We got excited about O.J. Simpson's slow-moving white Bronco chase and wondered whether Patty Hearst really became a murderous radical after being kidnapped. But many times, we neglect what is important. We spend hours of time and emotional capital being involved in long trials and dramas. (Google: Lorena Bobbitt) Even our episodic dramas on TV with storylines ripped right out of the headlines create a modified reality for us to digest. It's a lazy way to write, but it pays well, and we already know the back story. The fact that an average viewer knows the definition of "back story" sums up our media brains.

Is American life so dull and meaningless that we are lured into watching fake reality shows to validate our "normal" status? We get so close to the characters and competitors in these shows that we expect people in real life to behave in the same way. When we see something outrageous happening, even when it involves violence, we don't run away. We move closer to the event with our cell phone's video camera capturing the incident.

I remember a story from Miami in 1986. A couple witnessed a shootout on their street and, instead of calling the cops, they sat in their lawn chairs watching what they thought was the filming of a Miami Vice episode. Traffic continued to roll down 82nd Avenue through the gunfight, which was an actual FBI shootout. Four people died and five were wounded. We document many events as if it's our duty, even if it means we might lose our lives. WTF?

We fill our waxed cups to the brim with iced sugar juices and drink copious amounts of caffeinated beverages. We swallow profuse ounces of liquid "energy" drinks, concocted with a bunch of vitamin B, taurine, ginseng, gingko biloba and, of course, sugar. When the high wears off, we have another. We may be as orally driven as any other nation, but Americans get especially nasty when our mouths are empty. Just watch what happens when someone tries to break into a food line.

Scores of people spend entire days with earbuds jammed into their heads, effectively avoiding any interpersonal contact. Oh, sure there's a nod here or there, but many people choose to live in their own private Idaho without ever engaging another soul. Then there are others who can't pull themselves away from their mobile device. Such a person will turn their car around and backtrack ten miles to retrieve the cell phone they left at home. I had a major encounter with a woman in a movie theater the other day while she was watching another movie on her iPad and half-watching the movie we paid to see. This "second screen experience" is annoying and disrespectful of the actors and producers of these multi-million dollars works of art, as well as me!

We place ourselves in certain danger by text messaging while walking or driving. Our amazing mobile technology has become an addiction, and we should be aware the whole world will follow us. America sets the trends, so our curious habits eventually become the world's "new normal."

We love to blow things up. It's in our national anthem, And the rocket's red glare, the bombs bursting in air…" Sad to say we didn't invent fireworks. The Chinese claim that one, but we certainly know how to use them to celebrate a country that's never far from the next war, the next mass shooting or the next display of pyrotechnics. When we aren't in a war, we are prepping for the next one, focusing on the supply side and the nationalistic side of our brains.

The contrast between the Francis Scott Key song we use as our national anthem and "America the Beautiful" show the two sides of the American psyche. The words of *America the Beautiful* speak of amber waves of grain and purple mountain majesties, with a focus on the picturesque aspect of America.

The dichotomy between the war eagle image in our national anthem and our truly awesome land of plenty is a cross we are forced to carry. Let's add a biblical reference here, as did Katharine Lee Bates, the lyricist of the song, "God shed his grace on thee, and crown thy good with brotherhood, from sea to shining sea!" Well there you have a real "America First" message, but I guess "sisterhood" wasn't invented yet.

We Americans apply the Gold standard to everything that exists. You gain street cred when a possession is very expensive. All our medicines are clearly overpriced. We have let the pharmaceutical lobbyists run roughshod over our healthcare system, and they get richer while we pay more. They argue that all high drug costs are caused by the expensive research needed to push through regulation and approvals. I say, **"Shut up and enjoy your patents."** It's simply the cost of doing business in that industry where the best research flows from private universities and colleges which receive grants from both the private sector and government for their discoveries and inventions. There's no need to shed a tear for multi-national pharmaceuticals firms. They're doing just fine.

Our best colleges and universities signal that students without money need not apply. Even with some valuable scholarship programs, too few qualified candidates end up at a great school. When did we lose education as a national priority? Someone should point out that one of the most important priorities of our founding fathers was building universities and libraries.

We have some crazy people who think they can bring a peacock on a commercial airliner because of their claim that the large bird is an "emotional support" animal. What? As one of the other paying passengers on the plane, I'd like you to please keep your freaking peacock in the zoo. Don't get me wrong, I love male peacocks and their desire to impress, but we need to dial back this whole "emotion support" thing. Try some rosary beads and a good belt of scotch whisky to calm your nerves.

People sue companies for the dumbest things. A 79-year-old women won $3 million from McDonalds because she was burned after dumping a cup of coffee into her lap. Yes, it's hot coffee, but what part of "hot" don't people understand? The American judiciary system can't be a 24-hour-a-day guardian angel or an excuse factory for stupid human tricks. I'm truly sorry the woman had to suffer, but was it really McDonald's fault that she dropped the cup? I guess a judge and jury thought so.

When I get a bit crazy over my fellow citizens, I turn to the newspaper and I read the comics. Maybe I've become too cynical, but they are NOT funny. Come to think of it, they have never been funny. They are cute and corny at best. We need funnier comics here in the land of the free. I guess TV sucked up all the good comedy writers.

Our American parents messed up our minds at an early age when they put us to bed at night whispering, "Sleep tight and don't let the bedbugs bite." Really? First, is sleeping tight a good idea? Do I want the pain of muscle constriction while I'm sleeping? And why plant a seed in my soon to be dreaming brain that there are bugs in the bed? What a stupid parenting tradition!

American marketing brings us so many fatuous things. I just learned that we can now buy "pizza insurance," so if anything happens to our pie during the trip from the shop to home, we can get a replacement. Are we that stupid or careless that we need to protect our pizza against roadside attack? Who wants to go all the way back to the pizza shop and admit you screwed up? It's just another way for them to make more money, and since when does Papa John worry about people?

Attention visitors who come to America. I can't guarantee that this crazy melting pot will remain stupid-free while you are on our soil. We have these local fights between the federal government, the states, counties and cities. Perhaps your TV shows us as one big, happy country, but we have an ongoing churn of disputes and dilemma revolving around just about every aspect of life. For our visitors, you can smoke marijuana in Colorado, but I would avoid that activity in Texas.

Should you visit, try not to overreact to things like the Naked Cowboy in Times Square, or six-pound cheeseburgers or how fat our fellow citizens appear. NOTE: We are actually much fatter than we appear.

Because we are so overweight, diet program TV adverts dominate the first two months of each new year. We know we are obese, and someday we'll do something about it. One company makes us fat, while another sells us diet plans. It's a parasitic paradigm for the delivery of fat from farm and factory directly to our stomachs.

We disallow radio and TV advertising of certain things like cigarettes, yet those same cancer products are freely available for sale to any adult. It gives our local, state and the federal government a ton of Gold in taxes. Some say the federal government takes in more than $15 billion per year on the taxation of our most dangerous products, and Washington and Congress have been looking the other way for more than 240 years.

In North Carolina, cigarette taxes generate $300,000 annually, while in New York it's more than $2 million a year. It's not that New Yorkers smoke more, they just pay more. Smuggled cigarettes are one of the greatest rackets law and order deals with in the Empire State.

Florida ranks 33rd in the nation in terms of cigarette taxes, but because of the state's large Cuban population there are no taxes on cigars. Suck on that, New York! Every state has a unique exploitation of our poisonous habits. Nevada takes advantage of our risk versus reward impulses and makes tons of money on gambling.

The US is the biggest producer of killer tobacco, and the government Goofballs continue to allow its production and sale here and around the world. Each year, almost 500,000 Americans die from the use of tobacco. Now that may sound like a real problem, but if the people had to decide between the right to own a Gun and the right to be poisoned by tar, they would probably use their Guns to enforce their right to buy and smoke cigarettes.

We will continue to chew our beef jerky and gulp our energy drinks, wondering why we are so tired at the end of each day. We seem to be so unhappy and frustrated about things. The government should just hand us all Viagra, Xanax, Zoloft, Celexa, Prozac and, well, you get the idea.

The self-medication of America includes not only what we put in our mouths, but what we watch with our eyes. We are morphing into an unconscious and unaware group of oxidizing, then rotting, couch potatoes. Just imagine Mr. Potato Head dressed as an overweight Captain America to reach the visual embodiment of the idea of America freedom. Don't get me wrong, I would NOT want to live anywhere else. I mean, where else can you

DVR your life and see its playback while texting to a friend and watching a giraffe giving birth on YouTube? It's America, baby

Death by Cross

I daydream about time travel. I would love to go back in time and change history, but I would settle for simply witnessing an amazing historical event. When I'm asked what one moment in time I would love to observe, I say the trial of Jesus (Yeshua).

The Holy Bible's Book of Luke claims there was first a trial with the Jewish elders of the temple. Then, Jesus was brought before the fifth prefect of the Roman province of Judaea, Pontius Pilate. The elders claimed Jesus had proclaimed himself the King of the Jews, a grave offense in their doctrine. Before the second trial began, Pilate realized the defendant was from Galilee, and therefore his case should have been under the jurisdiction of Herod, not his court. Pilate took the case anyway.

The unfolding of events is in dispute because of the lack of evidence and many contradictions in scripture. Some say Pilate thought this man from Galilee was innocent. Others believe that Pilate sentenced Jesus to death because the elders and the mob wanted him dead. The myth describes Pilate washing his hands to symbolically demonstrate he was not responsible for the execution of Jesus. It's also not clear what law was used to put this man to death. I would love to have seen and heard what happened. Was Jesus a victim of perjury?

Today, we have more and more video cameras catching almost everything that happens. That doesn't necessarily give us the whole story but can be an effective tool for those who are counted on to protect us, dish out justice and write the laws of the land. Between the millions of security cameras and many cell phones capturing live events, there are a multitude of ways new technologies influence our court decisions.

That brings us to a new concept in law creeping across America. It's loosely called the "stand your ground" law. It started in Florida where it's officially called the "Home Protection, use of threat and use of deadly force" law.

You may remember hearing about this law during the George Zimmerman trial. He was found innocent of killing a young, unarmed black youth, Trayvon Martin, in Sanford, Florida. Zimmerman claimed he feared for his life when he confronted Martin, who was walking in his father's gated community. In Zimmerman's defense, the stand your ground law was cited, and the jury decided the killing of Trayvon was in self-defense.

There have been other applications of the stand your ground law with people not being charged with using deadly force. The person using force needs to prove they had "reasonable fear of imminent peril of death." The problem with this law is it serves to protect the person with the Gun, not the person who was shot. Sadly, but logically, the dearly departed have little say about what happened. After all, they are dead.

This is not a new concept, and in some states the basic form of the regulation has been around for more than one hundred years. It may have been codified into law to help judges decide cases where people had to protect their person or property from nefarious individuals. It originally focused on a citizen's home or vehicle. Refined definitions about location have crept into law and opened fierce debate.

When it was thought force was needed to prevent imminent death or bodily harm no matter where it occurred, this became a "he said — he said" situation. As the law expanded, the Goofball legislators thought their new wording would prevent future forceable felonies, but they were dead wrong. If you see a man attempting to rape a woman, the legal system permits you to use force, even deadly force, to stop this crime before it happens. In such a case, the testimony of the victim could help to determine the facts.

In most states the stand your ground law has a cut-out for law enforcement officers. If a cop breaks into your home for probable cause, you can't shoot the officer and use the stand your ground law as your defense. You would be tried for murder.

In states like New York, the "initial aggressor" in the stand your ground scenario has the right to say, "Okay, sorry, my bad. I'm walking away now," without fear of being tracked down and killed. It's doubtful that anyone in a heated confrontation knows the laws of their state or lawful recourse in that critical moment. In New York, you cannot use the stand your ground law if you shoot someone in the back. But I must ask, why would shooting someone in the back be legal in any state?

This whole stand your ground stuff is clearly a debate of "reasonable force" versus "deadly force" and how to legislate the difference.

Here's a case from 2018 that occurred in Pinellas County, Florida. An unarmed, African-American man named Markeis McGlockton parked his car in a handicapped space at a convenience store. He entered the store, and soon after a white man named Michael Drejka confronted McGlockton's girlfriend sitting in the car. He asked why she was parked in a handicapped space. McGlockton saw this conversation, left the store and returned to the car. You can see his girlfriend getting out of the vehicle and standing about three feet from Drejka. McGlockton approached the two people and forcefully pushed Drejka to the ground. We know all this because the events were captured on security video.

As McGlockton turned to walk back to the store, Drejka, still on the ground, pulled a Gun and shot McGlockton. Under the letter of the law, one could consider the man shot to be the "initial aggressor."

It was clear McGlockton had turned and walked away and not "standing his ground." The police didn't charge the shooter. Public safety officials claimed they applied the stand your ground law to this incident and no arrest was necessary.

Less than a month after the killing, Florida State prosecutors filed a manslaughter charge against the gunman, Michael Drejka. The system worked but law enforcement didn't look objective. The police aren't supposed to be the judge and jury, but why didn't they charge Drejka for shooting an unarmed man? Civil Rights activists ask another question. Would the police have handled this differently if a black man had shot a white man under the same conditions and video evidence?

Making this terrible incident even worse, after making it back into the store McGlockton, fell to the ground and died in front of his five-year-old son. How does a future generation of African-Americans believe in justice for all? The stand your ground laws in all states should be challenged. In some cases, the law protects the police or a criminal with a Gun, not the unarmed person.

The stand your ground law was created to protect us in our dwellings, residences and vehicles, but has expanded over time to protect those who use deadly force to get out of a conflict. Is that good for America and the citizens of a place where it's so easy to get a Gun?

Having a "reasonable fear of imminent peril of death or great bodily harm" is in the eye of the beholder. In other words, the only person who can claim fear is the person who holds that fear. How can a jury or judge ever claim to know both sides of such a conflict?

Of course, Trayvon Martin fought George Zimmerman because he had a "reasonable fear" of his own death. In fact, his fear was more than "reasonable," it was certain and real. Trayvon Martin didn't have a Gun, so he had only two choices, run and be shot in the back or "stand **his** ground" and fight. This is the best example of how the law and its application are totally flawed.

We need to figure out how to write laws that don't encourage more violence. I have a friend who is a judge and he said, "Florida's stand your ground law seems to motivate everyone in society to own a Gun." Someone must show me how more Guns help solve the misuse of too many Guns. Are stand your ground laws simply a "get out of jail free" card?

My cynical mind predicts we will see serial stand your ground killers surfacing once sick minds figure out how to use this law to kill. A bad man with a Gun could incite someone into the "initial aggressor" role, then shoot that person. How many times would this have to happen before courts would realize someone is getting away with murder by using a bad law as a loophole?

I'm quite certain that in the Roman court of law two-thousand years ago, the 33-year old preacher named Jesus had very little due process. Pontius Pilate was concerned only about the possible unrest that might occur if the high priests and elders of the temple stirred up the locals in protest of an acquittal.

Pilate was just another Goofball in government, worried more about how he looked and less about what was right and just. It would be good to know the truth of what really happened. Too bad there weren't security cameras back in the day.

Absolutely Almost Perfect

America is a funny girl. I have always been emotionally tweaked and philosophically torn over why we apply the feminine label to certain things in our society. Navy guys refer to their ship in female terms, "She's a well-made vessel." That timeworn phrase, "good old girl" pops up to depict the relationship someone has with their Subaru Forester, which also has a reputation of being the perfect car for Lesbians, though I'm not sure why. But let's talk about sushi.

Fifty years ago, I had sushi for the very first time with some friends in Los Angeles, California. The idea of eating raw fish wasn't really my cup of tea or something on my bucket list. When the food arrived, I was a bit mystified. On the plate was an artistic arrangement of foods rolled in, ah, seaweed? But my eyes quickly gravitated to a strip of fake plastic grass separating the rolls from a mass of green caulk and a pile of sliced white stuff. Now I know sushi is not American, but it's is a good example of how we adopt and adapt to other cultures.

I was schooled by my dinner mates that the green clay was to be carefully mixed into the soy sauce and the sliced pickled matter was to be eaten between bites to "cleanse the palate." It was pickled ginger and it did indeed "cleanse" what I assumed was the taste of raw fish. I then consumed more raw fish. It took only that one meal for me to fall madly in love with sushi, and I have been a big fan of her ever since.

What does this have to do with America? What does this have to do with Gold, God, Guns and Goofballs? Okay, you want me to stay linear and I get that, but please let me divert and it will soon make sense.

You might be tempted to think the amazing American success of Japanese cuisine, specifically sushi, could be attributed to World War II, but that would be unrealistic and reaching at best. Most of the cultural exchange between the USA and Japan flowed from us to them. From baseball to business techniques and manufacturing, we seeded their fields more than they did ours. When they started to sell us stuff, from transistor radios to refrigerators, Japan became a manufacturing power far beyond what we intended. We helped them build an economy based on our democratic principles and guided by that "shining light on a hill."

If someone served you a bowl of pickled ginger, you would hardly call it a meal and you'd certainly question your host's culinary etiquette. Would a plate of Sushi be complete without the wasabi mustard and pickled ginger? We will all agree the sushi chefs can do away with the fake plastic grass. There are many metaphors here, but America does employ fake grass in our Easter bunny baskets, so we aren't without sin. We also use artificial grass on our athletic fields. Who thought up the idea of artificial grass? Oh yeah, the Astro Dome, that is why it was called AstroTurf. But I digress.

Almost one-third of Americans has never tried sushi. Even the name is a misnomer. After all, sushi in Japanese simply means flavored rice. You know, the glutinous glob of white stuff they roll the fish in or around. As the isolationist Goofballs in power keep telling us how we want to make America more American, are we really, as the song goes, *Turning Japanese?*

Our country is a giant sponge that picks up cultures from around the world and slaps a big old red, white and blue sticker on them. It's not long before everyone here believes we invented it. We took a simple idea from the Italians and created an almost $6 billion industry called Pizza. We caught the concept of Chinese food and now buy more than $17 billion of the cuisine each year. Some say we eat $39 billion at Mexican restaurants annually but we only spend $3 billion on sushi in America. But, hey, it's a good start.

Although I love a good steak occasionally, I'm more than a meat and potatoes guy. Maybe because I've traveled a lot, I have a great desire for diversity in what I eat. American cuisine can be rather limited. Our country is great, but I'm not driven to dislike certain tastes because of politics.

I thought it was dimwitted when the Congressional snack bar in Washington, DC changed the name of "French Fries" to "Freedom Fries." Hey, they are French fries, not because they were invented in France, but because our soldiers went to France during World War II and were served "pomme frites." While we're on the subject, frying potatoes was a Belgium concoction, not French. They invented waffles as well. Hmmmm, does that make Waffle House a Belgium restaurant?

While you are getting back at France for all the things they did to offend you Mr. hand-in-the-pocket-of-a-lobbyist flagsucker, you might want to work on changing the names of French vanilla, French toast, French dressing, French kissing, French bulldogs, French horns and of course, French ticklers. I have no idea what those are, wink, wink.

We are a nation of misconceptions and bad receptions. We should realize that new ideas imported to our country make us better. Sometimes we Americanize things, like Chinese chefs coloring their hot and sour sauces red after realizing our people put ketchup on everything.

When we take the time to learn a culture and experience the true flavor of its homeland, we can fall deeper in love with her. If you want to taste a dish from a certain country for the first time, find the best, most accurate representation of that cuisine. Give it the best chance to succeed. You just might be amazed.

The late, great TV traveler and culinary explorer, Anthony Bourdain, showed us that once we break bread with another culture, we can become a small part of it and walk a mile in her shoes. That was his role in the world.

The story of two Macedonian brothers who moved from New York to Cincinnati, Tom and John Kiradjieff, dramatically shows how the influence of another culture can impact America. These two guys used Greek

Mediterranean spices to create a meat sauce they put on the hot dogs they sold from a street cart. Thus, the now-famous Cincinnati chili sauce was born. Along with typical chili spices, Tom and John added some cinnamon and unsweetened chocolate. Now for some it's an acquired taste, but America put its stamp on the concoction. We had to make it BIG!

We take simple things that are almost perfect and attempt to make them more perfect, like our nation. So, in Cincinnati, you can order chili many ways. You got your "2-Way," which is just the chili and spaghetti. Then you got your "3-Way," which is chili, spaghetti and cheese, that's "golden" cheddar, please. If you are hungry, you got your "4-Way," which consists of chili, spaghetti, cheese and onions or beans. And if you're truly ravenous, you got your "5-Way," with chili, spaghetti, cheese, onions and beans. Once we pilfer an idea, we own it, and then we supersize it.

You are probably wondering why I just made you so hungry that you are ready to put the book down and go eat, but I'm trying to make a point. This essay is pickled ginger meant to cleanse your palate and make you want more of my political vitriol and observations on the agonizing challenges we face in America.

We are a nation of immigrants and a melting pot of not only cultures but also cheeses from around the world. We are rolling around in spiced rice and evolving each day. We never stop. Even when we aren't smart enough to know the difference between a FAD and a TREND, we gravitate to new ideas and concepts. Sushi in America could have just been another stupid fad, like fidget spinners and reality TV show presidents, but once an idea gets ahold of us, we make it AMERICAN.

It doesn't take long for our land's smart people to exploit a brilliant new idea and reap large rewards. We aren't perfect, but we are the best test market for the world. That's why we should evaluate things for what they are rather than prejudging them. We should embrace cultures, ideas and belief systems. Stop with this blinding nationalism that makes us so ugly to the rest of the world.

If we just think about America as this "almost perfect" lady who keeps getting better with age, we'll be fine.

We become less great when we stray from the truth about who we are and our origin. This happens whenever we chase a "younger" version of America, when we were whiter, more isolated and less tolerant. If we continue down this path, we will be gravely disappointed. We are still evolving and changing for the better, and we should never go backwards.

License to Lie

While listening to the radio the other day, I heard the announcer pitching bedding sheets made of "organic cotton." Gee, isn't all cotton organic? It's a living plant. Doesn't that make it organic? But I was wrong.

It seems that organic cotton is grown without the use of synthetic pesticides. Producers are supposed to disclose the way they grow, handle and process their cotton and the rating they apply must be approved by a state certifying agency or the United States Department of Agriculture (USDA). Now here's something for my female readers. Companies that make tampons containing cotton aren't regulated. Why? Bad cotton could end up in a very private place and hurt you. Time to write some letters! Both men and women should be protected by our government.

The declaration of truly organic, natural ingredients is a good thing, but most of us don't read the fine print of advertising and packaging or pay attention to the disclaimers in radio and TV ads. The legal notices at the end of some radio ads are so fiercely fast that it's impossible to understand what's being said. And this brings me to the subject at hand, lying.

Embedded in the zealous marketing of most products and services, you will typically find a little hyperbole here and there infused with a smidge of creative license. It's a license to lie. As marketing speak becomes more the language of the land, the more lies we accept.

The next ad tells me that I can take a certain pill and I will be better able to satisfy my mate. Wow, it's an over-the-counter "drug" that will help me in the man department? Then I realize, it's not a drug at all but a supplement, a category not regulated in America. The disclaimer at the end of the ad clearly states the product has not been scientifically studied, evaluated or reviewed by the FDA and is NOT intended to treat any medical problem. Just what does this supplement do then?

The same myth is constantly thrown in our faces with the terms "natural" and "organic." "Organic" has some standing, while "natural" has no legal foundation whatsoever. According to the USDA, "organic" means that no synthetic pesticides, chemical fertilizers or genetically modified organisms (GMOs) were used in the making of the item. No growth hormones or antibiotics are allowed in "organic" meat, egg and dairy products. I don't know about you, but I get concerned when something has been genetically modified. We really have no idea what could happen over time with such alterations. Isn't that how we got the Ninja Turtles?

The term "natural" lands us in murky waters. As of this writing, the FDA web site admits they have not engaged in rulemaking to establish a formal definition of the term "natural." They state that nothing artificial or synthetic, including color additives, can be added to a "natural" food. Hey guys, once you say you have not engaged in rulemaking about a word you give everyone in the food business a license to lie. It would be like a town passing a law that says, "strip clubs" do not have to be located in "strip malls."

We are constantly manipulated by marketing language and vague laws that assume we will never make a claim. We hardly notice the fake promises rolling right by us. Did you see how I twisted that town law I mentioned a few sentences ago? It would mean that a strip club could be anywhere in that town. That's an example of the trick behind a marketing lie.

We see the word "natural" on a label and we assume it's better for us, like ALL-NATURAL turkey bacon. Taking a closer look, we see that it's high in saturated fat and sodium. One analysis showed a cup of gobble-gobble bacon contains 1,874 mg of salt!

It's like automobile manufacturers claiming their cars are safe. I get it. We test cars to determine how well they will stand up to a T-bone crash or a head-on collision, but no car is totally safe. We have faith in airbags and seat belts believing they give us a better chance of survival, but there are no guarantees. Someone who just drank a case of "natural" lite beer made from "organically" grown hops can kill you just as quickly as someone blowing through a stop sign while texting to his buddies suggesting they meet at the strip club in the strip mall.

The more our brains are bombarded with marketing and political horseshit, the more we lose our ability to discern what is real and what is fake. We believe some of the thousands of things we consume every day are good for us, while ignoring the facts. There was a time when anthropologists and social scientists calculated how many people were going to be living in the USA, and they wondered how we would feed them. There are still too many fields in America producing crops processed into chemicals that hurt us.

In the 1800s, the federal government realized that corn yields in the country were not improving. They got nervous and invested in dams and irrigation systems to increase the yield of corn and wheat crops. As we doubled and tripled, and then tripled again, our corn lab workers devised chemicals to help the crops grow faster and bigger. After years of polluting the land, which in turn poisoned the streams and waterways, we have introduced significant challenges to our environment.

There's an agricultural lie that chemicals and GMOs help feed America without doing harm. Most of these items have not been scientifically tested and many experts admit they don't know what they might do. In the sixties, farmers sprayed paraquat on their fields without knowledge of its toxicity.

The fertilizers used to enhance crop growth on our land create a problem when they drain into fresh water lakes and streams. It turns these waterways into a petri dish, where unearthly material grows and thrives. In recent years, an algae bloom spread across Lake Okeechobee in Florida. After large rainfalls, the impure sludge moved out of the lake and into streams and rivers, totally polluting them. This six-inch thick muck killed fish and marine life and smelled like the bowel movement of an extraterrestrial. So much for swimming and fishing in these densely polluted waters. Environmentalists claim that the state government in Tallahassee has been in the pocket of the powerful agriculture lobby for years, while politicians say this disaster is just a "natural occurrence."

One solution proposed in Florida was the creation of wider waterways to help divert the dank water into the Everglades. I guess they think that alligators, panthers, deer and snakes love sludge and won't care about the smell. The pounding of sugar cane fields with nitrogen, phosphorus and potassium created this deadly, foolish problem. Think about it. We want to grow more sugar, which is bad for us, so we polluted a lake, thus the gulf and ocean. The result is dead sea life, including dolphins, manatees and turtles, all for the sake of our sugar buzz.

The corporate criminals and lobbyists in Washington want us to believe we have too many laws and those regulations are keeping America from being great. They're ignoring the needs of the people and saying it's okay to lie. If we don't have safety and protection built into the laws that govern our way of life, we will destroy the value of our lands and properties. And, oh yeah, cause the death of living things. And let's not forget that we humans are living things, too.

We often justify our misfortune with the cynical phrase, "Everything dies and so that's okay." We cling to the misplaced belief we can always get another one. We must have the new this or that, partly because of peer group pressure and partly because we are just plain senseless. As the slogan in Huxley's *Brave New World* declared, "Ending is better than mending."

From the water we drink to the air we breathe, we have a lot of work to do. I love technology as much as the next guy, but I am not ready to put my stamp of approval on vaping, even though it eliminates tar. There is nothing worse than cigarettes. When the guy next to me blows smoke in my face and then puts out his cigarette in the sand at the beach, I want to kick some sand in his face.

As of this writing, there is no statewide smoking ban on Florida beaches because of what is called, "preemption," a law that says a local government action cannot conflict with state law. This means local governments are completely powerless to ban smoking, even if their community would prefer it. WTF?

The biggest lie in American democracy is the notion of majority rule. We are constantly beaten down by smaller groups of loud-mouth influencers, like Super PACs and legal political action committees who give money to politicians in exchange for "favors." If the majority wants to ban smoking, why wouldn't that be the law? Why should a lobbyist be able to influence a majority desire? While we're at it, let's dump the electoral college.

The license to lie is simple. We don't spend money on a stop sign because the research shows we don't need one there, until someone dies. Politicians say they want to protect us and keep us alive, safe and well in the United States of America, but their actions often demonstrate something else entirely. They take an oath to protect the Constitution, but often ignore their pledge. Some believe they must stay in office to keep a corrupt system in line. The Constitution is something they only talk about, and that is why there is a movement in this country to move to term-limits.

Maybe we need to deliver large containers of cigarette butts and lake sludge to the law makers at their next meeting. While we're at it, let's take all the broken dreams of the poor and disenfranchised, slide them into a Ziplock bag and drop those on the Goofballs' expensive, polished oak desks. Dead human bodies in black bags are the result of Goofball-supported companies ignoring warning signs. Really. The government waited a long time before busting a Japanese company that sold exploding airbags to American car manufacturers. By not demanding more, we give the Goofballs a license to lie.

OMG Society

The advances made in technology, fashion, and architecture in my lifetime are very apparent, though many of our big moves weren't without mishaps and mistakes. If we would only learn from our misfortunes, perhaps we would spend more time enjoying our new ideas. Sadly, we don't always use history to fix the future.

I remember when Columbia University was building its new Science and Engineering Library on the corner of 120th and Broadway in New York City. A friend of mine asked one of the construction project engineers working at the site whether he thought ice would accumulate on the decorative, slanted metal panels. He said, "No, that is not going to happen."

Well that engineer must have been quite embarrassed when the first icy winter storm hit. The school was forced to put up scaffolding to protect people from ice falling off the sloped panel. Sometimes the best-looking ideas simply do not work.

What appeared to an untrained eye to be a building problem, wasn't even considered by the veteran architect. There are many times when observational logic is lost on those closest to a project. Just because someone is "ordained to know" because of their previous work in an industry, institution or agency, doesn't mean they will get it right all the time. Consider the design of the first-class restroom door on the Boeing 727. It became blocked when the cockpit door opened. Oops!

We live in an OMG Society. We want to gasp at new ideas or breaking news, when slow, sure calm thought should instead prevail. Was the slanted siding intended to deflect sunlight from the building or was it simply decorative? Maybe they should have deployed a deicing system, but that would have cost more money. It's just cheaper to put up the ugly scaffolding every winter to protect the passers-by. They could admit they were wrong and remove or reengineer the inclined panels, but global warming might eventually fix the problem.

We have a deep thirst for knowledge but remain at the mercy of statistics produced by people and their agendas. Count the number of news stories on TV that continually change direction. First, it's "this" and then, it's "that," and the reports revolve around myriad, disparate topics such as how often to get a prostate or breast exam, whether vitamins work, or does taking an aspirin every day help or hinder heart disease.

One day the Food and Drug Administration (FDA) announces that something is unsafe, then later declares that same food or drug to be okay. If they took more time and care in their initial analysis, they might be able to get it right the first time. Most drugs are fast tracked by Big Pharma money so that profit comes sooner, while the public becomes the guinea pig.

Another problem with the FDA occurs when a drug's patent expires and generics flood the market. There are many complaints that the lower priced generics are not as good. The large pharmacy retailers, almost monopolies, negotiate side deals with generic manufacturers without any testing or knowledge of the potency or purity of those new, unproven medications. They claim their preferred offerings are exact chemical matches to the costlier brand names, despite the fact they sometimes are not, and the customers suffer.

There is high churn in the management ranks of the FDA, and this might explain the agency's ping-ponging decisions and policies. The Goofballs place lobbyists with ties to "Big Pharma" at the helm of the agency, meaning those who have been pitching new products and devices to put in your body are now in control.

If you want to learn more about the corruptive structure of the FDA, watch the movie *The Bleeding Edge* (2018). It sheds light on artificial hips and birth control devices, such as Bayer's *Essure*, which endangered patients. We seem to have more stringent controls over drugs than prosthetics placed inside our bodies. Why is that?

The Goofball who currently runs the FDA worked previously for a venture partner who invested in many of the devices and medicines seeking the agency's approval. He announced his intent to recuse himself for one year from any decision involving the twenty health care companies he worked with in the past, making one wonder that if he must recuse himself, how did he even get the job and why just a one-year recusal?

Many medical decisions in the US are based on insurance companies' mortality tables and algorithms. Gold is the prize. A doctor ponders whether he or she will be paid for the operation by the insurance company. I'm sorry to say that death panels are true. We have them, and they're called insurance companies. As you get older, your survival is based on having as much Gold as possible. Many poor people in America die simply because they can't afford the procedures or medicines needed to stay alive. This is a sad truth. Statistics are used to make every decision.

Political and opinion pollsters hold tough jobs. Having access to research in my radio career, I can tell you that people lie, maybe not knowingly, but they lie. I have seen radio station morning guys get mentions in the ratings diaries, even though they had been dead for years. When the radio industry switched from recall diaries to electronic monitoring, long-term winning stations became losers overnight. That tacky statement, "Opinions are like assholes, everyone has one," comes to mind. All surveys are based on a small sample of respondents, coupled with a mathematical equation to present a conclusion on what the whole population might be thinking based only on those sampled.

Statistics play a big part in our "Oh My God" society. Consider Hurricane Maria tearing through Puerto Rico. Not only did the Goofballs on the mainland not fully comprehend the extent of the damage, but those who traveled there lied about what was happening. Most of the studies done by the Federal government couldn't get a proper death count. Why wouldn't the people in charge be able to count dead people? Numbering them should be easier because they don't move.

Our constant attempts to know what people think is challenging. Since voting in our elections isn't mandatory, election results represent only the small sample of those who voted, not the total perspective of the nation. In the 2016 national election, only 60% of those registered to vote went to the polls. We don't know what the others think or believe. In the massive turnout of the 2018 midterm elections, some of the states couldn't handle the large number of ballots. Maybe it's time to rethink that one.

Pollsters use research samples to predict how people will behave or think, and so does our judicial system. Our courts depend on the opinions and thoughts of twelve jurors. They're supposed to represent our peers, the population at large, *a jury of fellow citizens.*

The US Supreme Court ruled that a potential juror cannot be excluded based solely on race or gender. We have a system in which both the prosecution and defense teams have a say in how a group of jurors is selected. Crafty attorneys and consultants now apply science to the jury selection process that attempts to give advantage to their side. So much for random selection being the fairest process, because that could mean an African-American defendant wouldn't have anyone who looked like him or her on the jury.

Because of the small number of jurors and research respondents, we never learn what the majority wants. Yet these results are blasted across radio and TV, shaping our opinions and, thus, our values. I'm constantly amazed at the story choices of news directors and show producers. Some days, they miss the most important stories because they have been instructed by the bean counters and social media analysts to focus on what is "trending" to boost their ratings. They fail if they don't come up with an OMG moment in their newscast. The true aim of journalism to get the truth out is many times lost due to the quest for readership and ratings. It's not "fake news." It's just bad journalism.

Our nation's narcissistic nature can be clearly seen in the trend to express ourselves with bumper stickers and car decals. As George Carlin said, "I think it's time we abandon sentimental, emotional kitsch as a prime means of expression in public." Yeah, he was talking about you with your bumper sticker telling everyone that your child is an honor student or stating your political position. I avoid applying any sticker to my car because some people are crazy enough to key it should they disagree with the words on my bumper.

There are those who display a bright red NRA sticker to show they are pro-Guns. Others display a sticker telling me they have an AR-15 or profess they are vegan. We get it. It's free advertising space and you own it, but did you ever think that most of us really don't care about your opinion? It's not quite the OMG moment I'm looking for, and that sticker probably lowers the value of your vehicle, but the bottom line is I DON'T CARE.

Some of us have a neurotic need to elevate daft data to a level of importance to force their viewpoint on others. An example is that social media person who posts research on something that has nothing to do with me. Some state I should die because I don't agree with their love of an orange-headed Goofball with small hands. Really?

Send me a video of alligators mating and maybe I'll set aside some time to watch it. Chatter like "I sat in the ER all night and all I have to show for it is 13 stitches," doesn't matter at all to me. Or, "My daughter just did her first flip at gymnastics class." How does this enrich me? I mean no offense, good for her, but we seem to be keeping better records on ourselves than the Nazis did during their reign over the German population. Our government gets all the information they want or need about us at no charge, because we freely supply them with a constant stream of our personal information. Facebook allows everyone in the world to know how we looked back in 1971. You know, because of *Throw up Thursdays*. Is that what it's called?

There's now a Museum of Failure (Innovation) in Los Angeles. I wonder if some of my screenplays are there? Here are some of its exhibits: Apple Newton, Google Glass, Nokia N-gage, the Kodak Digital Camera, Sony Betamax, Lego Fiber Optics, Harley-Davidson Perfume and Colgate Beef Lasagna. I owned a Betamax video recorder and loved it until it stopped working, right around the time it was declared to be dead. We honor things like Ford's Edsel car, which was ahead of its time, but are these true OMG moments?

We have glossed over massive failures, like creating a North and South Korea. I don't understand why we have a North and South Carolina and a North and South Dakota. Did we really need a Virginia, and then a West Virginia? That's as bizarre as the suggestion that West Virginia be named Lower Pittsburgh.

We never learn from our bad ideas. The Vietnam war was a total failure and we should have known the Afghanistan and Iraq wars would be similarly disastrous. We attempt to impress the world and control other people's lives by our stupid attempts to solve other peoples' problems.

It's depraved when someone like Syria's Bashar al-Assad kills 500,000 by bombing hospitals and gassing his own people. It's sad that the world sits back and lets it happen. We were attacked on 9-11, and we all felt the need for revenge and punishment of the bastards who did that terrible deed, but they weren't in Iraq; they were in Afghanistan.

History shows that the Goofballs at the Pentagon are being manipulated by people across the river. Or is it the other way around? Many times, even the smartest Generals do the wrong thing. Why would we ever wage one war on top of another? Is that an OMG moment?

There's lots of blame to go around. I'm sure the Goofball responsible for poor architectural design at Columbia will say the experts promised ice wouldn't form and fall. I guess someone at Ford failed to tell Henry Ford II that spending $250 million on research and development of the Edsel car wouldn't guarantee its success. We head to war chanting USA, USA, never thinking we might lose. We have unfortunately lost wars, tons of money and human life fighting unjust and unnecessary wars.

Just because some billionaire thinks I want a computer screen in an eyeglass contraption next to my eyeball, so I can surf the internet while walking around, doesn't mean I will buy it. Had that Goofball talked to someone with medical knowledge, he would have realized that all our vision problems can be solved with surgery. Why would I want to place eyeglasses back on my face when I can now see 20/20 without them?

We get bored with the same old, normal things, but can become obsessive with our speech patterns and clichés. Isn't there a better response than OMG? When you do something for me and I say, "Thank You" stop giving me the vacuous reply, "No Problem." It's okay to simply say, "You're Welcome." No one needs your judgement about the difficulty of doing some basic task. Maybe when we replace all our wait people with robots, we can program the droid with topics we find compelling. Then, we could say, OMG, that waiter really knows me!

Unnatural Carnal Fracking

We think we are smart, but we often miss the most obvious things. Maybe we need to scream louder when we believe something is wrong. Are we fearful of being labeled a kook or conspiracy theory fool? Speaking up and stating a case is very American.

It was 1978 when I first started to travel the country as a radio station consultant. My first trip was to Jacksonville, North Carolina, a small-town home to Marine Corps Base Camp Lejeune. The community's economy is driven by the military camp.

My client put me up at the local Holiday Inn, where the water in my room literally took my breath away. Opening the faucet in the bathroom assaulted my nose with what smelled like dead fish. I didn't even want to take a shower in that room. Of all the places I visited over 25 years, Jacksonville, North Carolina continues to win my "worst water" award.

So, I was quite disturbed to learn that NBC TV reported, "People stationed at North Carolina's Camp Lejeune while the water there was contaminated were more likely to die from several types of cancer, as well as Lou Gehrig's disease, according to an official government report released."

I immediately felt guilt for not saying something. I was sad for the men and women and their families who were exposed to this terrible water. I also thought about the kids in Flint, Michigan. I had assumed the bad water in North Carolina was only at my hotel, not the whole city or the base.

Medical irregularities continually pop up around America, and the Goofballs in power at the Environmental Protection Agency and the Food and Drug Administration stonewall the press or fling blatant lies about the causes of these problems. Even the Center for Disease Control (CDC) has been challenged about what to report to the public.

Conspiracy theorists believe that people in power hide things from us because they fear we will panic. It's downright hilarious to believe the Goofballs are protecting us with enormous coverups because they care about our feelings. When we find out they lied we simply cannot believe they would be that irresponsible, but their mistruths are not because of a concern regarding our level of panic.

It's not that they think we can't handle the truth. They don't tell us what is going on because they fear the bad news will cost them their jobs or land them in jail or, for my Mexican-American amigos and amigas, the *juzgado*. Make no mistake, negligence, carelessness or inaction that leads to harm or death can send people into litigation hell.

Just when you thought it was safe to go to college, a story claims more than 40 people who either attended or worked at Auburn University have been diagnosed with a unique kind of eye cancer. I'm sure the science and medical communities will have found the answer to this mystery by the time you read this, but it's clear we face unknown environmental dangers. We can't just pray things will get better. If it was that easy, God would have fixed all these problems before people had to beseech his help.

There are perils in the world that can't be defeated with an AR-15, and the amount of Gold scientists need to address our environmental and medical challenges can't be ignored by whatever party or religious group controls the budget.

It reminds me of the little crab named lybia that we fondly refer to as the "boxer crab." This tiny creature could be eaten by most large fish, but it uses other creatures, sea anemones, to defend itself from those who would do it harm. The lybia use the anemones as boxing gloves to punch big fish in the mouth. Those gloves look like flowers, but they have a ring of tentacles embedded with stinging cells. The predator swims away in pain after the tiny boxer crab knocks it in the face.

We can all wonder who or what taught these diminutive crabs to use another sea creature to protect themselves, but that is how they roll, I mean crawl. They're using instinct or learned action to protect themselves. If one of the "gloves" escapes, the crab simply rips the remaining anemone in two. The mutilation doesn't kill but rather causes another organism to form. Back to full protection, the anemones are carried around by their buddy boxer. Why can't people work together like this?

Humans often overthink things. If we can harness aspects of nature to help us, why shouldn't we? Are we not as smart as a boxer crab? FACT: We are killing the planet because we crank out too much carbon dioxide (CO_2). All those inscrutable Goofballs who genuflect to the corporate criminals who would kill a whole species or village just to make this quarter's budget are worthless creatures. They're blowfish, at best.

If we could only see life through the eyes of a tiny crab, we would learn that many of the chemicals we use to make crops grow faster and bigger are poisoning our waterways, lakes, gulfs and oceans. These actions may make it impossible to survive here on Earth, and remember there is no planet B. Yes, we need to feed more people, but we can find smarter ways to do it.

There are seaweed (kelp) farmers who are helping rid the oceans of the CO_2 concentrations. Even the oil companies are experimenting with seaweed to propel our vehicles. Maybe we can become as innovative as some of the fish in the sea, if only we live long enough to learn.

We need to come to terms with the ways we are polluting our world. We are constantly on the move, and our cars and planes aren't exactly helping the environment. If you think what comes out of a car is good for life, put your face next to the exhaust pipe and inhale for a few seconds. But please don't do it for very long, or YOU WILL GET SICK AND DIE.

Did you know the average temperature of North America decreased during the three-day period after 9-11, when all US and Canadian airliners were grounded? For all you chemtrail conspiracy theorists, NASA scientists confirmed that the hot air our jets produce help to create cirrus clouds which keep the planet hotter. However, it has not been proven that jet exhaust is making us gay.

Food production is another wonderful way we pollute the world. Our love of milk, beef and cows produces tons of methane, which is not good for the planet. Not to get too geeky here, but nitrogen oxides and volatile organic compounds mess with the environment and form ground-level ozone. Wouldn't it be embarrassing if aliens finally reached Earth after all us humans were killed off by cow farts?

We use many sources of energy for heating and cooling our homes and running household appliances. When I was a kid in Pittsburgh, hillsides in the woods had springs gurgling orange water, caused by sulfur leeching from the abandoned coal mines. There was a joke saying the discoloration was the blood of French soldiers. Was that because it looked like French dressing?

The fantastic 2010 documentary film *Gasland,* produced by Josh Fox, showed that tap water near fracking fields could be IGNITED with a match. Of course, the water wasn't drinkable after the companies forced tons of chemicals into the ground to retrieve natural gas and oil. The mining industry lied about the safety of the method and families have suffered greatly ever since.

In the state of Oklahoma, earthquakes have increased in areas where massive fracking and mining was pushed through by their grifter State Attorney General, Scott Pruitt. Can we really blame the destruction of land and property on one person? When history is written, Mr. Pruitt will be called one of many environmental terrorists.

According to a 2013 Oklahoma geographical survey, an estimated 109 earthquakes occurred, a substantially higher number than in any previous year as far back as 1978. When the scumbags tell you that fucking fracking has no effect on the Earth, hand them a glass of brown water and tell them to go to hell. It's warm there all the time and the air is unbreathable. You see, those same fracking chemicals we've pumped into the earth have seeped into hell and the bad guys will eventually get pickled by their poisons.

Let's put into perspective the debate about what is natural and what is normal behavior. When mating, a female praying mantis bites off the head of her male partner and then devours his corpse for nourishment. That's more than #MeToo, but it's nature at work.

In America, we use the acronym NIMBY as shorthand for "Not in My Backyard." It became an issue in the early days of radio when a station wanted to build a broadcast tower in a farmer's field. As soon as word got out that an erection was planned, the whole town got out their tiki torches and pitch forks to protest.

They said it would ruin their view. Not that a giant 500-foot steel structure with blinking red lights turns me on but, hey, it was a radio station belonging to an industry I worked in and loved. Then came the cell phone towers, and the locals raised hell at their town halls. The cell phone tower guys then spent extra millions of bucks on towers that attempted, but failed, to look like pine trees. Everyone knew they weren't trees. When the phone company threw them some cash, the city fathers forgot all about NIMBY.

And now, we've come to an idea the landowners should have done before they let those mother-frackers on their land. I've got two words for you, **solar farms**. Large public and private lands are being converted to solar farms, and as part of the deal some local communities are reaping as much as $40,000 a month. Electric bills go down and, in places like Florida, people are paying only $9 a month for electricity because of solar panels on their homes. Why didn't we do this in the first place? NIMBY has now become PIMBY, "Please, In My Backyard."

It's clear we are killing our planet a little more each year. We do bad things and hurt our offspring. WAKE UP AMERICA! In October of 2018, the United Nations' Intergovernmental Panel on Climate Change, a group of scientists convened to guide world leaders described a worsening world. They say that as early as 2040 we will have food shortages, wildfires and a mass die-off of coral reefs, so we have but ten to fifteen years to fix the problem. Sadly, the actions and statements by the US government within the last two years have essentially declared this report meaningless. Why are we accepting such poor governance? Can't we connect the floods in Texas, fires in California and brutal snow storms in the Northeast to the environmental mistakes we are making?

If we don't start biting off the heads of those people who lie to us, they will pull us over the cliff with them. We can't pray away global pollution. If it was up to God to save the world, wouldn't he have done it already? Not to be rude, but what's he waiting for? It's immoral not to care about our planet. Why should we trust mankind? God may be on the side of the environment, but he apparently doesn't have a vote.

165 Doors

You know what pisses me off about America? We have too many big mouthed experts and bullies who express themselves in ways that prevent productive discussion on controversial issues. Many people jump to talking points that have been blasted into their tiny, atrophied brains by propaganda machines and ridiculous people. They recycle retorts then walk away without hearing another view. I want an approach that considers facts and propels intellectual discussion.

I imagine you are wondering what the heck is up with those 165 Doors. Well, this essay is about education in America and how we should be ashamed of ourselves for the neglect of a sacred duty. Our lack of understanding about the challenges that schools and teachers face with your kids is appalling.

Which is the most important group in our population? Of course, it's the next generation. As the rest of the world gets better at educating their millions of young souls, we are constantly judged not only against an index we created within our institutions, but also against other countries. There are many metrics to evaluate a nation, from the number of its patents to advances in medicine and efficient use of natural resources. People drive these achievements and we must make smart choices when it comes to how we educate our children.

People with big mouths attack educators in many ways. First, they are hung up on the notion of tenure and political correctness born inside the ivy-covered walls of higher education. They also hold a belief that Joe Lunchbox should have a say on what is taught and how it is taught. These are the same people who complain about increases in local taxes to pay for education, which is necessary for a well-functioning system.

Tenure and political correctness are at cross purposes. Tenure is applied to protect the writings and sayings of experienced professors from being controlled by the institutions that employ them. Political correctness tends to inhibit open discussion, therefore muting the positive aspect of tenure. We all need to understand the workings of these dynamics on our college campuses.

Why do people often ignore historical facts when trying to spin things? The Goofballs who wave bibles above their heads while delivering political speeches need to shut the fuck up. All the writings from 70 AD had little sourcing, and while the babble from Babylon and missives from the Middle East might be a good foundation for parables and folktales, they have no scientific or academic grounding. During that early time people believed the world was flat, the sun rotated around it and God talked face to face with their brethren. And, oh yeah, homosexually was a crime worthy of a punishment of death. If your daughter was gay, would you kill her?

Let's say you have a fatal tumor that must be removed. Further suppose you have a choice between an esteemed doctor from John Hopkins University Hospital or a Greek physician who served in the Roman army around 50 AD and, while expert at removing soldiers' arms and keeping bleeding warriors alive, he lost 70% of his patients to bacterial infections and gangrene. Which of the two would you choose?

We have no problem seeking comfort for our heart, soul and moral being from a 2,000-year-old document, but we surely wouldn't trust the butcher-doctor medical procedures of that era to heal us today.

We are told that God created earthlings in his likeness and that he sent his only son to save us if only we would believe in him. Now think about a crazy ass kid who goes to school and kills innocent students with a semi-automatic weapon. What do we do? We send thoughts and prayers. Really?

Could preemptive praying keep our schools safe? Shouldn't we be praying to God to stop school shootings before they happen?

Do we have enough faith in the supreme deity to protect our kids tomorrow? And what exactly are those thoughts that we send to people who are grieving? Are they thoughts of sympathy, fast trains or puppy dogs? Why do we say such lame ass things to people during the worst time in their lives? So, let's get to the 165 Doors.

A good friend of mine works at a very large school and told me the school has 165 doors leading to the outside. The sad truth of school security in America is the vulnerability we face in keeping our schools open and free. Every time there is another mass shooting at a school we go through the most idiotic rituals. Media outlets cover everything with helicopters swirling overhead and horrifying social media streams of the mayhem inside the barricaded classrooms. We have the tweets and lip service of prayers and thoughts, and then we have the interviews.

A conservative pro-Gun person might make a ridiculous statement like, "This is not the time to talk about Gun control." That leads to a testy argument about Guns with folks on the other side. Then some politicians say we must do something, but soon they hear the warning shots across their desks from the National Rifle Association — and nothing happens. Next, it's an attack on the survivors, somewhat like saying a rape victim was "asking for it."

We are complicit morons. The Goofballs who worship the Second Amendment scream when any effort is taken to resolve the problems caused by that document. Now we have legally downloadable files to stamp out Guns on 3-D printers. What's next, grenades at 7-11?

When I hear someone say how unchangeable an amendment is, I usually ask, "You know, we've changed or added to that document 17 times, right?" If you look at the original text, you will find that women and people who didn't own land weren't able to vote and it was legal to own people. You know, slaves. When something doesn't work, shouldn't it be changed?

How do we protect our children in schools from a bad actor crashing through one of those 165 doors? It's certainly unreasonable to have a guard at every one. You might ask, "Why so many doors?" and that is a good question. Kids and teachers need to be able to leave the building in case of emergency. Building and fire codes have legalities about *means of egress*. Remember that schools often change. When the student population increases, we add trailers for classrooms. If the student enrollment stays high, we add to the existing structure.

The security at baseball games and rock concerts is better than what exists at most schools. It's because most professional athletic unions and music performers have riders in their contracts with specific security requirements. If only there was a student union that could demand the same. Oh, yeah, they're called student protesters or, to the mentally diminished, "crisis actors." So, what are we going to do?

Nicholas Kristof authored a productive, well-reasoned piece for the New York Times news service that described ten things we can do about Gun violence. One of his ideas was "universal background checks" **before** someone buys a Gun and the timeliness of those checks. He believes we need a national online database that could instantaneously show a problem before a Gun is purchased. Kristof says the databank must involve "red flag" laws and indications that give the authorities the power to seize Guns from any person showing inclination to violence or radical plans to do harm.

Kristof believes domestic abusers shouldn't be able to buy or own a Gun. He says people must keep their Guns under lock and key. Parents of an unstable kid who commits a violent crime with "Daddy's Gun" should face consequences and share legal responsibility for the crime.

Kristof writes about better serial number protocols and smart Guns. These are nice ideas, but anyone can build a firearm. We could enforce maximum Gun purchases by a single person, but anything pushing against capitalism in this country usually doesn't happen. Remember, this book has the words GOLD and GUNS in the title for a reason. Stronger federal laws can curtail the resale of weapons at Gun shows. Get ready Texas. We are coming to mess with you.

I suggest we erect giant chain link fences around our school perimeters, like we do with prisons. Everyone would enter through one of only two entrances, each with a 24-hour guard. Shouldn't we demand that every student have a picture ID worn on their person like airline pilots? Sadly, that wouldn't get to the root of the problem. Mental health issues are most likely the primary cause of violence in our schools. The lack of funding for expert medical analysis is the nemesis of a solution.

The 2018 budget proposed by the Goofballs in Washington sent a message to the country and the world that our educational needs are unimportant. Why shouldn't schools get the same focus as border security? Why do we scream and yell about our borders when our school perimeters are as porous as a porch screen?

Let me put this in perspective. The White House proposed that we spend more than $4 trillion dollars for all the things we need, but we only bring in $3.5 trillion. Wow, how do we handle that? According to the Education Week website, "Trump's proposed budget, would provide the Education Department with $63.2 billion in discretionary aid, a $3.6 billion cut or 5.3% for the budget year beginning October 1, 2018." According to the Center for Progress website, more than $200 billion was added for defense spending in the fiscal years 2017 through 2019. The increase in military spending is three times the total amount spent on education. Rather than dealing with our schools, we pour more money into the military industrial complex as we send our thoughts, prayers and body bags after each school shooting. Are we incapable of understanding that our domestic security depends on much more than taking our smelly shoes off at airports?

To be clear, there is a difference between money for educational purposes and a healthy dose of dollars for security. In November of 2018, the Washington Post ran this story, "Although school security has grown into a $2.7 billion market — an estimate that does not account for the billions more spent on armed campus police officers — little research has been done on which safety measures do and do not protect students from gun violence." We might be spending more money on security, but are we learning what really works and sending our dollars in the right direction?

We are failing our children. We care more about the Gold. Teachers should not be armed with Guns, Mr. Head Goofball. We need to be spending more on education. Praying to God won't keep our kids safe. We don't need fewer doors; we need smarter ways of keeping the people behind them protected without inducing fear. You never know when a federal Sky Marshall is on a plane. That's the kind of perfect idea that has protected us without producing anxiety and apprehension.

We the people, have failed to penetrate the gung-ho, military-might thinking in Congress and the White House that neglects the funding of education. The priorities of those in power is stunningly off course.

My heart hurts when I think of all the parents who have lost a son or daughter to Gun violence in school. I voted to maintain a higher budget for my district public schools. The budget included $5 million for security and more **mental health professionals.** That is a small step toward solving the problem of the 165 doors, but without ending bullying and dealing with mental illness in our schools we will never achieve safety.

X and Y Chromosomes

I'm a man and told I am a Y, as in Yes, chromosome. A female is an X, as in, well just go ahead and write your own joke here. We know men and women need each other. Liberated people are aware women can do anything men can do. In today's world, men have become mothers, daughters and wives. If you don't want to be a woman or a man you can change your gender. It wasn't always like that, but it's crazy we are still debating issues like homosexuality and transgender realities. God made people gay or transgender or whatever. God created life, right?

Let's look at an aspect of language as we address the battle of the sexes. I'm not sure why it has to be a battle, but here are some terms worth reviewing. A "male chauvinist pig" is a man who believes men are superior to women. For comparison, consider the term "racist" — a person who believes his race is superior to others. There is no American English term that is the opposite of male chauvinist pig, but we do have the term "misandry," which is the opposite of misogyny. The term misandry shouldn't be confused with feminism, which not only has political, social and ideological attributes, but has as its goal the mutual benefit of equality, an objective that appears to be slipping away in America. Misandry is a woman's general dislike of, or contempt for, men. I would call it an ingrained prejudice against men, whereas misogyny is a man's dislike, or hatred, of women. Men who hate women are just like Nazis, and there are some Nazis who hate women. When Hitler came to power, all women's organizations were forced to accept the policies of the party or disband. Notice when the Alt-Right or Neo-Nazis march in this country, we see very few women chanting with them.

We've all known men who we referred to as a "momma's boy," which might mean no woman can match the memory of his mother or he had a bad relationship with his father. There is a vast distance between hate for a gender and respecting someone. I call myself a feminist, but that doesn't mean I hate conservative women or hold chauvinist pigs in contempt. I don't believe a conservative woman, who might hold old-fashioned values, is a bad person. I want to believe even the most unliberated woman wouldn't blindly follow her husband's demands or beliefs. That would be submission of the highest order, much like we see in Islamic cultures.

I wonder if male chauvinist pigs are just trying to get a laugh or if they really believe they're superior to women. I'm tickled when someone says a man is "pussy-whipped," meaning the woman in his life continually criticizes and barks orders at him. It's somewhat of a reverse chauvinism. Some men look down on other guys who are being controlled by women with a belief they are inferior males. Ladies, good luck solving his inner man.

Now let's look at some terms American men think are okay to use. Because he is a celebrity, the Goofball in the White House said he can "…grab a woman by the pussy." Did he **really** say **that**? And we still elected him! Are we brain dead? Of course, the remark is offensive and repulsive to most women and a fair amount of men.

Perhaps you've read the Venus and Mars books about how men are different, but are we any closer to understanding each other? Not really. Judging by what we witnessed in the confirmation hearings of Judge Brett Kavanaugh, it's clear we haven't progressed much since the flawed 1991 confirmation hearings of Clarence Thomas. They are both on the Supreme Court now and, to the naked eye, it appears they both lied to get there.

When I was a young boy, I watched the movie *Goldfinger* and couldn't believe the adults didn't react to the female character in the film being called "Pussy Galore." I kept thinking the makers of the film really pulled off a fast one and helped corrupt millions of young boys. Not only did we get to say "pussy," but our hero was shagging more women in two hours than we would ever experience in our high school or college years. Okay, "shagging" is the British term for having sex, and Ms. Galore's name came from the book which was written by Ian Fleming, a former British spy.

I have my "man moments" when I think, "Gee, I'm different than a woman." There have been hundreds of books written that attempt to address the topic, but I have never read one that clearly explains what really divides us. I don't get decorative pillows, but many women do. Pillows are made to be pillows, but don't you dare lay your head on a decorative one. You will be reprimanded. Decorative pillows exist only to be stacked over other decorative pillows, to keep them safe from — what? I hate them.

And here's something similar. What strange gene misalignment tells women they've earned a master's degree on loading the dishwasher? I call it *Dish Order Disorder*. No matter how a man loads the dish "rinser," a woman will criticize his method. This disorder is just as bad as the way a woman treats her man about his perfectly legal use of the bathroom. Let's put it out here. Women think they can constantly berate men for the smell of our poop. Women are the reason for those noxious bathroom deodorant sprays, whose fragrances become seriously impaired when combined with fecal odor. I wouldn't be surprised if a future study uncovers the fact that those deodorant sprays have been giving men erectile disfunction.

Women have collectively created two myths; their shit doesn't stink and they never, ever fart. This is total bullshit! Women do fart and some shit like sailors. Oh wait, women can be sailors. Maybe I should just say a woman can perfume a room just as successfully as a man.

There is a consistent prejudice surrounding X and Y chromosomes, but it's a scientific fact that women have sharper olfactory senses. Females tend to perceive smells, colors and textures more accurately than men. Some researchers, probably females, admit they aren't sure why women have better senses, but they do. So, let's give them a pass, as in "pass your gas outside."

In part, I blame the Catholic and Muslim religions for keeping women down. There are no female priests and women aren't allowed to pray with men in Islam. If the churches, the Bible and the Quran say that men are the ones who talked to God, then how the hell does a woman get a place at the table?

This brings us to Mary Magdalene, who did have a seat at the table with Jesus. She's the only woman, other than the guy's mother, who seems to be part of the "mythical" Jesus story. What was Mary Magdalene's role? Why don't religious people hold her in greater esteem? Why didn't she become the motivation for all Christian followers to socially, economically and religiously equalize women and men? Shouldn't equality be the cornerstone of any religion?

Mary Magdalene was a witness to Christ's crucifixion, burial and resurrection. She is mentioned twelve times in the Bible. Some say she was a prostitute or, at least, a sinful woman whom Jesus forgave. Some speculate Mary Magdalene was the wife of Jesus and they had sex, but the very devout scholars deny this theory. The idea a man could have sex with a woman and still be the son of God doesn't ring true to them. Gee, why not?

If you believe the Gospel, you know she was there, and she had a special power within the group. Some religious scholars say the other disciples were jealous of her. Why am I bringing this up? We know that some of the other latter-day, post-Bible religious Goofballs, like David Koresh, thought having sex with more than one woman was a responsibility given to them by God. Charles Manson controlled women with sex and gave some of them to other members of his family as rewards. Manson said all religion was "Mother's death wish." Joseph Smith, the creator of the Latter-day Saints movement, declared a man could have more than one wife to insure there would be lots of Mormons. Some breakaway fundamentalist Mormons still preach a man must marry at least three wives in order to attain heaven. Most of the world has moved away from polygamy, but even where it's practiced the protocol says men get more than one wife, not the other way around.

If one takes a cynical eye to the idea of "tying the knot," it could seem bondage is part of the marriage ritual. The ownership of a woman by a man is codified in our laws. In the state of Georgia and many others, one of the factors in determining the sincerity of a woman wanting a divorce is whether she had sex with her estranged husband during their separation. The judge can ask the woman to seek reconciliation if she has had intercourse. There is no impact if the husband had sex with another woman during the separation.

Women in America have been traded for Gold, betrayed by God, held down by Guns and told what to do by grifter Goofballs long enough. If you aren't free now, what are you waiting for?

Think of it this way. If a man needs an artistic rendering of a fly in the bottom of a urinal to properly aim his pee, how can we possibly allow him to con a bunch of women into thinking that God told him to control how they think or handle their bodies? How could any American woman let a bunch of old white guys in Congress govern her medical needs or treatments? It's been happening for hundreds of thousands of years, it continues today, and you men like it. Believe me, I'm a man.

I have three daughters and I want them to be free and liberated. That means their happiness **shouldn't** be the responsibility of another person, just as I wouldn't want my son to think his total contentment must come from his woman. Men and women are different, and that's good. If I had to spend the rest of my life locked up and had the choice of being with a man or a woman, I would pick the latter with one caveat, she would have to leave the decorative pillows at home.

The Politics of Gender

Soon in life, we discover there are two genders, and we create an "US" and "THEM" reality from the time we can express ourselves. I remember my seven-year-old son declaring very loudly at a family Thanksgiving dinner, "Boys have penises and girls have vaginas." He got a laugh and we learned how those private parts can drive a narrative at a very early age.

This country changed dramatically when women were given the right to vote. Through the years, women have gained much, but its clear men are not ready to give up power so easily.

Women are still being treated as second class citizens. That's easily seen in our newspapers, media and boardrooms across America. Very few women have an equal shot at making business decisions that drive this country, and some men still have a problem with female bosses or having equal footing with women in the workplace.

In early times, men had lances, spikes, javelins, harpoons and spears, giving them the power to control the game. Infused with the power of weapons and the natural pumping of adrenaline and testosterone, men once killed animals and enemies for their women. This kind of male pride is out of place in our modern world.

From day one, man's agenda is based on the "owning" of another person. The very words of "taking a wife" designates a notion of possession. Men often follow a pre-conceived notion that a woman couldn't possibly exist without their help. The average male is taught to open the door, let the woman go first and carry those heavy suitcases for her. It's as if we have the word "chivalry" tattooed on our foreheads, without realizing chivalry was a medieval knightly system that codified a religious, moral and social code. You know, don't treat a woman like a man because the woman is weaker than a man. Oh yeah, that's from 1200 AD!

Then there's this stupid quip, "Hey, I'm not against women, my mother is a woman." Yes, if your mother could really get into your inner brain, she might see her little boy has been working against female empowerment at every turn. Maybe that notion of superiority is rooted in the way the father treated the mother in the home, or maybe the blame can be placed on the mother who demanded to be treated like a queen. Some men may hate their mothers resulting in the origin of their misogyny. Ask Sigmund.

Some mothers carry a uniquely female instinct that makes them believe no other woman is worthy of their son's love. We don't have time here to unravel those psychological imperfections and the mother-son dynamic that drives some Freudian behaviors, but the complexities of inter-familial relationships can shed light on the reason men treat women in certain ways.

Women have a competitive zeal and/or thrive on gossip. Those actions hinder women as a group. Yes, women can be very harsh on other women. There, I said it. By the way, men also love to gossip so it might be just a human-tribal trait.

The good news is that women in America are making encouraging advances and we should analyze this from multiple angles. First, what took us so long? Why did it take years for women to gain the right to vote? What is keeping women from achieving total equality in our society? Why isn't there an enforced equal pay law in the United States?

There has always been an underpinning of inequality in most interactions between men and women. In the strongest form of misogyny, real hatred or prejudice against women and girls might exist. Men must be regulated when they hold these beliefs, especially in the workplace. A common man may say he has no problem with women, but his actions might include social exclusion, sex discrimination, hostility, androcentrism, patriarchy, male privilege, belittlement, violence or objectification. These are deplorable ways to treat anyone, but we men hardly ever see our actions from a woman's perspective. I'm sorry to say, guys, but some of us don't recognize it even when we're doing it.

Social exclusion can range from a harmless "boys' night out" to a more disruptive tactic like excluding female co-workers from important business meetings and decisions. The old swipe, "She can't be there, we're fixin' to talk about her!" doesn't hold water anymore. Employee rights have been codified by law and working environments are not allowed to be hostile. This includes objectification, violence, discrimination and unwanted sexual advances. Nowhere in those last two sentences did I write the word, "women." These are rules for all people, regardless of gender. Although some states still argue what "sex" and "gender" mean legally, as can be seen in the recent cases of restroom usage, but most of corporate America would rather have rules than lawsuits.

The recent #MeToo movement has demonstrated the strength and determination of women. We heard their shouts of discrimination and realized they weren't half-baked. It alarms some American CEOs to learn women doing the same job as men get paid less. Bean-counters advance a belief that men arrived on the playing field earlier, take less time off (pregnancy leave) and have naturally progressed historically into higher salaries. In effect, they're saying women are still catching up. One expert recently asserted it will take women 100 years to gain true parody with men in America. Really?

Can you believe that some of our top CEOs say they do not know what is happening in their own companies because they never checked? The figures were always available at their fingertips but analyzing was never a priority. Profit is always king, not queen.

We now know that many powerful men in entertainment, politics and other industries have used their positions to commit crimes and harass young women and men. These slime balls demanded sex in exchange for employment, or worse, got the sex and then used it against the person in a brutal reverse blackmail scheme. Some companies went so far as to blacklist women who refused to provide sexual favors. When the perpetrator was an industry leader, they were able to ostracize a woman by their sheer power over an entire industry.

Some men, like movie mogul Harvey Weinstein, were brazen enough to demand silence or hire private detectives to dominate the abused women. Other men, like the late President George H.W. Bush, just did his "David-cop-a-feel" joke with furtive reach-arounds during photo opportunities. Of course, "Boys will be boys," or, as one First Lady said, "It was just boy talk." Thank you, old world philosopher and trophy wife.

Now you might ask, "Aren't you making things worse by calling a young woman who married a rich older man, a trophy wife?" I understand your point, but I am correct. The definition of a trophy wife is a young, attractive wife regarded as a status symbol for an older man. Her husband bragged publicly about her attractiveness and promoted her as a very good looking First Lady. I assume the President wasn't saying that other first ladies were ugly, or was he? And let's think about the term we apply to an older woman who marries a younger man. The word is "cougar," and the younger man is known as a "cub." So, does France has a cub President?

Some might say a woman isn't a trophy wife if she's deeply in love with her man. I say, "What's love got to do with it?" Tina Turner once asked that important question and then gave us the answer, "Love is just a second-hand emotion." Whatever that means.

Something in the news recently caught my eye. A teenage girl decided to go to school wearing a T-shirt and no bra. She was called into the principal's office, where she was instructed to put two Band-Aids over her nipples. The principal claimed her show-through nipples would distract the other students.

The first question I must ask is this, "Did a high school boy really complain?" Now that question might make some females uncomfortable, but here's some BREAKING NEWS: Men, especially young men, are extremely turned on when seeing a woman's nipples. This mysterious part of the female anatomy protruding through a shirt is something most heterosexual males will naturally ogle, thus the forceful comeback, "Hey, my eyes are up here!" Maybe it's all part of the male primal wiring. After all, my first experience with a nipple led to nourishment.

The mothers of many of today's young women helped invent the Woman's Liberation movement. Their daughters may be still learning the ropes, but they will certainly strive to be cooler and hipper than their mothers. The female students in this story announced a form of protest they termed a *Bracott*. Remember what I wrote earlier, once you've created a marketing hook you've got a movement.

Yes, hundreds of braless girls going to school isn't as daring as bra burnings on the college quads of yesteryear, but hey, it's a start. Amazingly, the male attendance for the recent "Bracott" set an all-time record. So, that was a successful promotion!

It didn't take but a few days for another story about women and the #MeToo movement to hit the airwaves. Two National Football League cheerleaders brought wrongful termination complaints against their teams and the league. One of the cheerleaders was caught with a showy post on social media, which the team said was in violation of the cheerleader squad rules. Really? Her counter complaint was since other employees — male football players — posted pictures just as raunchy or even more inappropriate, she was being singled out. Clearly, the right to post a picture of yourself in a teddy, you know, a cami-knicker, is a right that every woman should have. I hope this has been resolved by now, but I'll bet it would give twitchy-fits to the Supreme Court, a place dominated by males and Catholics.

A cheerleader from another team said she was discriminated against and fired because she's a Christian and a virgin. Now here's a case that seems like a violation of the First Amendment, but I'm not sure the Constitution covers virgins. This adds fuel to my statement that women working together can be extremely catty and self-important as they apply their "justice" to other women.

You see the squad members asked the cheerleader in question not to flaunt her virginity and talk so frequently about God and Jesus. This woman's gripe focused on being penalized for her outward love of her God and savior, while the male football players appear on national TV to thank God and Jesus when they win. I'm still not sure what they say to God when they lose, but that's their challenge. The maligned cheerleader also pointed out that Christian players from both teams kneel together to pray to God before and after a game. Her complaint makes sense.

I think the #MeToo movement is much like "affirmative action." President John F. Kennedy introduced the term in a March 6, 1961 executive order. This concept is also known as "Positive Action" in the UK.

While affirmative action attempts to promote positive opportunities for "defined minorities," the #MeToo movement is a declaration of wrongdoing. The former looks to the future, while the latter attempts to correct past wrongs.

Our legal system places "statutes of limitation" on older crimes, but our leaders attempt to equalize things with laws and orders. I fully recognize that women in America have never been a minority, but certainly know that women have been treated as such. I also comprehend that men who use their power and position to harass and sexually exploit women are scumbags.

The goal should be the elimination of affirmative action and the #MeToo movement. If a man knows he could be fired for bad or illegal behavior, maybe he will be deterred. With a real fear of penalty, the #MeToo movement could die in the near future.

An endless cycle ensues when men who do bad things are promoted and rewarded. It brings about more boardrooms and court benches with people who think they are entitled to domination and power. The #MeToo movement has changed that, forever.

America is better because of all the great women who have been here from the beginning. We couldn't have done anything without women, so why is this even a debate? It's because men have still not grown up or gotten beyond the point that all men and women are created equal.

A built-in bias exists that gives more attractive women better positions in a company. This will end only when more women are in management or when more liberated men run firms. Companies run by women do well or better than companies with no women at the top. Women are just like men, only stronger. Men should try childbirth!

It all comes down to respect. There are more mountains to climb, my sisters. Keep going and never give up. Always remember that you have the power! You have something every man wants. I'm sorry to break the news, but men are animals driven by an instinct to reproduce, or at least a drive to start the process. You must train an animal to do what you want, short of rubbing their noses in it. You must never be afraid to say. "No!"

There was a time when Human Resource (HR) departments were thought of as a luxury, not a necessity. They have a lot to cover and control in today's business world. Don't trust or work for any institution without a clear path to have any potential grievances heard. And to all you HR people, please get some solid training and know the rules. You have a responsibility to the people you work with. Of course, any HR employee needs to make sure that state and federal laws are followed.

Here's some more advice to all women in business, including my three daughters. First, get the Gold up front. Don't believe the male-corporate lie when they say, "Well, we need to see how you do. Don't worry, we'll take care of you after you prove yourself." Screw that! Get the most money you can when you're hired and don't be afraid to ask if you're being paid the same salary a man in the same position would earn. Keep "the man" on edge.

Next, you don't need to smoke cigars, drink scotch and go to strip clubs with the boys to be respected. You don't need a golf handicap to be accepted. You don't need to buy a Gun and hang with the NRA. I've always noticed some female broadcasters try to take on male gravitas in their presentation to fit into a previously male dominated press box. Just be yourself and talk like you would normally. You don't need to imitate a man to be a successful woman.

If your God gets in the way, ask him (or her) to stay home so that you can do your job without being thought of as a religious zealot. Above all else, remember that not all Goofballs are guys. There is an equal distribution of stupid people across both genders. Just because the manager is a woman doesn't guarantee that you'll be treated fairly. Keep your eyes and ears open, but never your legs.

Lawyers in Love

According to many sources, 25 out of the 56-white powdered-wig signers of the Declaration of Independence were lawyers. Of the 55 people who were involved with the writing of the Constitution, 32 were lawyers. It's an understatement that the United States of America is a country of law and lawyers. There's even a lawyer in my family.

In those early days, as we were declaring independence from Great Britain, it was important to make sure we crossed all our Ts and dotted all our Is. Those newly minted Americans were making history and writing law at the same time. They were building a framework for legitimacy and needed to be respected by other countries, like France, who had to see our efforts as legitimate before giving us Gold to help fund our revolution.

The concept of the average person being able to solicit help from a qualified person in a dispute was baked into law before America even started, but we took it to another level and perfected it. Injustices like debtor's prison, self-incrimination and being held without being charged for a wrongdoing were positive things that made America special, but there is a darker side.

According to the US Bureau of Justice Statistics (BJS), 2.2 million adults were incarcerated in US federal and state prisons and county jails in 2013. AmericaProgress.Org claims the prison population grew by 700% from 1970 to 2005, a rate that outpaces crime and population rates. The confinement rates disproportionately impact men of color: 1 in every 15 African-American men and 1 in every 36 Hispanic men are imprisoned, as compared to 1 in every 106 white men. It's a shameful legacy.

Some of the biggest TV shows, like *Orange is the New Black* and *Oz* have vast followings. Then there are successful movies such as *Shawshank Redemption, Cool Hand Luke, Papillon, Dead Man Walking, The Green Mile, Escape from Alcatraz* and *Escape at Dannemora*. While we sit in our comfortable chairs, sip sodas and toss popcorn into our pie holes, we seem to enjoy watching men and women suffer in confinement. America is happy glorifying the most despicable aspect of failure in our tribe. Isn't jail just another name for slavery?

It took us a long time to evolve and correct the wrongs those early white landowners had planted into the documents and regulations of our land. The fact the slave population was calculated by considering each member as three-fifths of a human being is highly despicable. The results were used when apportioning Representatives and Presidential electors as well as taxes, thus codifying racism for many years. The delegates at the Constitutional Convention of 1787 called it the Three-Fifths Compromise, and it remained in effect until the Emancipation Proclamation was signed by President Abraham Lincoln on January 1, 1863.

The 15th Amendment prohibits federal and state governments from denying a citizen the right to vote based on that citizen's "race, color, or previous condition of servitude." Ratified on February 3, 1870, it gave African-American men the right to vote, but not black or white women.

Until the 19th Amendment was ratified on August 18, 1920, American women didn't have the right to vote. After 100 years of female protests, the white men in control finally caved.

Sadly, it wasn't good enough. Many states continue to concoct stupid voting laws that discriminate against and directly intimidate Africa-Americans. Much to his credit, President Lyndon B. Johnson pushed through and signed into law the Voting Rights Act of 1965. It outlawed discriminatory voting practices, such as literacy tests, as a voting prerequisite. The tactics of bigoted and highly partisan state bodies continually look for ways to **disenfranchise** voters they don't like and to **suppress** the vote of minorities. This is the most scurrilous abuse of power in America. But let's get back to lawyers.

Arabella Mansfield became the first female attorney in the United States when she was admitted to the Iowa bar in 1869. Although Ms. Mansfield couldn't vote, she could represent clients in court. Strange! Women would not gain the right to vote until nine years after her death.

In 1872, Charlotte E. Ray became the first African-American female lawyer in the United States. She also died nine years before she would have the right to vote. We've come a long way baby, but you can't tune a person's DNA or make up for the psychological deficiencies of the Goofballs who kept people down.

Power is a funny thing. As Lord Acton said, "Power tends to corrupt and absolute power corrupts absolutely." There's another great line from this guy that's not often quoted, "Despotic power is always accompanied by corruption of morality." Not bad, coming from a late 1800s English Catholic historian, politician and writer. I can't help but wonder what he would say about the Catholic church today? But let's get back to lawyers.

According to the New York Times, "Women make up 50.3% of current law school graduates, yet they represent under 35% of lawyers at law firms." The struggle for justice and equality continues.

We have two kinds of lawyers in America today, lawyers in love with the law vs. loophole lawyers who grind the system for their clients and themselves. The dawn of attorney advertising brought big changes to the legal profession. Interestingly, that jump into commercial advertising had to be decided by the Supreme Court.

Lawyers must take a bar exam to get a license to practice in each state. In 1972, two new lawyers in Arizona ran into some problems when they decided to advertise their services. John Bates and Van O'Steen ran ads for their fledgling firm. After the state Bar Association reviewed the ads, both attorneys were suspended from practicing law for six months in accordance with regulations of the State Bar of Arizona that banned advertising.

Being smart attorneys, they took the bar to court. The case eventually landed in the lap of the Supreme Court, and it ruled the advertising ban was a violation of free speech, you know, the First Amendment. Advertising for lawyers blossomed throughout the land and forever changed the way we view lawsuits.

We have those "ambulance chasers" lawyers, blasting out their TV ads twenty-four hours each day. They encourage us to sue and get big settlements. When many parties are harmed by an action, inaction or bad deeds of a company, a class-action lawsuit with many plaintiffs, can provide some relief to each. Although recent Supreme Court rulings are slowly eroding those rights, states might prevail with class-action.

There are times when we make fun of lawyers, and there have been hundreds of popular TV dramas about the men and women behind law and order. In any given lifetime, there will be a time when legal representation is needed. From benign actions like making a will, to the frustration and pain of a divorce case involving child custody, sooner or later you'll probably be paying a lawyer.

Practicing law in America is an honorable profession. The self-regulating state bar associations tend to keep bad lawyers out of the system, so you should be confident that a lawyer will help you. Trying to defend yourself, which is your right, is a little like walking onto a professional football field and trying to carry the ball. You'll get crushed.

It's hard to determine if a given lawyer is good or bad. About ten years ago, a friend of mine won a case while being represented by one of the most famous lawyers in his state. Only later did he learn that his attorney was convicted of bribing a judge. Was that the reason my friend won the case? Someone might suggest that "the end justifies the means," but we should always understand our laws and the reasons they were adopted. Crooked judges and corrupt attorneys demean America.

We must respect the judgement of courts and juries, but we should never let them cheat. If America has learned anything, it's that the legal system doesn't always get it right. Ask all those men and women who have been acquitted after serving years in prison. It surely doesn't justify the death penalty, does it? Time to Google: Central Park Five.

Laws should be challenged, and legislatures should keep a watchful eye on the effects of the laws they enact. When law becomes policy, we find out the true outcome of the pronouncement. Lawyers should be in love with justice, not their self-worth and reward. Good lawyers do good work.

Smokin' OPs

After the future Native Americans came from Siberia 15,000 years ago, many millennia passed as North, Central and South America became populated. The early settlers had this hemisphere pretty much to themselves, until those smarmy Europeans landed with their Guns, horses and germs. But let's examine things before the "invaders" landed.

Every village had a dispensable person who was asked to eat each new mushroom the tribe found. If he died, word spread quickly, "Hey the red mushrooms are bad, and you'll end up like stupid Larry if you eat them." That's the origin of the term, *village idiot*.

With this simple scientific process at work, ancient man entered new lands and discovered new ways to amuse themselves. If you look at the movement of people, it was obvious they needed to keep on the go. Human beings not only ate things, but they also had a fascination with smoking things. One of the leaves they found was tobacco. The natives knew that smoking the dried-brown leaves eased the anxieties of running their tribe. The smoking also gave them energy which helped them get through long hunts without having to stop and muster some grub.

Chewing and smoking isn't exclusive to North and South America. It happened all over the world. At 2 PM every day in Yemen, the entire nation stops to chew "khat," while dodging bullets and bombs. In South America, people chew coca leaves motivating them to work harder and happier. Asians gnawed on the betel nut for stimulation. It wasn't long until Native Americans got into the jungles and found marijuana. Yes, they were getting high on something natural, but let's get back to tobacco which is the main topic of this essay.

When the Europeans came to the Americas, they got turned on to smoking. They were literally smoking **O**ther **P**eople's stash. They occasionally smoked the peace pipe with the "Indians," but more often they killed those locals. When the Spanish, Portuguese and English explored America, they took stuff back to Europe to show their sponsors that their investments had paid off. They brought back chocolate, Gold, silver, beads and, of course, tobacco.

So, here's a fun fact from 1560. A Frenchman named Jean Nicot was the first to introduce tobacco to France, and it wasn't long before the evil weed spread around the world. In 1828, chemists isolated nicotine from the tobacco leaves, giving them the fancy name *Nicotiana tabacum*. Thanks for the name, Mr. Nicot. It's great knowing that the French were involved in our national addiction and, of course, their national addiction, as well.

Tobacco became one of the world's biggest cash crops because the explorers and conquerors spread the leaves and hooked the populaces. The new world had an endless supply of the soothing leaf. The demand increased, and America needed a large work force to maintain the supply of tobacco. Workers had to pick the leaves, put them up to dry and then roll them into cigars. Our early farm managers were looking for people who could work in the sun for long periods without being as affected by the hot rays as those Anglo, white-skinned Europeans. So, they seized Africans and forced them to work without pay. Bingo!

The addictive nature of nicotine caused an ever-growing desire to smoke tobacco. As a result of the free labor of slaves, farmers got rich and bought more and more land. The economic bounty from cigars, pipes and, eventually, cigarettes motivated the southern landowners to inspire even more smoking to keep things exactly as they were.

It is said that Christopher Columbus found cotton growing in the Bahamas, and it wasn't long before that crop was growing alongside tobacco in the southern areas of the Americas. Slavery provided the harvesting of cotton and tobacco at no charge, and the power structure of the south reminded the abolitionists that this ownership of people was ordained in the Bible. They claimed it as a Christian right. This eventually led to the American Civil War, and don't let any misinformed Goofball tell you that the war was about anything other than slaves and Gold. More than three million of our ancestors used Guns to fight each other over this issue. 620,000 people died in the Civil War, more casualties than we've had in any war before or since, but let's get back to tobacco.

I hate cigarettes. I smoked in college because my asshole roommates smoked, and I thought I was being cool. Hey, it was the sixties. After two years of a pack of Marlboro's each day, I started to get pains in my chest. I thought, "What they hell am I doing?" Sometimes, something bad can lead to something good.

Because my wisdom teeth (why the hell are they called that?) were impacted, they had to be taken out. During the three days I spent in the hospital, I didn't smoke. After four of my molars were removed, something strange happened. The empty teeth sockets in my mouth became infected and my jaw blew up to twice its normal size. I had a fat face and needed to stay in the hospital for a week while they doused me with antibiotics. Not all drugs are bad, Nancy Reagan.

By the time I left the hospital, I no longer craved cigarettes. In fact, it hurt like hell when I sucked. I survived the curse of nicotine addiction and haven't sucked since.

During my life, I have honestly answered this question from several women, "Would you love me more if I didn't smoke?" I always quickly and loudly say, "Yes!"

I've had difficult working relationships with people who smoked and have ended friendships with some. I'm such an anti-smoker that I vacillate between looking down on smokers and feeling sorry for those long-term addicts. I've had co-workers die because of their use of cigarettes. Everyone knows how I feel, and I do not tolerate anyone smoking in my house, my car, or anywhere near me.

I read with great interest a very well-written article in the New Yorker magazine recently by Jia Tolentino called *The Vapors,* which outlines the option smokers have now with vaping rather than smoking. New vaping devices such as the Juul, provide a user's lungs with a high concentration of nicotine without the devil tar. In the article, Tolentino points out that "Cigarette smoking is still the #1 cause of preventable death in the country, killing nearly five hundred thousand people a year." Okay, call me asinine, but isn't that like fighting the Civil War each year?

The war against cigarettes and cancer doesn't get any help from the Goofballs in federal and state governments because of the revenue stream. According to the Tax Foundation, the highest per pack tax on smokes is in New York State, at $4.35 per pack, and tack on another $1.50 in local taxes if you buy in New York City. Lower taxes per pack are found in Missouri at 17 cents, Virginia at 30 cents, Louisiana at 36 cents and Georgia at 37 cents. Have we really gotten that far from the glory days of the southern plantations? Why do their statues and flags continue to honor the slave owners? Who are these people?

If we got rid of cigarettes completely, more than $15 billion in annual tax revenues would go up in (lack of) smoke, not to mention the incredible black-market that would develop after cancer sticks were banned. It would be like speakeasies and prohibition all over again.

It's clearly a mountain too steep to climb. Those who promote e-cigarettes as an alternative to smoking tobacco have a point. If you are going to be addicted to nicotine by smoking cigarettes, why not eliminate the tar? I say quit smoking everything. Try using THC edibles.

We are an addicted America. To get our high we consume sugar drinks and slam back endless ounces of coffee. We are addicted to our phones. We are addicted to obtuse TV shows. We are addicted to pain killers, and when we can't get them, we turn to a natural product with a higher high, heroin. We need to get smart by eliminating addictions which kill. Really folks, we need something more effective than lame ass slogans!

Here is a question for you. With the amount of money we spend on healthcare and the treatment of those who have contracted ailments due to tobacco use, aren't we the catheter bags for not doing the math and solving the problem? According to Reuters, "Using recent health and medical spending surveys, researchers calculated that 8.7% of all healthcare spending, or $170 billion a year, is for illness caused by tobacco smoke, and public programs like Medicare and Medicaid paid for most of these costs." That means treating tobacco cancers costs us ten times more than we make from cigarette taxes.

If smokers are costing the American public so much money, why don't they pay more for their insurance? Some plans do impose smoking charges, but that has not deterred smoking. Maybe we should just help tobacco users move to safer things to smoke?

By giving up $15 billion in cigarette tax revenue annually, we might be able to save hundreds of BILLIONS that could be dedicated to cancer research. In this case, we are the Goofballs. I would have no problem banning the cultivating and sale of tobacco in the United States. We could all just go and vape our lives away or replace the tobacco crops with fields of green marijuana plants. Now, that's a win-win!

Reality TV Syndrome

There was a time a person who saw their image for the first time on film would gasp and ask, "Gee, is that me?" In some cultures, people hold the belief that their souls are snatched when their picture is taken.

Powerful personal technologies allow us to shoot a 4-K movie from our small, handheld cell phone. For those non-geeks, 4-K is the same resolution used in theatrical movie releases. A greater number of pixels provides easier post-shooting editing and a much clearer picture.

Social media now allows us to instantly post video and photos, essentially publishing to the world, and often without a second thought. If only there was a built-in delay, many embarrassing posts might never happen.

There are some great uses of instantaneous video. Police departments now deploy body cameras to refute or corroborate what happened during confrontations. Because they're date-stamped, these videos can be offered as evidence in courts and can radically change the way law enforcement conducts its business. The combination of security camera footage and body cam shots gives a jury an opportunity to be more fully informed during decision making. Reality is the hallmark of justice.

Let's step back a few decades to see how a reality film played a part in a major historical event, the assassination of President John Kennedy in Dallas, Texas. A man named Abraham Zapruder used a 414 PD Bell & Howell Zoomatic Director Series camera to film the President's motorcade as a keepsake. It wasn't intended, but the video captured the assassination. Zapruder's camera was loaded with standard 8mm Kodachrome II safety film, running at 18.3 frames per second. He shot for 26.6 seconds, exposing a total of 486 frames. Had Zapruder been filming with a modern cellphone, such as the Samsung Galaxy S9+, he could have captured the assassination at 960 frames per second. That kind of technology would have provided evidence about the direction of the bullets and possibly eliminated or confirmed the theory of a second gunman on the grassy knoll. There have been entire books written on the Zapruder film and some claim there wasn't a proper chain of custody and offer reasonable doubt about the integrity of the imagery in the JFK assignation footage. But let's get back to reality TV.

Time has rolled along in this country and we have seen more and more reality TV. People are charmed into believing that all video, even doctored video, is real. I lived in New York on September 11, 2001, and vividly remember calling my seven-year-old daughter who lived in Atlanta. I wanted to talk with her about this terrible thing that just happened to America. She asked an intense question, "Dad, is the stuff they're showing on TV what really what happened or is that just a video they made to show us what they think happened?" I took a deep breath and explained that what she saw was real. Of course, she became a lawyer.

As the 9-11 events were about to unfold, a French filmmaker was on the streets of New York shooting a documentary on firemen. While making a test shot with his camera facing the World Trade Center, he captured American Airlines Flight 11 crashing into floors 93 through 99 of the North Tower of the World Trade Center. After that plane hit the North Tower, cameras from all the TV networks were trained on the buildings and they acquired images of the second plane going into the South Tower. Later, the cameras of all the TV networks caught both buildings crashing to the ground.

There were no cameras in Shanksville, Pennsylvania, so we have no video record of United Airlines Flight 93 going down. The only remains were a large scar in the ground.

Because the security cameras around the Pentagon used an extremely slow frame rate, we have only a blob-like image of American Airlines Flight

77 headed toward the building. This is just one of the many realities of that terrible day that has led to considerable conspiracy theories.

The Pentagon recording was shot at less than half the frame rate of the Zapruder film of Kennedy's assassination in 1963. The video is much like someone who looks away from the TV for a second and misses a major visual clue in the plot of a movie. It's not their fault they turned away. In this case, the lens captured only the plane, pretty much centered in the frame. The image is nothing other than a flash of a dark blob.

What I call the "Reality TV Syndrome" started, ironically, with PBS. They aired a show called, *An American Family*, and it followed the daily experience of the Loud clan. Yes, that was their real name. The 12 episodes aired from January to March in 1973. 300 hours of raw footage was edited into one-hour episodes that ran on Thursday nights at 9:00 PM. They had 10 million viewers, a major ratings achievement.

What started as a psychological experiment ruined TV forever because of major flaws in the production process. After the editing of the show's raw footage, viewers perceived negative character arcs. The family didn't feel that their personalities and interactions were accurately portrayed, and this set the stage for all future reality TV shows. There's a maxim in the storytelling trade, **"You cannot have drama without conflict."** To be successful, a production must show conflict, even at the expense of truth.

Any scientific value that might have been gleaned from the show was totally voided. Family members were NOT themselves for the seven months of shooting because of the presence of the TV cameras all around their home.

Nonetheless, this show paved the way for American TV networks, especially cable channels, to produce low-budget shows without high-salary actors. The programs achieve huge ratings and advertisers were socked with top dollar advertising rates.

In the 45 years since *The American Family*, TV has been editing footage, coaching Goofballs, sculpting conflict and creating the many white lies to make you believe that what you are watching is real. It isn't. Even the winner may be a lie. It's never claimed that the results are not manipulated. These aren't game shows, they're drama. Winners on a show like Celebrity Apprentice are picked before or during the shooting and the host is just a prop.

If we are led into hatred of a character seen in a TV show, what would stop people in real life from telling us who to hate? If we trust the host, then we believe everything that happens in the show. We don't see the behind-the-scenes footage that has been removed during editing. A similar thing happens with news broadcasts.

The master controllers at Fox News and MSNBC transferred or promoted conflict by slanting their political reporting. Their weaponized politics created a compelling entertainment lure to increase time spent viewing, thus breaking the sacred trust of professional journalism. They aren't "fake news" outlets, they are simply NOT NEWS. It's an expansion of the Reality TV Syndrome and viewers crave it, like a drug.

While we are on the subject, here's a note to all you TV executives who think you are fooling people. We know that in those ten episodes of a new show the network has ordered, your writers create an arc and a foregone conclusion. Should the show become a big hit and the network orders another season of ten episodes, you have the staff rewrite the last two shows to create a new story arc that will extend the drama and carry viewers forward into the next season. Then you slow-walk the plot for the next five or six shows, waiting for that third season contract. WTF? What you are doing is bad storytelling and bad TV.

The Brits produced 14 episodes of their version of *The Office*, then they were done. In the US, *The Office* ran for 201 episodes over nine seasons.

Even the showrunners were saying, "Hey, this is going too long." We milk things until all that's left is shooting the horse. The old TV show *Mr. Ed*, about a horse that talked, had 143 episodes in six seasons. That's *waaaay* too many.

The more we watch a show the more we get sucked into the dogma of its creator. We believe everything we see, but never stop to think if what we're watching are special effects or doctored video.

People died on September 11, 2001 and those who lost loved ones don't want to hear theories about how the US government orchestrated a conspiracy to kill its own citizens. They would like the facts. ALL DOCUMENTS SHOULD BE RELEASED.

When those assholes streaming on media platforms say the Newtown massacre of school children was a made-up story, they are sick humans. They should not be allowed to do this to suffering people. That is a violation of their pursuit of happiness.

Some of those who suffered on 9-11 have gone after the Saudi kingdom. A US court rejected Saudi Arabia's request to throw out lawsuits claiming the Middle Eastern nation helped plan the terror attacks. The judge said there was a "reasonable basis" to allow legal action seeking billions of dollars in damages for victims. Why was this not investigated more deeply?

When we no longer can see the difference between REALITY and a doctored television show someone is heaping on us, we are in trouble. Remember the TV show called *Columbo*? Peter Falk played a homicide detective with the Los Angeles Police Department. One of the many Columbo quirks was his unique way of interviewing people. Just when you thought he had gotten all he could from a suspect or witness, he would retreat from his move toward the door to slowly turn back to say, "Ah, one more thing...." That's when he would then ask the most important question which helped him solve the case. What great TV!

When you are suffering from Reality TV Syndrome, please stop and ask yourself one important question. Is someone trying to manipulate you? Had we only done this in 2016, we wouldn't be talking about how the Russians tried to turn Americans against Americans.

Even our fiction creates non-truths. In the fifties TV show Dragnet, we believed the character Sargent Joe Friday implored female informants to provide "Just the facts, ma'am." In fact, Jack Webb's character never said that phrase on the show. We just think he did. And in the movie Casa Blanca, Humphrey Bogart's character, Rick, never said, "Play it again, Sam." We just think he did. And that is true.

Whores & Prostitutes

One of my favorite writers is Hunter S. Thompson, famed for his great book *Fear and Loathing in Las Vegas*. He once said, "All political power comes down to Guns, pussy and opium pipes." The title for this essay was inspired by Hunter and celebrates his way of putting politicians and grifters in their place. I wonder if his coverage of those in power perhaps pushed him to a premature passing. At 5:42 PM on February 20, 2005, at his home in Woody Creek, Colorado, Thompson put a Gun to his head and killed himself.

With that visual in your mind, let's talk about the real Whores and Prostitutes in America. I could have titled this essay Republicans and Democrats, but some people wouldn't have read any further. We're now going to have a humorous and serious talk about the elephants and jackasses in the room as we look at our political system.

Politicians have only one focus, a continuous quest to get elected. This is reprehensible. Once they get to Washington, or your state capitol, they are prodded into the herd. They are tasered into submission not by a mysterious deep-state, but by elder, partisan statesmen who inflict rigid control of everyone in the party.

We know any politician's voting record can be blown-up and used against them, even when the reason for their vote on a bill was related to a specific part that would benefit or hurt their constituency. I would urge anyone who doesn't understand how this works to read a bill. The arcane structure, demanding that you read amendments located in different parts of the text, make it extremely hard to understand. Much fine print exists elsewhere in the bill and many politicians miss those bits before voting.

The people in Washington believe the loud squeaking wheels and think they represent the majority. Congress has succumbed to party lines and minority rule. With daily battering by the alpha males in the club, even the most certain representative will bend to the mob-think of Congress. Herd mentality is the only rule in a self-governing body.

The newbies, who might have a sense of being more competent than their tenured associates, lose their convictions and purity soon after they step off the plane. They quickly discover that getting things done within our government is not easy. All the party challengers who were decried and pushed aside during the campaign are not the demons they were made out to be. The verbal abuse and castigating simply creates a long-lasting effect of a negative feeling inside the political ruling class.

The statistics are terrible. According to a recent CNN poll, just 18% of voters approve of Congress, while 75% disapprove. Lying in Washington is political sport, and those who finally get there don't care what people think about them. If they did, wouldn't they have embarked on PR campaign to improve their ratings? The talking heads on TV say, "Well, that is simply how political races are won and lost." Really? We can probably cure some of this insanity with term-limits, but my cynicism dictates caution. Look at what happened when all those "Tea Party" people got to DC. They didn't have time to learn how things worked and, their lack of knowledge slowed things down.

Political elections and appointments happen in a strange, filtered, acted-out manner. My analogy is digital compression. I'll try to keep this simple for our non-science readers. The sending of large digital audio and video files around the internet presented a challenge. We've all seen the message, "This file is too big to send." So, the smart guys in technology invented a concept called compression.

Everything in the digital world, including pictures, videos and music is broken down into a data element known as a byte. And a byte is simply a number but, when combined with other bytes, can yield a representation of a picture, a video or a song. Compression is a process of finding patterns in the arrangement of the bytes and expressing them in less complex ways that uses fewer bytes. Upon viewing or listening to a file saved with compression, the process is reversed, and the simplified patterns are expanded into their original arrangement. Compression schemes known as "lossy" delete some of the bytes. This forever degrades the quality of the picture, video or music in the compressed file and can never be reversed. Most lossy compression schemes allow the user to set the degree of data loss. Less lossy settings create larger, higher quality files, and vice versa.

Flagsucker politicians are adept at lossy compression. In their quest to simplify and make us swallow things, they throw out the bytes that disagree with their messaging. When the political lossy compression is delivered to citizens, their dogma should be doubted because the playback is distorted, and clarity is lacking. People who attempt to control messaging tend not to answer any hard or insightful questions. They disregard facts and divert to talking points. This misinformation can knock voters off the scent of truth. What really stinks is TV newscasters and commentators let them get away with it. There are few Mike Wallace's in today's media landscape.

How many times does a well-known interviewer ask a question and the politician instantly switches to something else? Even when the host says, "You didn't answer the question," the elected official leaves out the bytes they don't want to talk about. When it doesn't serve their purpose to answer the question honestly, they just make up shit.

The talking points of both Democrats and Republicans are designed to keep the stench of the lies from voters. Many times, the people repeating these points have no facts to back them up. When you get into an argument with a right-wing Second Amendment wacko about reasonable Gun control, they may switch to talking about how people are using knives to kill in other countries. What does that have to do with it? When confronted with another tragedy, these idiots restate the cliché that the way to solve a problem created by Gun violence is to use more Guns. WTF?

By the time the large file of facts on Gold, God, Guns and Goofballs gets compressed into little, bite-sized, digestible slogans, phrases, half-jokes and falsehoods, it's too late. The more they talk; the more conspiracies and myths are created.

The only way to stabilize the fault line in American politics is to **eliminate all parties**. While we're at it, let's **dump the electoral college**. That Constitutional safety net is no longer working. Whoever gets a simple majority of votes should win an election. And we must **outlaw gerrymandering**. It's a shameful, corruptive cancer on the system.

All these excuses for not fixing things reminds me of a story from baseball. When he hit his 100th homerun off the Phillies, New York Mets' Jimmy Piersall ran bases in the correct order, but he ran backwards! Nothing in the rules said he had to face forward. As long as he touched all the bases, he was good. This stunt was so embarrassing the league felt compelled to clarify the rule. It was not in the spirit of the game and, unlike gerrymandering, it was thwarted immediately. Gerrymandering's "excuse" is that it has always been done and there is no rule against. So irresponsible! Just change the damn rule. If the Supreme Court can't get it right, maybe there's a way to appoint better judges to that bench.

We need to ask each person running for election in America to face the citizenry and clearly explain their plan for making things better. We can eliminate the true bigots, assholes and miscreants through the primary elections to find three or four qualified people to run for office. Remove the notion of a party platform and demand each candidate tell us exactly where they stand and what they believe in. Let's make them sign an agreement with the electorate!

All candidates for any office, dog-catchers and judges alike, MUST release their previous four tax returns. We know the number of grifters, douchebags and dingbats who run for office is increasing, and this will be a huge step in the right direction. Just look at he who currently sits in the Oval Office.

We also need to eliminate all corporate contributions and Super PACs. When we take away the giant paydays for these self-serving bastards, we will regain control of our country. Why should a billionaire or multi-national company have power over our electoral process?

We all know a prostitute is one who offers sex in exchange for payment. We also know a whore is a person who would debase himself by doing something for unworthy motives, typically to make money. Most government participants in Washington are guilty. Once an interest group promises or gives a bunch of money to a candidate or elected official, they will articulate what they want in exchange. It's called bribery where I come from. For some reason, this isn't against the law unless the money goes into a politician's personal bank account. What is the difference? A large contribution helps them get elected and earn a pension we created with our tax dollars. It's simply long-term quid pro quo.

Few people see the complete picture and examine every byte to know what is truly happening. In May of 2018, the state government Goofballs in Oklahoma passed a law authorizing any adult to carry a firearm without a permit. If you are counting on a national database to warn us when a crazy person wants to buy a Gun, it isn't going to happen. Without a permit for a firearm, and many states are considering a *Constitutional Carry Law,* we will never know who has the Guns. This is the hogwash from the Russian-funded National Rifle Association. The good news on this one is that the Republican Governor, Mary Fallin, vetoed the bill, thus dodging a bullet.

The quest to polish partial information into certainty could be the demise of our democracy. When a lie becomes the repeated mantra of the masses, we are no better off than the happy faces in *Brave New World,* going through their days, watching the screechy, fear doused rhetoric of a misinformed zealot on Orwellian telescreens. We know they are whores, yet we make them legitimate with our silence. In the back of our minds we suspect they are prostitutes, yet we keep praying for them and paying them.

You might think we could fix it all, by electing new people. But they will slowly get lured by the pimps and the devil's bargain that says you can have massive Gold by taking care of the right people. Whores and Prostitutes who lie or remain silent when things matter most are one major problem in America. Another is politicians forgetting that the reason they were elected was to help people.

Carbon 14

I take comfort in using science to defend opinions, theories and thoughts. When someone rebukes true facts as "fake news," I immediately lose all respect for them. Let's not get weighed down by heavy people with no brains.

Carbon 14 is radioactive and has a half-life. Think of it like a date-stamp on something in your refrigerator. In the case of living matter, it takes 5,730 years for the Carbon 14 to lose half its potency. This is important because we often need to know the age of anything, from a petrified bone fossil to that old limp wiener in the fridge.

Our holy books were composed primarily to commit oral histories and long held myths to written words. This process has always been important in the development of men and women. Without a written history, we would know little about the way people lived during certain times. However, there is a flaw in this method. Like Carbon 14, a written account of a current event is simply a snapshot of one moment in time. We need to know much more about what occurred in the time between creation and now. It's called "context."

People who thought the entire world consisted of the area between western Europe and Asia, also believed the Earth was the center of the universe and completely flat, like a map or pancake. The writers could address only what they knew. Very little was understood about medicine, the human body and plant life. Knowledge about the timelines of animals, plants and humans can help us keep our planet alive.

The writers of the Holy Bible didn't know then what we know today. They didn't know the history of the world, whether Noah's Ark existed or, perhaps, the validly of the resurrection. There were few eyewitnesses to Biblical reporting. Most of what we read there are recollections of second and third parties. John of Patmos, while he was in prison around 70 AD, allegedly wrote the book called Revelation. Some experts claim he composed the Apocalypse prediction while suffering from mental illness. Others say it was a crack cocaine addiction. So, the Christian world revolves around the writings and predictions of a convict on death row? John of Patmos never met Jesus Christ. He was born six years after Jesus was executed.

I'm perplexed when world archeologists say they have never found any evidence of Jewish tribes existing in Egypt for any length of time. Was the story of Moses and the Ten Commandments a myth? We are certain the writers of these books did not know the age of the world or how it was scientifically created.

According to the scriptures, the Earth was only 6,000 years old when written. Far from it. We know the Earth was created 4.543 billion years ago. If you believe God made the Earth through some kind of "big bang," that's fine, but its creation took place a long, long time ago.

Man has been flopping around and walking on the Earth for at least 200,000 years. Through the discovery and research of bones and artifacts, we've been able trace the movement of people from Africa to every continent. All our steps can be tracked as we moved from hunter-gatherers to farmers to industrialists to whatever we are today. Moochers, I think.

In Poland, researchers recently discovered the oldest human remains ever found, the bones of a five to seven-year-old Neanderthal child. They were located among animal skeletons and scientists say the bones are 115,000 years old. Wow, there's more key information about our progression!

Even having photographic evidence and eyewitness accounts, some people want to believe certain events in history are just a huge, made-up hoax. BREAKING NEWS: If you think you can deny the truth about science, then don't get pissed off when someone of reasonable intelligence denies that God is real.

Could it be that Carbon 14 was put here by God to give us a path to gain knowledge of our creation? How can anyone doubt God invented the periodic table of elements found throughout the universe? They just seem so orderly and logical.

The cynical conspiracy types bother me a ton, almost the atomic weight of uranium, because of the wasteful use of their minds, morphing historical events or facts into a narrative comfortable to them.

A friend from North Carolina asserted that the South had won the Civil War and the rebels were nice enough to bring peace to the nation. His brain never connected the statistic that the end of the war brought freedom to approximately 3.9 million slaves. That's evident in the 1860 Census. It took five years for all the slaves to be freed, yet there are Goofballs like Kanye West who say that slavery was a choice. You know, being a Goofball is a choice, too.

Roy Moore, the Senate candidate from Alabama, once waxed poetically about slavery by saying, "I think it was great at the time when families were united — even though we had slavery. They cared for one another. People were strong in the families. Our families were strong. Our country had a direction." Oh, Really? Was is it a good time for families who were separated, tortured, shackled and made to work for free? Who are these deniers? They would be correct if they claimed, "Before 1863, 100% of the African-Americans in this country had jobs." Wake up Goofball, they were slaves!

The Civil War has been documented with historical facts and figures, photos and written accounts. Conversely, the man from Galilee walking on water and curing the sick with prayers is chronicled solely by 2,000-year-old word-of-mouth narratives. Our traditions bang into logic with the notion that Jesus was born on Christmas. It was probably a pagan compromise to land the birth of the savior in December. Jesus was probably born in the summer. It would probably be tough riding a sleigh in June.

Life today gives all of us vast opportunities to understand what has happened to our world in the past. Ken Burns, the famous documentarian, has covered everything, from war to jazz through baseball and on to the Central Park Five. After I have experienced one of Burns' works, I have a better understanding of what really happened. I encourage every American to spend time with his films.

We must stop denying historical facts that are based on proven Carbon 14 discoveries. This science does not have a political bias, as some Goofballs would like you to believe.

It's a sad truth that men and women are always going to fight over land, money, religion and weapons. The Gold we extract from our citizens is used to fight and exploit human capital, here and abroad. The God we pray to has been totally unsuccessful at stopping war, death and destruction. The Guns we endlessly produce kill innocent people. The Goofballs, who think they know best, get manipulated into war by generals, Neo-Cons and "hawks" who have no sure purpose other than inciting conflicts or wars. It's an insane loop, but it's good we have the Pope to explain it all to us.

In the movie *Pope Francis – A Man of His Word,* the highest figure in the Catholic Church tells us that children must suffer in this world because God so respects man he can't go against his own gift of human freedom. So, mans' freedom trumps compassion? When the leader of the largest church in the world says God cannot stop what free men do, there is certainly a problem.

Francis has fallen short on logic, science and orthodoxy by letting God off the hook for all the children forced to endure terrible lives. That explanation, coming from a man who could become a co-conspirator in legal cases against the Catholic Church, holds no water with me. Crimes against children caused by humans should be dealt with harshly. Will Pope Francis do the right thing about the pain and suffering his church has imposed on young Catholics over hundreds of years? You cannot blame God for what men have done to harm children any more than you can castigate a deity for a hurricane that takes lives.

Human beings are more than 200,000 years old and we have suffered some of the worst possible things imaginable, but more nastiness might be coming soon. The use of Carbon 14 dating could warn of us of future scientific peril or environmental exposure. What if all the lowlands of the world were covered in water? The people who would have to flee those areas would create a human refugee crisis far beyond what we can comprehend. Look at Bangladesh and you can see what water can do to a country. We know the age of the world's glaciers and we know they're melting. We need to study and observe the lessons of science.

We must use data to chart the future. We know our carbon footprint is creating larger storms, bigger fires and deadly floods. Are we blind? Isn't it the number one priority of humanity to protect the planet and the humans who live here?

If we can agree to look at science and be openly curious about the data gathered, we just might be able to make the world a better place.

The American Dream

We have all heard the expression *The American Dream*. What does it mean? Who started this idea? Was it Jefferson, Washington, or Hamilton? No, the credit goes to historian James Truslow Adams, who first talked about the American Dream in 1931. Here's his quote, "The American Dream is that dream of a land in which life should be better and richer and fuller for everyone, with opportunity for each according to ability or achievement."

Are you reading this book in your beautiful house, with your beautiful wife or behind the wheel of a large automobile? WTF? You may ask yourself, well, why is this guy stealing the lyrics of the Talking Heads' song, *Once in a Lifetime*? Do you believe in the American Dream? What does that phrase even mean? Does it mean that you get only one dream fulfilled, "once in a lifetime?" It's more than buying a house.

There is a misconception of life in America. It's not our fault. We don't even realize how well off we are. If you are over 50, you will probably remember your parents telling you how hard they had it. After all, if they experienced "the depression," not the sadness that pills defeat but the economic depression that knocked this country for a loop and our parents certainly reminded us, over and over. They told us about October 29, 1929, known as "Black Tuesday," when the stock market crashed and 16 million shares on the New York Stock Exchange were sold in a single day. Billions of dollars were lost. People jumped out of windows and killed themselves. They also remember the day we finally won World War II. Those who were not killed in the war returned to a country still rebuilding from the losses of 1929.

Savings and Loans institutions played a part in that recovery. Easy money helped people borrow at good rates to buy cars and homes. The GI Bill provided free education to returning veterans, so they could experience the American Dream. We thought "everyone" could make it, but at the same time we still had wretched segregation laws and customs denigrating minorities. For many, the American Dream lived up to its name, just a dream and not a free passage to wealth.

The post-World War II era was positive, and we didn't even think about inflation. We were growing and building and there was a job for everyone. We did have some bumps along the road, however. Under President Nixon we suffered wage and price freezes. Toward the end of his reign, we waited in "gas lines" to fill our tanks. That prompted every president since to declare our goal of energy independence. Back in the 70s, the Organization of the Petroleum Exporting Countries (OPEC) controlled the world's oil supply. If money was available to buy a home, feed a family and put gas in the car, most Americans stayed happy and believed they were living the American Dream.

We have taken punches to the gut that have cast doubt on this dream of ours. Let's talk about the rich Saudi Arabians who had close ties with a very prominent American family. Former President George H.W. Bush was a member of the Carlyle Group. Coincidentally, this organization happened to be hosting a conference at a Washington hotel on September 11, 2001, you know, the day now known as 9-11. One of the guests was investor Shafig bin Laden, brother of Osama.

Well, what the heck is the Carlyle Group? According to their web site, it's a global "alternative asset manager" with holdings of $201 billion and more than 1,500 employees in 31 offices around the world. They are, in fact, the organization that churns money around the world, and the World Bank is highly involved.

The fact that Osama bin Laden's brother was in Washington that day, was not part of a master plan. The theory the family of bin Laden were whisked away on a private jet after the FAA had grounded all planes in the

North American airspace is untrue. The far-flung conspiracy theorists would have you believe the father and the brother of bin Laden were somehow involved with Bush in a poppycock scheme to frighten America. The dreamed scheme is nothing but far-flung horseshit.

Beyond the death, terrorism and conspiracy theories, September 11, 2001 had a devastating effect on our economy. Wars and conflicts make investors more cautious, which impacts the stock market. There was another financial warning sign before 9-11, it was the dot-com bubble pop created by Goofballs in high tech who sold dreams and phantom-ware. Many of these mid-1990s internet services were just dreams and wishes, not real products. Soon, investors learned the need for more research before plopping down their millions in venture capital. The Dow-Jones industrial averages were stable compared to the hit taken by NASDAQ (the tech sector), and many investors turned to something they thought was more stable, real estate.

The Federal Reserve is the central banking system of the United States. As the new millennium began, the Federal Reserve, also called, "the Fed," was trying to guard its security. This central bank is not funded by Congress and its monetary policy decisions do not have to be approved by the President or anyone else in the executive or legislative branches of government. We count on the Fed to act responsibility and to prevent any upheaval of the US monetary system. Recovery from the dot-com bubble appeared to be going well, until events in New York, Washington and Pennsylvania changed everything.

Because of 9-11, the stock market had its biggest one day and one week drop. According to the Labor Department, 1,735,000 million jobs were lost in the US. The American Dream became a nightmare and it was important to get the country back up and running. There were bankers who thought they knew all the answers. They were at the poker table, down but not out. Instead of being prudent, they went "all in." They were Texas hold 'em poker players with no limits and hands full of number cards, while dreaming about face cards.

The nation's largest banks walked a path of destruction between 2007 and 2010. They traded in subprime mortgage, which led to their demise and created a serious mortgage crisis.

Instead of detailing the minutia surrounding the "housing bubble" that was created by "mortgage-backed securities" and "collateralized debt obligations" offering higher interest rates than government securities with very attractive risk ratings, let's cut to the chase.

The collapse of several major financial institutions in September 2008 disrupted the flow of business and personal credit and created a severe global recession. You see, these wolves in lambs clothing at the banks were handing out loans to people like a rehab leader passing out coffee stirrers at an AA meeting. It's probably one of the big reasons Barack Obama defeated John McCain in the election that fall.

Some in the financial sector were quick to state, "There's a lot of blame to go around," in an attempt to explain the massive failures of oversight, but that phrase feels more than a bit disingenuous. Institutional lenders, like the Fannie Mae and Freddie Mac government sanctioned monopolies, were handed a large part of the US secondary mortgage market. In fact, they were established so the government could bail out either the buyers or the banks if things turned sour. This *implicit guarantee* clearly linked the government to the collapses, because these ordained lenders are governed by the United States Department of Housing and Urban Development (HUD). As an aside, Freddie Mac paid Newt Gingrich $1.5 million for consulting services or, should I say, lobbying activities. The tentacles of politics and Goofballs are everywhere.

The tons of debt were bundled up like Christmas presents and sold to other banks. High-risk mortgages were hidden in collections with many better than average accounts. The victims took seconds and thirds on their loans, thinking they could continue to live the lifestyle the so-called "American Dream" promoted.

There are some in the banking and lending industry who equally blame the collapse with the right hook of "let the buyer beware." Yes, unaware or uneducated loan takers having no professional guidance might share some of the blame, but when are we going to stop accusing victims? One of the responsibilities of this country's consumer protection agencies, like HUD, is guarding unsophisticated people from bad decisions. The freaking bubble burst caused home values to take a deep dive, and the term *underwater* cut off the air supply of home owners.

The American Dream was stolen from them in the broad light of day and only one nefarious banker served jail time. Some homeowners abandoned their houses and left them to rot. In Arizona, people rented their neighbors foreclosed homes, so the renters' kids could stay in their schools. The grass grew so tall it almost covered the foreclosure signs in the front yards of many American Dream houses.

Aside from the lack of accountability and lack of revenge dealt in this case, our latest government of Goofballs is now working to eliminate banking rules and regulations. This whole disaster could happen again, and they know it.

We need to work on uncovering real conspiracies, like the hijacking of the American Dream by wealthy people in our country. It isn't that rich Americans don't love America, they merely love their money more.

We all want to see the stock market do well. The bankers clearly see how your American Dream has given them yachts, multiple homes and trips around the world on private jets. They care more about cash flow and profits than protecting our banking system or your 401-K. They are distracted by margins, bonds, interest rates and what the Goofball in the White House promised to do. Their American Dream is not your American Dream. **The power of the American corporation is increasing, while the power of the individual is diminishing.**

Members of Congress care only about staying in power. Not every one of their decisions is made for middle-class taxpayers. Some members of Congress love only notoriety and power, and if their constituency turns away from them, they often resign. When they see they can make more money outside of government, they run away. Ask Sarah Palin.

When trying to convince your boss you need a raise, remember that the average person in Congress makes $174,000 per year and the Speaker of the House lands $223,500 a year. As you try to make ends meet on a retirement pay of $35,000 annually, realize that every congressperson gets a taxpayer-funded yearly retirement package of $139,200 for the rest of their life. Did they work harder than you? Why do they get so much money?

If one more person tells me that God is watching over the US Government, then I say God is complicit in lack of a fair distribution of wealth in the United States of America. Why didn't God stop the bankers from pushing families from their houses? How is it moral for men and women to con Americans out of their own homes? Read the news and learn that Wells Fargo has admitted to errors which led to disaster for many families. Little late guys.

Frustration may have motivated those affected to buy more Guns, but that doesn't change the economic reality of the middle-class. Congress took our Gold, and left us on the beach with a stinky, rotting American Dream. It's not a reality, just a dream.

Whom Do You Trust?

In his well-written and illuminating book titled, *Elements of Taste: Understanding What We Like and Why,* Benjamin Errett points out this stark truism, "Teenage rebellion is generally rooted in the realization that adult society is full of lies and propaganda that do not make any sense."

On February 14, 2018, we all watched the horror of another school shooting unfold at Marjory Stoneman Douglas High School in Parkland, Florida. 17 lives were snuffed out on that tragic day. It also led to a first-time, genuine openness by adults to listen to the survivors and hear their calls for Gun reform.

We even witnessed a television intervention of sorts, hosted by the President of the United States. Parents of victims, survivors and people of political power gathered in the White House for a discussion about what to do next.

Events in my home state at first seemed encouraging. The Florida Legislature passed a law to raise the state age limit for the purchase of semi-automatic weaponry, but that was the only result of all that preceded.

Many Americans believe that the Second Amendment is a sacred promise made by our founding fathers to allow American citizens to form an armed militia against tyranny.

Other Americans hold the radical position that our country would be safer if we got rid of all firearms. That Second Amendment genie will never be put back in the bottle. There are experts who say there are more than 300 million Guns in the United States, basically one for every man and woman. Recently a man who had more than 500 Guns in his collection was arrested. Was he a one-man militia?

The youth of our nation have a right to feel disenfranchised by adults. Mr. Errett was correct; adults do say stupid things. For a few weeks after the tragedy, the students from Parkland, Florida and millions across the nation thought something would finally be done to make students safer. Not only was nothing done, but on May 18, 2018, ten people were fatally shot, and thirteen others were wounded, at Santa Fe High School in Texas. In this case, a teenager used his father's legally purchased Guns to shoot up the place.

America struggles with the divide between privacy and security. Even the court system seems to take a male chauvinistic view of spousal abuse. Look no further than Phoenix, Arizona and this story about a guy named Dwight Jones. His wife raised a series of complaints about violence against her and their son. Jones, after being divorced, was not only able to maintain supervised visits with his son but received support payments of $6,000 a month from his victimized wife. It's the old "she makes more money than he does" loophole. What happened next proves that the court system, cops and mental health professionals aren't keeping America safe.

In Phoenix and Scottsdale, Jones systematically gunned down members of the legal community who were involved in his custody case. He also shot and killed his tennis partner. In all, six people lost their lives before Dwight Jones killed himself. Don't tell me the system worked. It didn't keep people safe and the ex-wife and son are lucky to be alive.

How can we give reasonable privacy to people while also keeping the rest of us protected? Times have changed, but are we wasting our lives being paranoid about the "deep state" and "big brother?" We all care about free speech, but we must also keep our eyes and ears on the whack-jobs out there. Let's stop generalizing and start focusing on the important protections. The First Amendment is being eaten by the Second Amendment.

Not so long ago, a radical Berkeley student who was instrumental in the Free Speech Movement said, "Don't trust anyone over 30." Jack

Weinberg gets credit for the quote, but he's now more than 80 years old. We all get older, but do we get smarter?

From the dirty deeds of Charles Ponzi, the con man who is the namesake of the scheme, to the more recent scams of Bernie Madoff, we always fail to see it coming again. Madoff used a pyramid scheme to defraud unsuspecting rich people out of their savings, more proof that the world is full of adults who can't be trusted. We must find honesty again.

Then there are those people under 30 who can't be trusted. The personal digital data of millions of people have been collected, used, sold and distributed without their permission. The founder of Facebook was called before Congress to explain. It was 34-year-old Mark Zuckerberg who testified, and let's remember he started his information gathering empire when he was only 20-years-old. So, today's teenagers must keep their eyes on more than the adults.

Elizabeth Holmes, a wunderkind in the healthcare business, was only 20-years-old when she founded the company Theranos. It raised more than $700 million and, at its peak, was worth $9 billion. The device she was selling was supposed to bring low-priced blood testing to the world, but it ended up being a massive fraud.

In the Summer of 2018, former Theranos president Sunny Balwani was charged by both the Security and Exchange Commission (SEC) and the Department of Justice (DOJ) with allegations that Holmes and Balwani engaged in one scheme to defraud investors and another to defraud doctors and patients. These cons could have killed people.

The concept of trust and whom one can trust is being diluted by government Goofballs and flimsy "intellectuals" on TV. It's amazing how many magazine cover stories featured Elizabeth Holmes, the blood testing fraud lady, without any reasonable investigative reporting. The new generation is a bit too trusting. We need to think like slime balls when trying to figure out if a person is distrustful or perpetrating a fraud.

Willa Paskin has a great quote, "The internet's default mode is obsession." The need for instant gratification and reinforcement of self-importance keeps us tuned into the internet. We return again and again, sometimes within seconds, to see what has happened since we were last there. We consume news, our granddaughter's latest song and our friend's funny cat videos which give us a sense of belonging. We trust people who think like us, but I admit that I keep two or three right wingnuts in my Facebook friends list just to see what the other side is up to.

In his book, Benjamin Errett also talks about, "the dark appeal of bonding by exclusion." Some of the people we push away we should be trusting. We have lost some basic tenets of trust by thinking we know best, and we have adopted false protective shields to keep logic out of the equation. By excluding the opposite, we become more entrenched in one-way thinking.

The rage in Washington is Goofballs who think they know everything, but their vomit is usually just self-serving and mostly unproven. They hide truth and change the meaning of words. They are playing with your mind by telling you the government is getting too large and eliminating certain government jobs, while they are expanding the government in other places, giving their friends jobs and creating a greater deficit. WTF? Never trust an old, fat, rich white guy who says he's working hard for minorities and middle-class America. He's lying.

I grant you, certain organizations are there to help us, but there doesn't seem to be a way to spot the good guys from the bad guys. When you gut the part of the government which is supposed to make sure the banks don't rip us off, should you be surprised when another bank crisis comes? When you take money away from an organization that researches diseases, you are endangering the world. When you stop thinking that Global Pollution is a problem, you should probably invest in life preservers and sell that island resort.

In 2018, more American students were killed by mass shootings than US soldiers were killed in our country's many conflicts around the world. We must ask if we can we trust the Goofballs making our military budgets. Are they truly on our team?

My generation was once focused on why our country was sending us youngsters and our friends to fight in Vietnam. We learned the truth because of brave souls like Daniel Ellsberg. He released the Pentagon Papers and revealed the Goofballs' lies, which sentenced thousands of our sons and schoolmates to death in southeast Asia. The falsehoods that were exposed should have never been forgotten, but they were. Thousands of lives could have been saved if it wasn't for the egos of generals and the devious motives of politicians. Before he was president, Richard Nixon committed treason by colluding with the Viet Cong to keep the war going a few more years. You see, we were right to not trust big brother then, nor should we now.

In a newer iteration of distrust, we saw a man named Edward Snowden take the radical step of disclosing the illegal spying on Americans by the National Security Agency (NSA). We learned they were monitoring our phone calls, making the large telephone corporations complicit in the eavesdropping. They are still doing it. For his whistle blowing, Snowden landed on the FBI's Most Wanted list and he now lives in Russia. Why does everything bad involve Russia?

The Supreme Court used an 18th century document to guide their judgements about the use of high tech to tap your phone. They even decided whether police needed a warrant to obtain location pings while your cell phone is on. I'm sure they made the right decision.

In the last decade, we learned that American forces and the Central Intelligence Agency (CIA) tortured enemy combatants considered to be terrorists. Those acts, whether taking place at "black sites" located off US soil or in military prisons, directly violated the Geneva Convention war rules we signed in 1949. This agreement is an International Humanitarian Law put in place to protect our soldiers and fighters who might be captured. Who will rely on us if we disregard our own agreements?

The concept of trust is a large part of who we are as Americans. We talk about the trust and will of the people, and we trust in God. We must reestablish trust through honesty and transparency if we want to narrow the divide in our country.

Remember, Bernie Madoff made people lots of money before he was exposed. If an attempt at transparency delivers only more lies, then we are doomed. People who give you a tax cut might not have your back for the long term. The same people say that mandating an increase in minimum wages will hurt the economy. Really? Tell that to the single Mom working two jobs. Listen carefully to the words of the Goofballs and ask lots of questions. Demand commitment and real answers. Whom do we trust?

Take a Knee for America

America was built on protest. We have a right to speak up and those who do don't always get what they want, but the fun of making a big old demonstration poster and walking around chanting a slogan against some bad person or thing feels damn good.

Let's start at the beginning — this part of our First Amendment: **"…the right of the people peaceably to assemble, and to petition the Government for a redress of grievances."** When the founding fathers wrote those words, they did so recalling an incident in Boston that didn't involve a football, baseball, hockey or a basketball team.

Most Americans know this story. Much of America was controlled by Great Britain in the late 1700s and the King of England had a say in what happened here. In 1760, at the age of twenty-two, King George III took the throne and, judging from historical writings, he was a totally spoiled brat.

The Brits decided to exploit the new world for their purposes, so in 1765 they enacted a stamp duty on newspapers, legal papers and commercial documents. Colonial opposition (that's us, the Americans) led to the act's repeal in 1766. The Stamp Act was hardly forgotten when the British bastards came back with the Townshend Act of 1767. These were import taxes on glass, paint, paper, lead and, of course, tea. You know, the drink you serve at a party.

If those taxes or tariffs weren't bad enough, the absentee government across the pond also introduced what they called *writs of assistance,* which were just bloody blank search warrants. It gave the British soldiers the right to arbitrarily, and without notice, enter and investigate anyone's home, office or hotel room.

On a snowy night in Boston on March 5, 1770, a bunch of punks and rowdies were messing with the British soldiers who were sent there to assist the customs officers collecting the tax. The young whippersnappers started throwing snowballs at the redcoat British soldiers. Like many nervous military types, the soldiers shot into the crowd, killing three people and wounding others. Two people later died of their wounds. The bad news is five people died, but the good news is AR-15's hadn't been invented yet, or the death count could have been worse.

Eight soldiers were arrested and charged with murder. Future President John Adams defended the soldiers in court. Six of the British soldiers were acquitted, while two were convicted and given what we would call a slap on the hand. Our newly developing country surely had a sense of humor. The guilty soldiers were not given jail time or hanged. The court ordered their thumbs be branded.

Six years later, the young American troublemakers in Boston used this event to muster support for the Declaration of Independence. People like Paul Revere, a silversmith and a guy who liked to ride horses, along with his buddy Samuel Adams, second cousin to John Adams, remembered what happened that fateful night in 1770. By the way, Sam Adams did work for his father's malt house and sold grains to brewers, but Sam himself didn't make beer.

Events during the next six years set a course to independence for our 13 colonies and the formation of the United States of America. Did politicians and statesmen exploit this protest gone bad? Of course, they did. They also felt that dissent should became part of who we are as a country. When someone who disagrees with another is accused of "being political," I must chuckle. From its early beginnings, everything about America has been political.

My first protest was against the Vietnam war. The insight of my limited college education told me this was an ill-advised war without a possible positive conclusion. Plus, some of my friends were going away to war and never coming back.

When I marched in the streets, I felt a connection with my generation and had a "patriotic feeling." I was speaking out and doing something. It was a non-violent, non-destructive display with TV coverage. I was pleased with myself, until I stepped off the sidewalk and tried to cross the street. A mammoth Pittsburgh Policeman raised a large nightstick over my head and screamed, "Get back on the sidewalk or I'm going to smash in your fucking skull." I backed up and stepped over the curb. Nice guy.

Many protests are called "marches," but back in those days we also had "Sit-ins" and "Love-ins," which were peaceful public gatherings focused on meditation, love, music and sex. People dropped acid and laid around in protest of, well, I'm not sure what. And by the way, "acid" is Lysergic Acid Diethylamide (LSD), and after taking that drug it's doubtful anyone would know what the hell they were protesting.

America witnessed some protests that turned ugly and sad. On May 4, 1970, four unarmed college students were shot and killed by members of the National Guard at Kent State University in Ohio. The students were protesting the Vietnam War and illegal incursions into Cambodia by US troops. No soldiers or commanders of the State Guard were ever charged in the murders of the four dead kids.

Days later, on the Mississippi campus at Jackson State University, two students were shot to death after a small protest of the Vietnam War. Perhaps the killings at Kent State had given the police and guard in Jackson the green light to murder some more students.

Throughout American history we have used protests to make those in power aware of things we thought weren't right. The recent March for Our Lives was organized by students from Parkland, Florida after another school shooting. Some say as many as two million people marched that day but, sadly, nothing changed.

We've had Million Man marches and we've had a March for Women's Lives. Would we still be a Democracy if we didn't march? What do we say to those people who become frustrated when nothing happens after a protest? Well, I would remind them of the Moratorium to End the War in Vietnam on November 15, 1969. The Vietnam War did finally end (six years later), and I truly believe our demonstrations made a difference.

If you are conducting a March for Science, or a March Against Global Warming, you will need to give it time. If you are impatient like me, let's just kick the Goofballs out of office.

There's a potential danger with protesting caused by people who support a cause but attempt to force the issue with destructive behavior. These are anarchists who break things, turn over cars and light stuff on fire. They tend to join protests in cities with economic forums. They are not helpful and have only given protesting a bad name.

There are times when you know you are right and feel a need to march against a march. Look no further than on the night of August 11, 2017, with the "Unite the Right" rally in Charlottesville, Virginia. Neo-Nazis, white supremacists and KKK organizers chanted things like "Jews will not replace us!" The poison continued the next day when a White Supremacist drove his car into a crowd of marchers killing Heather Heyer, a peaceful protester, and injuring many others. A year later, the driver of the lethal car was sentenced to life in prison. Some small justice.

This rally was organized by right wing crazies dissenting the plan to remove a statue of the Confederate General Robert E. Lee from a city park in Charlottesville. So, you see, one can protest a protest just like one can protest an elected President. At this writing, the statue of the loser of the war, General Lee, still stands in Charlottesville. Even Robert E. Lee said there should not be a statue commemorating him. Why are these things still standing on public land?

We must always remember that our First Amendment covers everyone, meaning we must let the Neo-Nazi sleazebags assemble peacefully. They have the same rights as the rest of us. That's what America is all about.

Ever since Abraham Lincoln signed the Emancipation Proclamation on January 1, 1863, there have been questions and concerns of racism. We know what the law says, and we know every law has a spirit behind its words, but we can't legislate the banishment of hate in America. It will slowly work its way out of our systems, but there are those who have totally misinterpreted American movements based on the tenets of equality. Black Lives Matter would be seen in a more objective light if the word "Black" was changed to "Native American" or "Irish American" or "Polish-American" or "Asian American."

Some Goofballs and misinformed humans face off against the National Football League. The protesting players in the NFL are not opposing the flag or America, they are protesting bigotry and hate. If you think they are against our country, then you haven't taken the time to listen to what they are saying.

Many white people fail to understand the reality of African-Americans, who often feel uncomfortable in their own country and skins. "The forgotten white majority" is a nauseating phrase used by the right-winged loonies as justification for segregation, school vouchers, cutting all state aid for higher education and other discriminatory actions. If you are a white person in the United States and you think you've been forgotten, you are an imbecile. I also don't appreciate a person of color in power who accuses their co-workers of "white privilege." You will never make things better in this country by putting your foot on the neck of another American.

Nonetheless, we must all deal with reality. According to the Guardian newspaper, "Twice as many unarmed black people in America are shot by police than unarmed white people." That is a single fact that exposes many problems.

White America often sees black people through a filter, as innocent as it may be. When confronted with a need to determine who is in the right, the white cop or the black guy, many white folks will automatically believe the black man must have done something wrong. And I must snicker when the white person claims that, "Race has nothing to do with it."

Neurobiologists have studied our brain chemicals using magnetic resonance imaging (MRI), and know the specific tints of a hateful brain. Bigotry can be measured scientifically. We slowly lose prejudices when we spend more time with those who look different than we do.

If you are white, you may think the guy writing these words must be black. Well, I'm not. My opinions and thoughts aren't based on the color of my skin.

Some white people were offended when they saw African-American football players taking a knee during the National Anthem. I get it. We all have a patriotic belief that everyone living here should respect the country, the flag and the National Anthem. But don't miss the point. Remember that **protesting is a primary part of our country**. It's who we are. The African-American football players are not protesting America, the flag or the anthem. Even late Supreme Court Justice Antonin Scalia argued that flag burning is protected by the First Amendment. Look it up.

Upon the death of a sports team member, the league allows the team to wear patches on their uniforms with the initials of their fallen teammate. WHY? The team wants to honor their dearly departed, even though the league disallows using the uniform to promote personal sentiments or business interests. The team and league own the logos and uniforms, but those corporate monopolies don't own their employee's opinions.

The NFL President recently said that a professional football player may stay in the locker room during the National Anthem, but if they are on the field of play then they must stand during the song. Isn't a player staying in the locker room just another way to protest? It's a compromise to safeguard the business, not necessarily to protect a highly skilled millionaire's right to protest. This controversary was boiling up again as I finished writing this book, and I'm convinced this mercurial issue will continue to be debated without a desperately needed solution. It reminds me of the "don't ask, don't tell" military ruling, which was one of the stupidest policies of the Clinton administration. We are either free to express who we are, or not. We should never relinquish our freedom of speech and expression.

I find it ironic that a little league coach tells his team to, "Take a knee," after a game, so they can talk about the game. If NFL players were praying while the National Anthem was playing, would that be okay? Does religion trump nation? We should ask Mike Pence. When did taking a knee become so disrespectful? I personally would have gone with the Black Power fist in the air.

I wonder what they would say if we asked those young people in Boston who lost their lives back in 1770 what they thought about how we protest today. Would they ask, "Is Roger Goodell a King?" You know, it does seem like he is the king.

One of the protesters killed back in 1770 was a freed black slave. Crispus Attucks, a dock worker born in Framingham, Massachusetts in 1723, spilled his blood for a country not yet formed. Would Crispus take a knee if he were alive today?

If you are confused, you should be. Does it matter that a football player wants to say something about the lives of black kids in America? Why did this become such a big problem? Does anyone have the right to judge your motives and ask you to prove your patriotism? To protest is patriotic.

Things Used to be Better

Some Americans get a warm, fuzzy feeling when looking back to their early years. We often hear these nostalgic words, "Back in the good old days." It's a natural, regressive impulse. Today's shortened version is, "…back in the day." We feel comfortable being retro because, as they say, "Things used to be better."

I wonder if a founding father on his deathbed thought, "Gee, things were so much better when we suffered from gout and had to deal with those British bastards." Do you ever hear first generation European immigrants saying how much better it was to move to New York and live in tenements?

Even our parents, the ones belonging to what television calls the "greatest generation," had to deal with starting families while Daddy was overseas fighting the Nazis or Japanese. They reminded us often how bad things were during the depression and how they had nothing to eat. Now they sport a beer belly or, in my father's case, an ice cream belly.

Occasionally we get a funny email reminding us about how things were when we were growing up. It was a time when "swipe" meant stealing and not paying. We used products like "Wite-Out" to correct the mistakes we made when using a manual typewriter. Oh, how things have changed in our lifetime.

While I was a radio consultant, I preached that most people established their musical tastes between 12 and 18 years of age. We carry that profile for the rest of our lives. Yes, my older sister grew up with Elvis and I grew up with the Beatles, while my younger brothers loved Kiss and Led Zeppelin. My kids listened to Eminem and Incubus.

In radio, we were always on the lookout for new artists who fit the demographic and social profiles of the listeners we wanted to attract to our station. It didn't always work. The common "wisdom" was women disliked heavy metal and white people hated dance music. Stereotypes with music are unwise. Michael Jackson enlisted rock genius Eddie Van Halen to play guitar on the song *Beat It*, and that was a trailblazing change. What was the world coming to? Generalizations are a perfect way to miss the next best thing, even if it appears right before your eyes, or ears.

You would think a positive environment would produce a confident human being. Some believe that one who works through struggles and stress is more grateful for their success, but that's not always true.

Ask any undocumented worker in our country if things were better in the old days. They will probably tell you that as tough as things are here in America for immigrants, they have no desire to go back to the old days or their home country. Why is this such a big mystery to the Goofballs in the White House and Congress? People who walk 800 miles to get to America are escaping murder and mayhem. They do not come here to join up with the thugs and cartels in this country. They could have done that back home.

I recently visited the 1903 train station in Venice, Florida, which is now a museum. The historical sign in front of the building points out that the depot was built at a cost of $47,500 and included segregated waiting rooms, ticket windows, baggage and freight rooms. So, both the waiting rooms and the ticket windows were segregated. Were those the good old days in America? Well, not for African-Americans who are still treated to real racism right here in their own country. Despite that, ask any of those families if things were better back then. Ask them if they want to go back to Africa. That was once their country, but no longer. They are now Americans living in America.

Recycling is proof that America loves to return to her past. We remake movies and TV shows. We resurrect styles and looks with the hope we will find peace and love, if only we could place a little more paisley in our lives. Can we truly find happiness in the past?

We are proud when one of our countrymen comes up with something new. To make sure we would have communication during an all-out global war, the pentagon invented the internet. Universities quickly jumped on this electronic gateway to have instant, constant connection with other college researchers working on similar projects. Thank you, America, for making the internet.

Occasionally, I think about how long it took to get things done without the internet. Mailing a letter to someone meant that you probably wouldn't get a response for more than ten to twenty business days on even the most critical matters. Those certainly weren't better times for anyone. Technology also moderates the marketplace. I remember 1970, when some of my college friends ran up hundreds of dollars' worth of long-distance calls to their girlfriends. Now, our cross-country phone calls cost nothing extra.

Is there any truth to the idea that certain foods were better back then, or was that just our imagination? It's thought provoking when someone pines for the used-to-be larger size candy bar. We've all heard, "Man, this used to be so much bigger when I was a kid." Yes, that is true, and your hands were smaller back then, but does that make the candy bar better?

I remember a Mexican restaurant on Ross Avenue in Dallas, Texas that had the best Mexican cuisine I ever ate. It was one of those straw-on-the-floor cowboy places always being shut down by the board of health. Regardless, the food was tremendous. Eventually they lost their lease, moved up the street and opened a new, clean, well-lighted place. It had the same name, but the food was mediocre. What happened?

Sometimes we change the way we do something because we want to put our own unique stamp on it. Sometimes our ancestors did not follow the rules when they cooked food or made products. The inventors of the combustion engine didn't care about pollution, they probably didn't even know what was coming out of the exhaust pipe.

The people who make food are also at the mercy of their vendors. I knew a small hot dog shop in upstate New York that served the best Coney dogs with chili. The owner retired and sold the property. The first thing the new guy did was to buy different buns. Then he changed the chili meat slightly, perhaps thinking cheaper beef would help reap a greater profit. It wasn't long before I stopped going there. It simply wasn't as good. What were they thinking?

On the other hand, my high school hang-out was a hoagie-pizza place located in South Park, Pennsylvania. To this day, watching the South Park TV show brings back memories of pizza and Italian hoagies from DANNY'S. On a trip back to Pittsburgh, I decided to return to the scene of the crime and see what the experience was like today. I managed my expectations by assuming it wouldn't be nearly as good. Such a "Debbie-Downer," right?

Well, much to my delight, it was exactly like I remembered it. Even down to one guy who I saw as a kid in the 1960s, sliding those hoagies into the pizza oven. There he was, roasting the meat and bread to a buttery golden brown, before putting the lettuce, tomato and Italian dressing on the concoction. Change doesn't occur very frequently in Pittsburgh. It's why people stay there.

Is looking back to your memory for a brighter time a healthy way to live? Americans have so many things to recall, both good and bad. If you keep thinking everything was better back then, be careful. You might start to sound like your parents. When things get declassified and we learn what really happened, we are typically less impressed with the past. There is a vast difference between a great memory and the next moment.

My parents were happy through most of their lives. They had "sacrificed" for their country, therefore our family suffered tons of conflict when I was protesting the Vietnam war. They truly believed in the government. Is that what people remember about the 40s, 50s, 60s and 70s? People today have no trust in institutions. My barber said to me the other day, "There is no sense of truth anymore. It's lost forever." Because he had a sharp object in his hand, I wasn't about to disagree with him.

Perhaps this is the real problem. When we look at today with a strong cynical filter, the past seems so much better; everything shimmers like a bright light at the top of a hill. Wait, who said that? Ronald Reagan, that's who, "America is a shining city upon a hill whose beacon light guides freedom-loving people everywhere." And, of course, Ronald McDonald said, "Two all-beef patties, special sauce, lettuce, cheese, pickles, onions on a sesame seed bun." Both Ronalds wore make-up. One is the face of a charity that helps families with terminally diagnosed children. The other was an actor, who was once the president of the Screen Actors Guild, a union, who then went to work for General Electric to help break up the unions. Did he evolve into a conservative, or was he just acting like a liberal when he was an actor?

Later, President Reagan fired all our air traffic controllers when they went on strike. We remember the quote about tearing the Berlin wall down, but we forget about the Iran-Contra Deal (look it up). He claimed he didn't know what Oliver North was up to. Gee, I wonder whatever happened to that North guy who became a convicted felon? NEWS FLASH: He now heads the NRA.

Ronald McDonald was put on the bench when we had these creepy clown sightings all over the country. What is America coming to? To save their PR face, most of our institutions make changes and decisions based on the internet mob and what's trending. We generally succumb to the small, misguided bunches of people with loud mouths and nimble fingers. Are we losing our moral fiber, our backbones, our individuality or our righteous compass?

Sitting in my office in New York on 9-11, watching the World Trade towers fall to the ground, I could see the fear and angst in the eyes of my co-workers. I called my mother in Arizona and told her I was okay. I remember her voice, "Oh no, we can't have another war. I remember how bad it was last time." Don't fool yourself. Not everything from the past was better.

I realized the United States had entered a new phase on that glorious-blue-sky September day. It was a time we knew we had to get back at them and do something. I was offended we were attacked. I was angry that we didn't spot the conspiracy before it happened.

In that specific moment, I needed a warm and fuzzy feeling of security with something from my past. I took a walk around the block and saw McDonald's. I went up to the counter and ordered a Big Mac. I hadn't had one in years. Nothing more American than a Big Mac, I thought.

It wasn't as good as I remembered it. My stomach was full after the meal, but my heart was still empty. Face it, America, we can't go backward to find meaning and gratification. We must move forward. Can we just make tomorrow better? Let's no longer dwell on the past. Let's make a better memory tomorrow.

Disagreeable People

We open with this rich quote from Matt Taibbi, "We live in a country where people believe implicitly in their right to bore the living shit out of absolutely everybody within haranguing distance with tales of their miserable, lonely, and inevitably self-deluding searches for personal fulfillment in the emotional desert that is our crass commercial culture."

Many conversations in life go nowhere. If Matt were asked to analyze his message, he might say it's rather harsh. Aren't we all involved in some kind of "self-deluding searches for personal fulfillment?" A better question might be this. Who determines if these searches are self-deluding or merely outcries for love?

The human vocal response mechanism is always prepared to discuss the weather, current events or ailments and disorders. Regarding the latter, many will respond by matching your pain to something in their life. It might seem rather disrespectful, but that is just how regular people think. It can feel heartless when someone renders your latest tragedy irrelevant by talking about themselves, but they'll do it anyway.

Some people try to make things better, seeing situations as half-full rather than half-empty. The simplest things can create division between people. Some see advantages, where others suffer through disadvantages. Take the fact we are born either right or left-handed. Learning to write might be hard for a leftie, but if they can throw a fastball, they could find a valuable career in baseball.

Because most people are right handed, baggage claim carousels in America typically turn counterclockwise, making it easier to grab bags with the right hand. 10% of the population is left-handed, so one could make the point baggage claims are designed for the majority without regard to the lefties. A hard-core lefty could say the whole world is against her. Ask a left-handed person to tell you the struggles they have endured in a right-handed world.

My brother is ambidextrous, which helped him play hockey and lay bricks. Lefty, righty, or both, we are all human.

During a discussion with another person pontificating away, I might ask, without sarcasm, "How do you know that?" It drives me up a wall if they get uptight and start to argue. I like to engage on an intellectual and logical level. Hey, I was simply asking, "How do you know that?" I would like to know the source. Is that too much to ask?

If I ask someone how they are sure there is a God, they might quote one book or a friend. Sometimes they claim an out-of-body experience, in effect claiming that God or Jesus appeared and talked to them and, thus, the term, "born-again." A declaration of faith in God should never keep anyone from getting a job, but if the same person claimed a sincere belief in a giant lizard, who talked to them and protected them from evil, the perspective employer might take a second look. The applicant could pull the reptile out of their bag and introduce the lizard to the interviewer, but even with the reptile and applicant right there, the interviewer probably wouldn't believe the person's claim unless the lizard spoke. When did "Can you prove it?" become a rude question? Would the lizard be God if he talked? To the half-full people, he wouldn't be God, he would just be a talking lizard. And by the way, it's against the law for someone to ask about your religious beliefs during a job interview. It's none of their damn business.

I enjoy open discussions with a person ready to debate any issue. You may like someone a lot and still disagree with them. There are people who make good points on either side of an issue, but if we see them as slimly little lizards, we don't hear what they say. A true breakdown happens when a person disagrees with you, and then simply declares you stupid and walks away. They've made up their mind that you aren't worthy of any interaction. Those are disagreeable people.

We must all work together, but the older I get the more the general population seems to be less capable of doing so. There are volumes of proof showing that we are a divided nation. The more diversity we create in the United States, the greater the challenge for small minds to comprehend that our "one of many" country is richness, not a curse.

There are many dogmas, religions and political perspectives in the United States, but a problem arises if we hold only one small opinion. We can survey thousands of taxi drivers of Sikh decent and never believe **they aren't Muslims**. Their turbans are an accessory of their culture. We can talk to Irish shipbuilders or Italian marble workers but know that a person doesn't have to be of a certain heritage to do a specific job. Not all Vietnamese women work in nail salons, nor are all Koreans dry-cleaners or grocery store owners. Some of these folks are doctors, lawyers and teachers.

Generalizations and prejudices can lead to painful suffering. Sometimes we are quick to judge a person by the way they look or what they do. It amazes some people when they learn that Mike Rowe, TV spokesperson and host of the TV show *Dirty Jobs*, is a trained opera singer. There are certain people who look like someone you like, so you like them. Other times a person might be the doppelganger of someone you highly despise, and their look-alike probably won't get a fair shake from you.

I'm reminded of a story the late author Timothy White told me. He was assigned to interview Johnny Carson for a cover article in Rolling Stone magazine. After weeks of negotiations, Tim was invited to Carson's California home for an hour interview. When arriving, White was a little nervous not knowing if an hour would be enough time to garner thorough information for a cover story. Johnny himself came to the door and invited Tim into his home. They talked for several hours before Carson realized he needed to get to his show rehearsal. As he showed Timothy out, Johnny asked if he could come back tomorrow to continue the interview. Tim was beside himself and certainly took up the offer.

Through their long interviews, Tim learned that Carson felt the Rolling Stone writer looked like one of his sons. That was great for Timothy and was probably the key to having more time with the king of late-night TV.

When I began working in Atlanta as a radio broadcast consultant, my boss gave me a crucial piece of advice. "Remember," he said, "you are going to work with some clients you will really enjoy. You will also be working with people you absolutely abhor, but you have to do your job and help all of them do well." Because of that planted seed, I always found a way to work with the occasional assholes one encounters in business.

I grew up in a typical American middle-class family. My father came from a farm in Knox, Pennsylvania, moved to the big city of Pittsburgh, played baseball, found work and got married. He put life on hold for five years to fight Germans in Europe and helped bring peace to the world. My mother was a hard-working woman who raised five kids. She was a secretary at the local elementary school for a few years, but my father asked her to be a stay-at-home Mom. Dad was an old-fashioned guy with values to match. If the truth be told, Mom ran the family finances.

I vividly remember those times. We never went hungry because $15 would net five large bags of groceries. We had a happy home suffused with a keen sense of humor. We were Presbyterians and there was never a question about our patriotism. We were American through and through and the flag was sacred. My little mind was molded by these wonderful parents who made it through thick and thin and helped us be good kids.

I was affected forever by an event in elementary school. During the early grades, many students lost things like gloves, scarfs and lunch boxes. Things just disappeared from classrooms. Money, baseball gloves and even gym shoes went missing. These things were being stolen and this really bothered me. I started to become paranoid, my feelings of mistrust so foreign because I was raised in a safe home environment.

About the time I was 12-years-old, a kid who lived right next to the school befriended me. I wasn't sure why he did what I'm about to tell you, but maybe his approach was more an outcry for help rather than friendship.

We went to his home after school one day. Both of his parents worked and were not there. After getting bored with whatever TV show we were watching, he suggested we go out in the backyard and catch some baseball. I saw it when we went down to the basement to get his baseball glove. Along the wall was a long table filled with dozens of lunch boxes, pairs of baseball gloves and all the other items that had been stolen from the school over the years.

I felt guilty seeing this, feeling dirty simply by being so close to his thievery. We went outside and caught baseball, and I eventually left with an understanding that this kid was a kleptomaniac, despite not knowing the meaning of the word at that time. I never met with him again. I mentioned this to my mother, but nothing came of it and the kid's family moved away next fall. Looking back, I believe his parents were aware of their kid's disorder but chose to move along rather than getting him professional help.

Sadly, there are many bad people in the world. Along with each you'll typically find an enabler, someone who either permits them to be disagreeable or guides them to be a bully with a punk attitude. They must share the blame for polluting the world with such people.

A lack of religion or the misuse of medical prescriptions aren't always the causes of disagreeable people in the world. There are merely people making **"self-deluding searches for personal fulfillment"** which, at times, conflicts with the common good of the tribe. Everyone in the world needs love. Some get it, some don't. Maybe we need to find better ways to share our love?

UR what U8

Why are we the way we are? I read an interview with a European who had just returned from his first trip to America and I had to shake my head. When asked, "What was America like?" He answered, "It's just like you see in the movies, except all the people are fat." So, we begin this essay right here. Why are we so fat?

While writing this book, I had the pleasure to read Robert H. Lustig's tome *The Hacking of the American Mind*. My first thought was it must concern the 2016 US election, but it was much more encompassing. Lustig is a doctor and a lawyer and his book is written from both a science and political perspective.

Lustig's illuminating work points out that pleasure and happiness are two different things, controlled in the brain by dopamine and serotonin. Serotonin helps us achieve a feeling of **contentment**, thus happiness. Dopamine keeps us linear, logical and less angry, but also produces a short burst of **pleasure**. Dopamine is a large diet coke, while Serotonin is a fuzzy Teddy Bear.

Dr. Lustig stated there are major, long-term consequences to laws passed by Congress, Supreme Court rulings and presidential executive orders. Now, I don't want to sound like a conspiracy theorist or some bullshit activist, but those confederate-flag-waving, neo-crazies totally miss the stark reality surrounding the government's poisoning of its citizens.

In *The Hacking of the American Mind*, Richard Nixon was portrayed as a real enemy of the people because he worried about fluctuations in food prices affecting his approval ratings. Never be fooled. The Goofballs care only about what's good for them. Nixon didn't understand why the government was paying farmers NOT to grow certain crops. Policies were designed to control what farmers grew and brought to market. The government was artificially inflating the cost of certain crops, thus giving farmers a better living. Our government always does more than they admit.

This farming manipulation was codified in the Agriculture Adjustment Act of 1933 (1938), and then undone in 1971 when Nixon ordered Earl Butz, his Secretary of Agriculture, to end the payments to farmers. Lustig's book points out the order from Butz focused more on the quantity of what was produced rather than the quality of farmers' harvests.

With this move, our government pushed farmers into growing tons of corn, the biggest cash crop at the time. We produced so much corn it was challenging to figure out what to do with it. We exported some of it, but we also discovered another cash cow, high-fructose corn syrup. Thus, came the end of a healthy American diet and the beginning of a grand experiment to use the population of America as laboratory test rats. Nixon changed the biology of America without realizing what he was doing.

To make food taste better, the "scientists" at the food processing plants added sugar made from corn into much of what was sent to market. Food containing a little sugar always scores better in taste tests, so more and more high-fructose corn syrup was added to the foods we bought.

According to the CDC in Atlanta, 1 out of 3 adults has prediabetes and 29.1 million people in the United States have diabetes, but 8.1 million may be undiagnosed and unaware of their condition. About 1.4 million new cases of diabetes are diagnosed in United States every year. Why is this happening? Could it be the changes in our food processing?

Pounding our systems with sugar has changed our metabolism. We have wasted billions of dollars because of the monumental mistake the government made back in 1971. In effect, Richard Nixon and Earl Butz poisoned us, and you thought Watergate was bad. This is far worse.

Lustig slipped an interesting statistic into his pages, 65% of all healthcare costs are payed by the government's healthcare bank. We are all compensating for this disaster and it will only get worse.

Why is sugar bad? It makes us feel good. It gives pleasure. Sugar quiets a screaming kid in a car. The truth is, sugar is dope and you know it. We feel good when we put sugar in our coffee. We feel pleasure as sugared caffeine wends its way into our brains. Nicotine in cigarettes provides another drug running around our brains. We self-medicate, then go about our business without comprehending the long-term effects to our bodies.

Hey, I get it. My father suffered from Attention Deficit Disorder (ADD) and never knew it. He drank a pot of coffee every day and just kept working. It didn't affect his sleeping, but eventually he had a heart attack after an accident at work. No one back in the early 70s blamed the coffee. To top of it off, my father loved butter. He slathered it on everything. Dad became a walking time bomb, devouring the gristle from tons of steak and bacon, but what killed him was the misdiagnoses of several doctors. They thought he had a bladder infection and gave him lots of antibiotics, when he was actually suffering from kidney disease. He died of renal failure at age 66, six years after the initial misdiagnosis. Each doctor in the string believed the other doctors' analyses. Lemmings. With today's medical science, my father's ailment would have been diagnosed properly and given him a complete life.

Times have changed, and almost all of us are eating better. The wealthier of us shop at Whole Foods or other farm to table grocery stores, while others less fortunate buy large containers of drinks from box stores and feed their families bottle after bottle of liquid sugar. You'll see large women at Walmart loading their carts with sugar laced products, never bothering to read the labels. Maybe it's too late?

Lustig believes we are in a death-spiral, and there is little anyone can do to stop these bad food choices from making us sick. Watch some of the incisive documentaries like *Food, Inc.* (2008), *King Corn* (2007) and *Super-Size Me* (2004) to gain insight into the games played by big agriculture and food corporations driven by profits rather than nutrition. They will never work to make us healthier unless we the people demand it.

The conspiracy can be blamed on both political and farming forces. First, politicians believed agricultural price wars would result in hungry, angry people, and they gladly accepted money from agriculture and fertilizer lobbyists to put them in office and keep us on the path to chemicals.

The other conspiring force was the processed food industry. They wanted bigger, fatter animals and larger, bug-free fruits and vegetables. They processed these with just enough salt to be tasty, or lots of high-fructose corn syrup to make us feel pleasure, then sliced them and stuffed them in cans and packages for sale.

With the rule of law tilting ever closer to the power of the corporation rather than individuals, we must learn more about how this works, so we can survive. In America, we are now forced to spend wads of money to buy healthy food. Cities, counties and states are now adding sugar taxes, a regressive taxation that places the burden on the consumer instead of the food giants who got us hooked on fat and sugar. Why is this smart? It sounds like drug addiction to me.

When Mike Bloomberg, former Mayor of New York City, tried to pass a ban on the size of sugared drinks, it was viewed as a draconian action instead of a progressive solution to a serious problem. We consume too much sugar, but banning large cups is foolish.

We live in a country where the Gold people selling sugar have more influence than your A1C, a measurement of the amount of glucose attached to the hemoglobin in your blood. The higher your A1C level, the less efficient your blood sugar control, which brings about a higher risk of diabetes and all its complications. If you have diabetes, you know all about this.

If you give your kids lots of sugar, they will eventually become little drug addicts. They will want and need more to maintain their sugar high. Parents become enablers when they give in to their kids moaning about the sugar they want. Our Halloween tradition perpetrates a pagan myth and celebrates the harvesting of crops with pounds of sugar and chocolate for our children. We revel in our addiction with its very own holiday.

There are those who say there is no harm in letting the little kids have some fun with free candy. Years later, when not so little, they will dull their brain receptors with painkillers, a fine substitute for the sugar high taught to them by Mom and Dad. Bingo: Opioid Crisis.

Beware of other enablers in America. When your kid has pain after a terrible accident, your family doctor may give them medication to get them through the pain. With each pill those receptors keep saying, "I want more." After the doctor pulls the prescription, your kid might start looking for something on the street to dull the pain. If found, it's probably cheaper than what your insurance company previously paid for the legit medication. Some doctors overprescribe, and you need to be watchful and responsible. Congress is finally investigating the distributors and manufacturers of painkillers. What took them so long?

Research tells us that kids who get a free breakfast at school do better academically. Our minds need nourishment, and we now know how our bodies process the chemicals in food. Medical science is far advanced from the voodoo and soothsayers of the Bible era. Even the Goofballs in Congress and the White House drink their diet Cokes to keep focus, while they are doing damage to society because of their lack of awareness. Inaction is being complicit in the poisoning of the next generation. It's not just the drinking water in Flint, Michigan and ONE THOUSAND more towns where the water is even worse. The food and water supply in America need to be put under a microscope.

It's not just Big Pharma that convinced doctors there was nothing wrong with using Oxycontin for long-term pain treatment. There's also an ongoing lack of discipline about things people put in their mouths. We are raising a country of overweight people who are unable to focus on anything, including the truth, without sugar, caffeine, nicotine and pain killers. We can't seem to face each day without self-medication.

We grew up in America and it's not our fault that we've been brainwashed by pictures of food that say, EAT ME AND ALL YOUR PROBLEMS WILL GO AWAY. You are surely *lovin' it,* America, but you might want to start practicing pricking your finger for those daily blood tests you'll have to do in the future. We are what we eat, and it's high time all of us work on the goal of making America healthier.

American Parents

I love my parents. My father lived until age 66, while my mother stayed on this planet for 95 years. I have millions of great memories and, for sure, those wonderful times upstaged whatever minor disturbances took place over all that time. I was conceived and born in the late 40s, grew up in the 50s and 60s, got wild in the 70s, settled down and raised a family in the 80s and 90s and reinvented myself in the 2000s. Even though I hate the term "reinvented" I don't have a better way to express it. I'm not a machine and wasn't invented, I was born, and I cannot say I was "reborn." Someone else owns that terminology.

I have dedicated myself to writing in the second and third decades of the new millennium. I find more contentment in not having a boss, although, all of us has a boss, except God, but they say he has a fierce competitor. This is my beginning point of discussion about the American parent.

With the arrival of your first child, you are totally unqualified to have one, and even less experienced in raising one. The best way to know this is to talk to someone who has never had kids, especially if they grew up as an only child. They think every adult should be able to control a child like you control your media center with a remote device. So, how does one become qualified to raise a kid?

Oh, you can read books and take classes, but nothing will prepare you for your first child. Some of them are reasonable little campers and don't kick up too much dust that first year, but don't be fooled about how a little life starts out. Things can change. On the other hand, you could get the kid from hell who doesn't sleep through the night for the first 18 months of their existence. Google: Baby colic. Regardless of their beginning, there's an indeterminate lifetime of possibilities about the eventual characteristics of your precious newbie.

It is true that what you and your offspring experience in those early days will be carried by both of you forever. I was given a satin blanket when I was a baby, and to this day, I love the feel of that fabric. It totally calms me down. Okay, sorry, that's a bit creepy.

Good things happen, and bad things happen. Your job as a parent is to make sure you provide much of the former and little of the latter. We all remember the emotionally driven events of our lives better than cold, impassive events. When a bad thing happens, a child stores its painful thoughts in their subconscious forever. Hey, no pressure, but every child is different. When my five-year son fell headfirst into a jacuzzi, I rescued him; but who could possibly know how that affected him?

I remember a dirty trick my cousins played on their sister, Betty Jane. They told her that a giant fluffy mass of white stuff in a bowl on the table was icing for a cake. She went over, picked up a large tablespoon and took a large gulp. It was mayonnaise. That was it. She could never eat mayonnaise again. Imagine memories of all the other possible things a child can feel, hear, see, taste or smell which can never be doused.

American parents come in two basic flavors. The first is the over-protective "stage-mom-type," clinically known as a "helicopter parent." Parents of this flavor not only control the child's life at every turn, they attempt to manipulate anyone who encounters their little jewel.

Then there is what I will call, for lack of a better term, the "Hippy Parent." These liberal parents are found in big cities and in small towns throughout this land. Their goal is to raise "free-range kids." If you are the least bit uptight, you will find yourself asking them, "Oh my God, you let them do that by themselves?"

There's no proof that one type of these extremes is better than the other, but an American kid's path to adulthood is scattered with a lot of broken glass. If you're overly protective of your kids, you probably already know that. If your kids are free-rangers, I hope you work with them to make sure they are at least street-smart. After all, a little paranoia and readiness aren't so bad. For the most part, kids are kids. Sooner or later they will break an arm or slash their lips on something sharp. They might even try to shave their hairless seven-year-old face with a razor. Maybe that was caused by a head first fall into the jacuzzi?

Cute stupid little pranks and small accidents pale in comparison to the challenge parents face with one important subject. I remember a discussion my wife and I had about whether we should address sex with the girls. At first, there was the suggestion they are good girls and will make the right call. I was quick to ask my then wife if she remembered how horny we were at that age. That conversation didn't end well. Neither did the chat I had with my 14-year-old daughter who got drunk on copious amounts of vodka given to her by older boys. I was direct with her on a phone call, "You know, they are just trying to get into your pants?" I was attempting to raise free-ranges kids from afar. This brings us to drugs.

Is America safe? It depends on who you ask, and the latest survey results you choose to quote. According to Center for Disease Control (CDC), "Drug overdose deaths rose above 70,000 in 2017, an increase of almost 10% to a record high." I can't believe people in high places are still against the legalization of marijuana. It's a substance that doesn't kill you, and some say it's a good treatment for PTSD, or helps those with cancer keep their appetites. We should field extensive research on whether pot could be used with medical supervision to help people with hard-core opioid addiction.

While you're raising your precious little bundles, think about another sharp edge of reality out there. Every day in America, 19 kids are either wounded or killed by a Gun. According to FBI data, there were 11,000 Gun-related homicides in 2016, up from 9,600 in 2015. And this just in from CNN, 23,854 people died in the US from suicide by Guns in 2017. I will try to make this more positive, so please keep reading.

The Center for Disease Control (CDC) says, "Every day, 28 people in the United States die in motor vehicle crashes that involve an alcohol-impaired driver. That's one death every 51 minutes. The annual cost of alcohol-related crashes totals more than $44 billion." And in true American statistical form, we love to include the associated costs. You know, to make the numbers more meaningful. As if we can't be moved profoundly enough by the deaths of children and adults, let's make sure we state the full depth of the cost.

We give our kids training wheels on a bike and then, one day, we remove them. We teach them how to drive and then, one day, we let them go it alone. Every parent's greatest fear is something will go wrong on that first night a kid takes the car out alone.

Sometimes while driving a two-ton-plus vehicle, our kids feel a need to text and post on social media. This will soon give us a new statistic of deaths caused by using a cell phone while driving, to complement the research results that show the potential mortality of taking selfies.

Life isn't all booby traps and landmines, but we must teach children to know danger when they see it. America is still more safe than Syria, but we ought to be smart enough to figure out how to end distracted driving and foolish activities. How about an app that prevents texting while the car is moving? The kind of technology is already in the car.

Parents have, for the most part, tried to stay on top of latest trends and ideas to raise good kids. Yes, we let them watch too much TV and they spend way too much time on their tablets and cell phones, but what are we supposed to do? How can we lecture them about looking at screens when we as adults are just as addicted to social media? It's not demographic specific. The makers of games and software have won the war and they are slowly reshaping the way we think.

My kids will tell you that there was a time when I felt compelled to yell and scream when they did something wrong. I could list all the things that drove me crazy, but that would probably get me arrested. My kids will soon have the same power over their own kids, and I wish them luck. I do regret that I wasn't patient enough during their developmental periods. Okay, I admit it, I was an asshole sometimes and I hope they are a bit more tolerant with their kids.

American parents plant an early seed about the necessity of keeping up with the Joneses. Kids aren't stupid, even when they get bad grades. Every mind processes information differently, and many American kids learn by watching their parents. Really, think about it. How many kids of diehard, far right Republicans end up becoming right-wingnuts? (Google: Liz Cheney) Or how many children of smokers, become smokers?

Neither one of my parents drank alcohol or smoked cigarettes, so drinking became a giant part of my revolting against them. I smoked for two years until I realized I hated cigarettes.

Environment is one thing, but DNA is all powerful. Genes are the reason I have no hair, and maybe the reason I might have a longer life than the average person. My kids are separate humans, with their own combination of A, C, G, and Ts that determine who they are and what will become of them. More people are getting those DNA tests and attempting to peer into the future. Will the causes of my death be like those of my parents or is this person my true biological parent? Yes, we can get those kinds of insights. We have caught killers based on DNA results.

I wonder if anyone consciously thinks their job is to make their new kid a replica or clone of themselves? Not only are my kids visually different from each other, they aren't at all like their parents. They showed very early signs of being individuals. Each of my four kids is unique and special, and I love that about each of them.

Too often, Americans get sucked into generalizations about how kids should react. After the terrible school shooting in Parkland, Florida, students started a movement and created massive protests, while the kid survivors in Santa Fe, Texas, turned to God and thoughts and prayers.

One group held the belief that the solution was Gun control, while the other group was fortified by their parents' need to protect the Second Amendment, saying more Guns was a possible solution. Neither approach has fixed the problem so far, and the myth that equal armament will save lives is bullshit. The result of more Guns on either or both sides will be more deaths. We might not want to test that theory, other than having a quick study of gang warfare which clearly indicates lots of Guns usually ends with lots of death. **Body count is never a moral achievement.**

The safety of our children is a major concern in America. Let me restate an honest and true observation. We protect football games and museums better than we protect our schools. One could also argue that we protect people in other countries with our military presence better than we fortify the security of kids in our schools here at home. Why aren't American parents screaming about the overkill of military spending and the annual decrease in funds for education? Children don't learn very well when they are dodging bullets. Whether you are a "helicopter parent" or a "Hippy free-range parent" you need to stand up and fight for your kids' safety and education.

Those who know me can't help but notice my keen sense of humor. I cynically say to new parents, "Don't worry, you will make tons of mistakes with your new kid." That's when they stop, look at me and scrunch their brow. I laugh, they laugh, but I must insist that I'm telling the truth. Nothing can properly prepare you for bringing another human being into this world.

Something that drives many new mothers and fathers crazy is every grandmother, grandmother-in-law, next store neighbor and nanny thinking they have the only correct recipe for raising a kid. One of our nannies said that placing a drop of my kid's urine in each of their eyes would take care of pink eye. Can you believe that one? Just what a wretched case of conjunctivitis needs, more bacteria. WTF?

The mother-in-law says, "Let them cry it out," while the grandmother jumps over a sofa to check on any peep heard from the baby monitor. Which side are you on? That's an argument you will never win. They are both right and both wrong. Wrong, like forcing a boy to play sports because his old man was a super jock when the kid wants to play with his dollhouse and design gowns. Let him be.

Your kids didn't pick you as a parent. They just happened to come out of you. You had your few minutes of fun nine months before, and now you think you own them. You don't.

I remember a good friend in high school. This guy was not only a ranked cross-country runner, he was brilliant and a scholarship candidate for many universities because of his amazing chemistry projects. He was a bonus for any college recruiter and, sure enough, he was offered great opportunities at several major colleges. Sadly, his parents had promised his grandmother that their first-born male child would enter the priesthood. The commitment wasn't what my friend wanted. It was what his parents wanted.

I felt so lost and sad the morning when they announced my friend had passed away over the weekend. It seemed that he ran his 10-mile workout, went back to his room, cooked up some cyanide and took control of his life.

As much as we want to do a good job with our kids and protect them from all the bad things that could happen, we must never believe we own their souls. My friend didn't want to die; he simply wanted to make the point he didn't want to become a priest. It turns out his worst enemies were living in his own home and mind.

Listen to your kids to find out what they really want. You may not like the guy she wants to date or believe playing poker is a viable profession but hear what they want. Talk with your kids and, as crazy as some of the things they say are, listen to them. Some of those moments are life changing, explosions of truth making destiny.

Kids are sometimes compelled to reveal a dark disturbance. You should be relieved if your kid tells you something before handling it herself. Help her before it's too late. Don't overreact, and always remember that sometimes kids do the exact opposite of what you suggest just to piss you off. That's why they are called, "kids."

Military Madness

Graham Nash is a talented musician, a politically aware human being and a very polite Englishman. He has been living in the United States since 1978 and has dual citizenship here and with his native home, Great Britain. As a member of the Hollies and then Crosby, Stills & Nash (& Young), Graham has revealed his thinking to the world via the many songs he's written over the years. It was Graham who composed and recorded with his bandmates the 1970 song *Ohio,* mere hours after the shooting of students at Kent State University.

This essay's title comes from his 1971 song *Military Madness,* the lyrics of which have never escaped my mind:

> *And after the wars are over*
> *And the body count is finally filed*
> *I hope that the Man discovers*
> *What's driving the people wild*
> *Military madness is killing your country*
> *So much sadness, between you and me*

Let's put this in perspective. As of 2017, the United States government had 1,281,900 uniformed service members, with an additional 801,200 people in the seven military reserve components. That's a total of slightly more than two million people protecting our country in the armed services. Now that's far less than 1% of the US population, but the *"military might machine"* spends nearly $700 billion every year. In 2019, we are planning to spend only $63.2 billion in discretionary funding of schools, which will be a $3.6 billion decrease from 2017 level. It's clear that the Goofballs believe education is far less important than war.

We can all agree that protecting our country from outside attack is important. Most informed citizens also know we need well-trained, domestic police forces to protect us from wickedness originating inside our country. Local police and county sheriff departments usually run on tight budgets, but they still need to properly educate and train new recruits. Are we wasting money on military equipment for the local police departments without investing in the ideals of local police? The Goofballs in local enforcement say they need bigger Guns because the bad guys have bigger Guns. I wonder if there is a way to control this. The irony is we can never, ever do anything to curb the purchase of Guns by good or bad guys. **As a nation and government, we do nothing positive about the negative aspects of weaponry in America.** We simply stand on opposite sides of an issue that is taking lives and ruining American families.

We are looking for the right answers in the wrong places. There is a theory that showing strength and authority is a deterrent, but in real life it doesn't always work that way. Anger is the driver when it comes to criminal actions and grudge killings.

Being prepared is good military business, but that deterrent theory goes out the window if both guys have nukes. I mean, how many atomic bombs do you need to destroy the world? And if one country is attacked with a nuclear weapon, surely the other would launch their own weapon of equal measure. Why would that be good?

I apply what I call the "Use it or Lose it" syndrome to the top brass in the military. At the Pentagon, you'll find some small minds with loads of spaghetti on their chests who want to take some of those bombs, drones and missiles out for a test drive. Military "might" doesn't mean "we might use them." There is reasonable proof there is a cadre of army men who are waiting and prepared for war. We try hard to avoid war with our United Nations seat and NATO membership, but the risk is always there. It's one of the reasons why presidents have more gray hair when they leave office. Our treaties, summits and economic councils still haven't mastered peace. In my life, there have been four or five major conflicts, along with the Cuban Missile crisis when we thought we were all going to die.

To help blow things up, we have diluted diplomatic efforts and cut aid budgets to many nations. Then we get to spend even more money to restore peace. If you are interested, Google: The Marshall Plan.

We can no longer afford wars. The Congressional Budget Office predicted that between all the military madness in Afghanistan and Iraq, we probably emptied $2.4 trillion from the US Treasury. Some estimates say more than 210,000 Pakistan and Afghanistan civilians have been killed. Another dire statistic is almost 500,000 deaths in Iraq. Our bombs and bullets have annihilated three-quarters of a million people since 2000. And what did we get? Well not much, other that inner turmoil that, as of this writing, is still not settled. People continue to be bombed, shot, raped, tortured and enslaved. Great job, America!

As Ronan Farrow pointed out in his book, *War on Peace: The End of Diplomacy and the Decline of American Influence,* the United States has given the military more power while lessening the influence of embassies and diplomats. We are doomed when we remove aid from countries and create the next ISIS or Al-Qaeda. Economic stress produces armies of angry young men. The military madness ailment has infiltrated the mental state of America.

Veterans should be proud of the service they have given and continue to give to the nation. Vietnam veterans were treated incredibly poorly when they returned from southeast Asia and we now have a collective, national guilt about veterans. Even with all the grandstanding and promises of our elected Goofballs, we still haven't done the most important things for our returning heroes. We have not made them feel cared for, honored and, in some cases, whole.

Medical "care" for our soldiers is a disgrace. The Veterans Administration (VA) is a fat bureaucracy mired in tons of inefficient paperwork, procedures and particulars. We're told that any healthcare system is "complicated," but those in charge have created a monster. Despite changes in leadership, the problems remain. The smartest experts are not working on this issue. They're far too busy making tons of money running "for profit" hospitals. Have you ever wondered about the constant expansion of our hospitals? The highly experienced people running them are raking in the money and don't want to get anywhere near the VA disaster.

I don't blame our returning warriors for needing to label themselves with bumper stickers, baseball hats and T-shirts. They want you to know they fought for our country. The MIA and POW flags and posters remind us that some troops never came home. Our veterans must fight to keep us honest. It's a badge of honor my father didn't need to wear. After the fact, he avoided the subject of World War II. He was glad the atrocity was over and just wanted to be respected, not given an award. When I see a license plate holder on a car that says, "I support the Troops," I have to ask, "Who doesn't?"

War does long term damage to human beings. It causes disorders and diseases. "Shell Shock" first became "Battle Fatigue," then was refined to Post-Traumatic Stress Disorder, or PTSD. So, we now have clinical nomenclature for a very personal hell. There are those who think the medical name makes the disorder less stigmatized. Maybe so, but it's a terrible, horrific by-product of war, no matter what it's called.

Let's make sure we aren't blind to what our military-industrial complex is all about. There are people and industries out there making millions and billions of dollars on military contracts. When I learned parents had to send their sons and daughters bulletproof Kevlar vests to the Middle East because the military failed to deliver them, I went ballistic. Who the hell is running the army, the three stooges?

I lost friends in Vietnam and I will never forget the time I went to see all those names at the Vietnam War Memorial in Washington, DC. It was heartbreaking. Our troops fought long and hard to keep communists out of a southeast Asian land, but along the way we lost our morals, values and diplomatic honor due to government inspired fear of communism.

We deployed napalm in Vietnam to burn to death hundreds of thousands of human beings. We created hell on Earth for all the non-combative citizens who lived there. On what moral ground were we standing? Vietnam was a mistake. Iraq was a mistake. War — what is it good for? Vietnam is a communist nation now and we buy T-Shirts from them. Why did we fight that war again? *War — what is it good for? Absolutely nothing!*

Since World War II, we've become so incoherent that we don't even realize our engagement in warfare comes not because we feel threatened as a nation but because we endlessly stick our noses into other peoples' stuff. Aside from the retaliation for 9-11, the reason for most of our recent wars was a dislike of the governments we battled. We had no intention to make settlements and end those wars quickly. We didn't even use our biggest weapons. Maybe that is the only moral high ground we kept?

Despite dropping two of our atomic bombs on Japan, I disdain the use of nuclear weapon. Are we this morally corrupt? President Harry Truman claimed that killing so many people on one day saved thousands of American lives in the Pacific theater of war. We never used atomic bombs again. Why? Because killing with a nuclear weapon is considered immoral by civilized countries. They are swords to be rattled, but many irresponsible people are running countries with nukes. We must be careful because we apparently have no power to stop a good guy or a bad guy with nuclear weapons.

America brought the fissionable beast into the world and we should suffer the guilt that so many people were killed in such a sinister way. Due to the impact of the bomb, plus the ensuing radiation poisoning, we probably eradicated 200,000 or more Japanese people.

In the three yearlong Korean conflict, nearly three million people were killed. China claimed that 180,000 of their soldiers died in the war and it's the reason they have a vested stake in the Korean Peninsula.

According to the BBC, "In Vietnam, the US suffered more than 58,000 dead and an estimated 2 million Vietnamese civilians were killed, while another 5.3 million were injured." Take a minute to think. War is immoral, and no matter which weapons are used, war kills people.

Death is death, and, as Martin Luther King, Jr. said, "I refuse to accept the view that mankind is so tragically bound to the starless midnight of racism and war that the bright daybreak of peace and brotherhood can never become a reality. I believe that unarmed truth and unconditional love will have the final word." This is why people like Mohammed Ali and Martin Luther King, Jr. were so against the Vietnam war. Now we must ask ourselves why they were both investigated for holding these beliefs.

Between Korea and Vietnam, more than five million people were taken from the Earth. Are we proud of this? Why are we killing so many civilians? Oh, silly me, it's only collateral damage in a "just war," at least that is what a military general or a soulless person like Richard Nixon would tell you. The dark guilt every commander takes to the grave comes home with the final body count. People died on their watches. If the number of enemy body bags determines the success of a war, the military leaders are complicit.

And as I have preached before, the cost of the Afghanistan and Iraq wars could have bankrolled a college education for every high school graduate during those years. The amount of money we spent on those senseless and unmerited wars could have totally repaired our healthcare system.

Let's make it clear; the result of our "trying to help out" has made all those countries worse. Vietnam got better only after we got the hell out. For 9-11 revenge, all we needed to do was to kill Osama bin-Laden, which we eventually did. How much did that Seal Team 6 cost, and what was the cost of all those bombs we dropped on Afghanistan and Iraq?

We think we should be the world's police department, but that role demands a lot of blood, sweat and money. We should protect our country at any cost, but we need to get smart and understand the culture, government, customs and people we think we can change. Some places aren't so easily transformed.

If the Goofballs in Washington end up wasting money on a big ass wall on our southern border, they will once again be throwing away money and hurting the middle class of our nation. It would be yet another travesty, more money spent on wrong things. **The wall is a monument to racism.** It will never keep people from trying to come to America. It might have the opposite effect, an enticing challenge to be breached. Warehousing migrants in Mexico will produce more cheap labor for them and eventually eliminate American jobs.

The drugs will come across the border the way they always have, in boxes, tires, cheese boxes and bras. This just in from CNN, "Most drugs are smuggled into the United States onboard fishing boats, trains, tractor-trailers and ordinary cars that come into the country at legal ports of entry, according to former cartel members who've testified in the trial of notorious cartel leader Joaquin 'El Chapo' Guzman." And of course, he's an expert on the subject.

Our leaders use fear to sell wars. They always have. Their mantra is "OTHERS" are coming to take our Gold and Guns. In the Goofballs' claim of Judeo-Christian unity, we see a little bit of *Onward Christian Soldiers.* Can you hear them singing it? The second verse declares that those who fight against us are not human, but the devil himself:

> *At the sign of triumph, Satan's host doth flee;*
> *On, then, Christian soldiers, On to victory.*
> *Hell's foundations quiver, At the shout of praise;*

Brothers, lift your voices, Loud your anthems raise.

Does that mean that every one of our conflicts is, in some way, a holy war? And after we conquer them in the name of our God, will they be singing our anthem?

The Goofballs in power constantly try to manipulate us into spending more money on bombs, tanks and boats. When all of our precious American institutions and infrastructures become infected with neglect and fail in disrepair, we will only have only ourselves to blame. The fat orange man in the large suit and long tie will spend your money. You will never see it again. The military madness continues.

Cockamamie Classes

Why do we have a class system in America? Why do some people think they have the right to tell other people what to believe or how to act? Who are these people attempting to dictate what we feel or who we should love? What proclamation gives them power over someone else's business? They patronizingly say, *All men are created equal,* while I quickly counter with, "Would you please get out of the way of my *pursuit of happiness*?" Remember, both phrases are in the Bill of Rights.

The United States of America is arguably freer and more liberal than many nations. In the lands of totalitarianism and devout Islamic states, homosexuals are legally executed. In other places, people who criticize those in power are poisoned. We don't do these things here, but we sometimes stay silent when they happen elsewhere. Look no further than the recent lack of accountability when journalist Jamal Khashoggi was murdered in Turkey, apparently by Saudi agents on orders from their Crown Prince.

Human Rights violations occur everywhere. In Buddhist controlled Myanmar, more than 6,700 Rohingya Muslims were killed in one month, including at least 730 children under the age of five. The exact totals are elusive, but some experts claim nearly 700,000 Rohingya have become refugees and moved to Bangladesh to escape the abuse of the Myanmar military. The Rohingya forces have now started to kill Hindu men, women and children. State Counsellor of Myanmar, Aung San Suu Kyi, lied about these atrocities to UN inspectors. Can we sit back and ignore these violations of human rights? It's a real mess and we can only hope they will find peace without suffering. Hey Aung, it's fucking ethnic cleansing and genocide! We are watching what you do.

After 9-11, much of America believed someone had to pay for the death and destruction. Since all the 9-11 hijackers were Muslim, some narrow-minded people decided that the Islamic faith was the enemy. 15 of the 19 hijackers were from Saudi Arabia, yet we kept buying their oil, selling them armaments, dancing around with their swords and looking the other way when they murdered people. Who are we?

I have written about this issue in my other books and I have not found any link between American Muslims and a grand plan to destroy our country. In the Middle East, however, the threat to Israel is real. If the radical jihadists had their way, Israel would be wiped off the map.

According to the Pittsburgh Jewish Chronicle, "The annual funding Israel receives may be increased by $200 million in 2019. The US fiscal year budget request indicates Israel will receive $3.3 billion in 2019." These figures imply that we already have picked a winner. Wait, according to the Times of Israel, "Since 1994, Washington has provided the Palestinians with more than $5.2 billion through US aid. This money is used for developing and sustaining the Palestinian Authority." Are you confused?

United States foreign policy might be summed up like this, "If we can't buy you, we are going to bomb you." At any given moment, we have a simmering conflict somewhere in the world. An expert uses facts and science to shape important discussions, but our elected Goofballs drive their framework by hearsay and loudmouth ideologs. This isn't advanced calculus. We invest in some countries the careless way we sometimes pick racehorses or stocks, betting the farm that nothing bad will happen. After inserting our man or government into a country, we pray that it doesn't fall to radicals. We know when the "death to America" guys take control, they're fighting with the weapons we supplied to the "good guys." It's a crap shoot, at best.

Israel gets more money from us because all the nations around it are Islamic, and the small country needs to defend itself. Without US support, the region would be in never ending war. But wait, isn't that exactly what's happening?

Hardcore Christians and Muslims agree on gay people and how they should be treated. The denouncement that being gay is unnatural has seeped into the politics in America. Over the years, some asinine Goofballs with large megaphones and TV coverage, like that bug-eyed lunatic from Minnesota, Michele Bachmann, have made things worse. Her husband, Marcus, owned a clinic that pushed a "pray away the gay" therapy. Of course, if you believe God created everything and everyone, then the logical conclusion is God created gay people.

Now, I know, you can cite Leviticus 20:13 from the Bible, "If a man lies with a male as with a woman, both of them have committed an abomination; they shall surely be put to death; their blood is upon them." So, just like a natural disaster that kills millions of people, God seems to take no ownership for creating gay people. I guess God made a mistake when he created gay men and women and now refuses to do anything about it. If you consider homosexuality a mistake, then who's side are you on? By the way, the scriptures give lesbians a pass, so go for it, girls!

Our attitudes, laws and policies have overtly and covertly created classes of people. We just refuse to admit it. We go about our business in the belief that this person is a snob and that person is a slob. One highly talented baker, a snob of sorts, decided the art of his cakes and pastries affords him the right to dictate who may buy his creations. I'm sure the US Supreme Court agrees with the baker and, most likely, the candlestick maker. A maker's First Amendment rights are more important than those of the buyers. If a baker said his religious scriptures deem that he not serve African-Americans, isn't that discrimination based on race? You might be tempted to say, "Hey that would never happen," but think again. Before 1978, the Church of Latter-day Saints, prohibited *black people* from holding any position in their church. Brigham Young, the LDS leader, was instrumental in legalizing slavery in the state of Utah. In 1947, the state banned interracial marriage. Black people were not allowed to enter the Mormon temple. LDS controlled the state legislature, and most of the state's money, through the Zion National Bank.

Discrimination was ordained by Mormons until 1978, when church president Spencer W. Kimball declared he had received a revelation to end the restrictions. I wonder if that revelation's timing was much like in 1890 when the church leaders ended polygamy? Was it Gabriel who visited them, or could it have been a manifesto by President Woodrow Wilson? By 1890, the Federal government had disincorporated the church, taken its assets and imprisoned many prominent polygamist Mormons. Washington works in mysterious ways. We hope that freedom and justice can coexist.

Here's a scenario to demonstrate that premise. Let's say a publishing company hired me to write a book about Barack Obama and paid me a big advance. When I delivered the finished manuscript, they showed me the proposed cover art in which Obama was made up to look like Hitler. I certainly should have the right to say, "No," but let's further say the contract's fine print stipulated the publisher had the final word on the cover art. I would then have two choices, pay back the advance and take the book to another publisher or simply publish the work myself. After all, a book is my art. It's not always easy living in American and it's even more difficult to get a "big fat" advance.

Lots of people give me crap about the way I talk. It's not only the direct Pittsburghese approach, but also my gratuitous use of profanity. If one more person calls me an East Coast elite, I'm going to scream, "I'm from Pittsburgh, you jagoff! I'm not from either coast and Pittsburgh is not the Midwest, which begins in Ohio where everything gets flat."

The Goofball in the White House, no matter which party, always attempts to manipulate public opinion. I would prefer you call me an erudite fool, but I'm far from elite. I put Heinz ketchup on everything, including hot dogs. So, it goes, Chicagoans.

Catheter bags like Mike Pence think they get to decide my beliefs. That's pure bullshit. I know the word "bullshit" bothers him because he has constructed a class-oriented pyramid where hardcore Christians sit on top. Why?

Michael D'Antonio and Peter Eisner have written a book called *The Shadow President: The Truth About Mike Pence*. In it, they claim that Vice President Mike Pence is a "Christian supremacist," who is amassing power and wealth behind the scenes which he will eventually use to attack the LGBQT community. That's not only an interesting claim, it's quite believable and more than slightly frightening. If Christians claim supremacy over all others, haven't they become something other than Christians?

If I ever get the chance to meet Mike Pence, I will have to ask him, "Why do you fear gay people?" Seeing his reaction would make my life complete. Of course, he would deny it. I would then ask, "If you have nothing to fear, why do you condemn gay humans to a lesser class?"

Mike Pence is the kind of anal-retentive, Bible-thumping politician who wants to place all the things he dislikes into hermetically sealed plastic bags for disposal. This essay isn't only about Mike Pence, the guy with that phony radio voice. He's just another symbol of intolerance in America. I'm including all the Goofballs who think that being gay is a choice. While the world is slowly trending toward the LGBQT community, we Americans have a lot of work to do at home.

We have closed-minded corkscrews who need to learn that there are millions of things that occur in the womb to determine the kind of human a baby will become after birth and growth. When a fetus is developing, switches and chemical processes unfold in certain ways, and those of us on the outside must deal with it. Gay humans have been around, well, since men and women have been in existence.

If medical science could determine that a given fetus was going to be born gay, I'd like to ask Mike Pence if he would let the mother terminate the birth. If he said no, then one could say he believes being gay is a normal and natural process of life. If he said yes, then he would be trampling his argument that every life matters. Truth is, it's not this Goofball's decision to make, neither now nor ever. It's a woman's decision.

According to a 2015 Gallup poll, 3.8% of Americans identified as gay lesbian, bisexual, or transgender. I used to think it was more like 14%. I'm not sure where I came up with that number, but we know many people are still "in the closet." Speaking of which, what a strange expression! It began life in the 1950s to describe a secretive alcoholic, but by the 1970s the expression became popular for men and women who believed they were gay but didn't disclose it to others. So, I now drink openly.

Many Americans are afraid. They are afraid of gay people. They are afraid of a man dressed like a woman. They flee people who wear turbans. They balk at two men kissing on the street, but some men can't take their eyes off two women kissing. Dual standards, dudes!

We make fun of the way people dress or walk or talk, but we have no problem inking hideous tattoos all over our bodies. I'm confused. Would someone please explain why getting ink injected under your skin is a way to express yourself? As George Carlin said, "It used to be you got a tattoo because you wanted to be one of the few people who had a tattoo. Now you get a tattoo because you don't want to be one of the few people who don't have a tattoo."

Now understand that I love a great, artistic tat, but some of what I see reminds me of the lady who tried to fix the ancient painting of Jesus in

Borja, Spain. I can't believe in this age of tattoos that botched restoration is now a tourist attraction. WTF?

Some tattoos make me ask, "What the fuck is that?" Then there are those who have the text of a complete book inked onto their bodies. Hey, if that makes your cat purr, go for it. Maybe some have a desire to make themselves more unique than God was able to do.

We disparage women wearing head coverings and demand they be removed if they want to live in America. France passed a law to ban head coverings. Don't we see what we are doing? We are creating a caste system based on visuals, dogma, gender, sexual orientation and political alliances — all bullshit.

It's like those who fat shame. I'm guilty of that, and I'm sorry. In my defense, though, obesity isn't a birth condition. To attain that massive tire around their waist a person must eat tons of the wrong kinds of food. If it's not the food, then they need to see a doctor ASAP. I see guys walking out of the 7-11 with two 24-packs of beer in the morning. I know, it's hard to live in America and stay thin. Some people read the ads for grocery stores like I used to read Playboy. I can see the moisture forming on their lips when eyeing a rib-eye steak. You can almost hear that piece of meat taunting them, "Come and get it big boy! You know you want me."

We drive people away when we put them in cockamamie class boxes. There are still churches and preachers who try to convince young people they should seek a cure for their gayness. This is truly reckless. Hey, where's the love or, more importantly, WWJD (What Would Jesus Do?).

Maybe Pope Francis gets it. While meeting with a victim of the sexual abuse scandal rocking the church, Pope Francis said, "Juan Carlos (Cruz), that you are gay does not matter. God made you like this and loves you like this and I don't care. The pope loves you like this. You have to be happy with who you are."

After the Pope was critical of the current Goofball in the White House, devout Catholic and former Senator Rick Santorum said, "The Pope has his right to an opinion, but he should stay out of politics." REALLY? So, Ricky, the Pope is infallible, right? But you can bust his rank when he disagrees with you politically? Santorum, a confused grand flagsucker from Penn State probably has some disconnected wires because he says stupid things all the time.

Human nature drives our need to feel special. Most of us love "status elevators," whether an airline frequent flyer club or a magic plastic card for store discounts. It's only when we start to look down on someone else that we get into karma trouble. When we create an "US" versus "THEM" mentality, we step dangerously close to the brink of discrimination. With the least provocation we can slip off the ledge into full-fledged hate. If that happens, what moral ground do we own?

I spent almost half of my life in the south, and being the "Yankee" that I am, I was quickly recognized by the people northerners usually derisively call "rednecks." These two classes of citizens are as divided as Alabama and Georgia football fans.

After living in the south, I came to understand why these "necks of red" feel compelled to fly their large confederate flags on big ol' pickup trucks with mammoth wheels. I think they want to belong to the cult of civil war or, more ominously, like being a member of the neo-Nazis, White Supremacists or the failing KKK. I don't know everything, but I can tell you Southerners hate to be called racists even if they talk, walk and smell like one.

If you see a person flying the "Don't tread on me" Gadsden flag next to the Stars & Bars (the Confederate flag), ask them why they aren't flying Old Glory. Oh, they will tell you that they want to go back to the good old days. They want to take back their country. It's just more US and THEM. Anyone can define a THEM. That phrase, "my heritage" is simply bigotry wrapped in sheets of fear and racism. A town wanting to remove the Robert E. Lee statue is simply a representation of change, and some people just can't deal with it.

Why would a southerner want to be a loser? They want to win just as much as all other Americans, so why are they looking backward and glorifying people who fought a civil war they lost? When will the idea of being against the obliteration of slavery end?

People often generalize about those they don't know, but not all rednecks are Nazis. Some are just BBQ-lovin' souls who think *Gone with the Wind* was the best movie ever. Tons of people living in the south are from the west, Midwest and north. I can testify that there are just as many "rednecks" in upstate New York as there are in Atlanta.

Instead of wasting your energy and time trying to ban a little boy who wants to dress like a girl from entering the women's room or fighting for your right to discriminate with a ban on gay wedding cakes, think about who you are. Are you a person who truly fears gayness? Why? Do you need to see a doctor for conversion therapy? Maybe you should become gay for a day to see if you like it. Hey, you never know until you try. Okay, if you are laughing then you get the sarcasm. Just like you cannot be converted to someone you aren't, you cannot "fix" a gay person. He or she isn't broken; they become free only when they are finally out. You should honor them. God made them that way they are, just like he made some people brown. Why are you dishonoring your God's work?

The fact is that not all people are created straight. Some are shaped to be gay, and they are equal with all other human beings in the world. God created them, so why are you looking down on them? There are many ways people pursue happiness and, provided it does you no harm, just let them be. Remember what the Pope said, "God made you like this and loves you like this." If God says it's okay, and the Pope says it's okay, it may be high time to disregard those portions of the Old Testament written by homophobes.

269

True Transparency

I read with great interest a recent article in my local paper about state agencies and town halls attempting to keep the press and public away from what, one would assume, are public records. This is happening frequently, from local to federal government, and it should disturb all Americans.

Instead of turning over the requested records, these cities, counties and school boards are suing those who are seeking them. These records could be the minutes of meetings on environmental issues, salary disputes or harassment claims in the workplace. It seems that someone is always hiding something. The cost of defense in these lawsuits is intended to silence and deter anyone from getting to the bottom of bad governance.

Are you familiar with the saying, "See how the sausage is made?" It's an expression used in some industries when allowing a customer deep access to the process or development of a product or service. There is an implication the witness may be somewhat appalled at what they see. This brings to mind a major literary work by Upton Sinclair, *The Jungle*, published in 1906. In that famous book, Sinclair exposed the dreadful working conditions in the meat-packing industry. He told the country how diseased, rotten, and contaminated meat was being packed into sausages and cans for sale to an unaware public. Transparency is important.

We Americans love to gossip, much to the humiliation of the politicians and evil Goofballs on Capitol Hill. Deep down inside, we also thirst for truth, but sometimes we get confused along the way. We have no problem believing Edward Snowden, because he had to leave the country to tell his story. Being on the run has given him credibility. What? Well, think about Bonnie and Clyde. We knew what they were doing was wrong, but what they were doing, was, well, cool and compelling. Snowden is a modern techno-cowboy version of Clyde Barrow.

Our current government has a keen interest in blindfolding the public. Are the Goofballs embarrassed of their work, or are they trying to keep citizens in the dark, so the world will never know they are making up stuff as they go along? Most of the politicians in Washington play a zero-sum game. They decide first, "Will releasing this information to the public give me an advantage in the next election?" or, just as importantly, "Will it hurt my opponent?" There's no consideration about whether having the facts would be good for the nation. That's why Goofballs hate free speech; they can't control it.

If the Secretary of State, Colin Powell, goes to the United Nations (UN) and says he knows, without a doubt, Saddam Hussein has "weapons of mass destruction" in Iraq, the UN will believe him. He is, after all, our representative in government. He plays on our team. Why would he lie to the whole world? The more lies get exposed, the less we think our elected or appointed Goofballs are honest. A lack of transparency hurts more than too much transparency. It's a "Catch 22." Once a person is exposed in a lie, many then believe everything they say is a lie. Only 18% of the people in America approve of Congress. They deserve it but, to be fair, the campaigning protocol teaches them to lie. Following those teachings is how many of them got elected.

Recently, we have seen reporters turned away from certain Environmental Protection Agency meetings and seminars. What do our elected officials fear? Are they worried the American public will find out that the "clean" water distribution system in the United States is old and failing? Will our officials be outed as incompetent executives and lousy caretakers of our country?

Shouldn't all meetings and all records be available to the public? Why is it necessary for us to wait for an in-depth investigative reporter to show us that something is wrong?

Would the kids in Flint, Michigan have been exposed to tainted drinking water if the public had immediate access to the results of the water tests? The slimy grifters in government would rather create an elaborate coverup than face the loss of their jobs for telling the truth. Not only are kids hurt for life, but more credibility is chipped away from the fragile veneer of truthful governing.

The rule of law stipulates that if I lie under oath, I can be charged with perjury or contempt of court. Lying is not okay in our judicial system. Then why is governmental lying or hiding facts okay? The truth might hurt the politician, but the transparency will make sure others don't do the same later. The fact that we can't trust the most powerful and important people in America is our grave challenge. How the hell did this happen? I truly believe when a politician takes an oath of office, they remain under oath until the next person is sworn in. **Every lie spoken by a politician while under oath should be a felony crime,** one I would call "Contempt of the Nation." We need to find a way to make officials accountable for their lies.

The creation of fake news or facts not being revealed might not seem significant at first but lies layered on top of lies ruin America. Office holders gain a belief that they are all powerful. They buy expensive furniture, add unneeded security guards and book expensive, first-class airplane tickets. They justify their abuse of power and lack of transparency simply with their self-importance. Soon, this kind of misbehavior becomes normalized. Why? If we had a governing body capable of imposing a large penalty every time representatives lie, maybe those liars would straighten up. This is third-world bullshit corruption and we should be utterly embarrassed. Lying to the public you supposedly serve is UN-AMERICAN.

We are faced with a dilemma far greater than any other in the history of America. We are slowly losing the ability to know what is true and what is false. We have too many bad people in power, and now we have foreign governments joining with our criminal actors to cast a shadow on truth and democracy itself. The internet circulates more lies than truth. Have we lost all desire for honesty and transparency?

Someone during the 2016 Election, most likely Russian operatives, hacked the Democratic National Committee email server and released thousands of messages to the notorious Wikileaks site. This isn't a debatable issue. It happened, and we have plenty of evidence to prove it.

We now see a string of misstatements or exaggerations intended to deflect attention from the real challenge. When an official spokesperson from the White House lies, they should be sanctioned by the Congress. He or she isn't a private citizen but rather an employee of the taxpayers. When asked a question about a statement he or she made, we often hear a representative say, "The statement stands on its own." What the fuck does that mean? The question was whether the statement was accurate, and it needs a direct "yes" or "no" answer, Goofball.

We should demand that representatives of our citizens who lie or obscure facts be replaced by honest people. If someone in government who is paid between $100 and $179K per year lies or, worse, hides records from the public, they need make retribution to those harmed and then leave office.

If a public official blocks transparency and then uses the power of government to sue the press or the source of the request, they should be made to pay the legal fees out of their own pockets. Maybe that will make them think harder before wasting taxpayer money on damn lawsuits.

The attitude we are seeing today is straight out of the novel by the late, great author, Philip Roth, called *The Plot Against America*. It's is a story about World War II politicians who took our naïveté and nationalism to the next level. In this fictional account, America sided with Germany and our government rounded up Jews. And you said it couldn't happen here.

Fortunately, the book has a happy ending, but it does offer a serious warning for all Americans.

Strangely enough, calls for transparency are sometimes made by the very people who are keeping things from you. They claim they want openness, but they are working behind the scenes to get rid of all the laws that could be used to find out what they are really doing. The Patriot Act was just one of many giant leaps to keep us little guys from discovering big truths. They passed a law giving the government the right to spy on us.

They say they want you to know what is happening, but they don't let you watch the making of the sausage. Their political deals and promises are negotiated behind closed doors. They claim a right to privacy just like you do, but the outrageous end results are damaging to the people those policies affect most.

When they get caught in a sexual harassment situation, they dip into the taxpayer bank to pay the victims for their silence. Why are these payments invisible to the American public? Who are these people? The more we learn, the more we know we need much more oversight.

One of the great reveals of the Watergate scandal was the exposure of the true nature of Richard Nixon and all his men. We got to hear the Oval Office tapes and clearly understand the complicity of everyone involved.

Roosevelt started the practice, and President Lyndon Johnson recorded over 800 hours of conversations, mostly on the telephone. Take the time to watch the fantastic 18-hour documentary, *The Vietnam War* by Ken Burns, and listen to Johnson's revealing phone calls. NEWS FLASH: We had a bigoted President whose every action was guided by appearance, not what was right.

Isn't it time we learn the true nature of these people in the White House, the Cabinet and in Congress? Let's end the capricious use of "national security" as an excuse for lack of transparency. To any person who says that people would misinterpret what was being said, I say, "SHUT UP!"

Let's remember the scene in *A Few Good Men*, where Tom Cruise's character (Lt. Daniel Kaffee) is questioning Jack Nicholson's character and says, "I want the truth!" Nicholson's Colonel Jessep then screams, "You can't handle the truth!" When someone else becomes the judge of whether we can handle the truth, bad things happen. The new slogan of the Washington Post sums it up nicely, **"Democracy Dies in Darkness."** I couldn't have said it better.

Social Media Menace

Could you imagine any country other than the US inventing social media? On one hand it's the tip of the American narcissism sword, but on the other it can also be a little puppy warming your heart. It can be a smiling face of someone you haven't seen for years or could be the cruel rebuke of a post you meant in jest. Dichotomous is the best word to describe it.

What this "fun" tool has created is not only a vast cottage industry of vendors who help us use it, but also many dark networks of hackers working hard to exploit our information. Not surprisingly, pornography was one of the first industries to launch itself on the early world wide web through a plethora of websites. It was, in a sense, the test case that the internet could generate money. Yes, people willingly gave their credit information to hustling strangers to see people naked.

At this writing, most social media providers are under fire for not protecting our personal information. The underbelly of the internet threatens your freedom, and if you are NOT at all concerned, you just might be brain dead. Some psychologists and neurologists have advanced the theory that social media are changing the way we use our brains or, worse, changing our very brains in ways not yet fully understood. It's way too soon to medically, physically or chemically disprove this theory, but you may know someone who spends more time looking at their phone than looking into your eyes. This level of disconnection is affecting many personal relationships.

Some people must check their tweets, push their posts and make their likes and opinions known, while their loved ones are pining for a few mere sparks of their attention. These social media addicts don't even realize they are isolating family and friends, because they have been enticed and sucked into this evil force. No, this isn't a cry for help, but if *Words with Friends* payed a salary to its players, I know someone who would be filthy rich.

Social media platforms were designed to give users a way to connect and reconnect with others. Once Facebook established itself and pulled ahead of the other platforms, it became the most powerful communication force in the world. You can send a picture of your granddaughter, a video of the final run being scored by your little leaguer or a picture of a much-needed operation, complete with a detailed description of the procedure. Did I ask for this? Do I need to count every stitch in your leg? Really? Who takes selfies of their body parts?

Most of the stuff on social media is good clean fun, but the Goofballs who run these giant social media companies are flying high and loose monetizing their technology at our expense. Ironically, users of the platforms have an illusion of power. They can say things to someone they would never say directly to their face. However, there is a serious flipside to this. Words matter and can come back to bite. Some people are simply too transparent with social media.

In May of 2018, we saw a drama played out in front of our nation which demonstrated the power of the pen or, rather, the might of the keyboard. When ABC TV star Rosanne Barr decided to tweet about a former African-American Obama adviser, it wasn't invisible, and her intent was utterly obvious. Everyone saw it within minutes and reaction was fierce and fast. Here was a painful lesson of personal responsibility. When someone mass distributes a creed, opinion or joke, the author is in plain sight. One quick stab at your glowing keyboard in the dead of night may gratify you, but it can just as easily hurt others and boomerang back to you. It's bizarre that the "liking" of another's words can do as much damage as if you said them yourself. A ratification of hate has become something that now needs to be owned by the endorser.

There is a great separation between cult of personality and the need to operate a business. ABC runs a network that produces thousands of shows, events and movies each year to entertain the public. The bigger the hit, the more they can charge for each commercial that runs in that program.

After being off the air for more than twenty-years, the reboot of the comedy TV show *Roseanne* attracted 18 million viewers. That's a huge audience! Even the head Goofball of the United States recommended the show and told his Twitter followers the show was all about them. That was probably insulting to some, don't you think?

After airing the first nine episodes, ABC knew they had a smash and ordered another season from the producers. What played out on the star's Twitter feed tested the entertainment giant, but before we continue let's observe a bit of history.

The movie *NETWORK*, Paddy Chayefsky's fabulous screenplay, gave us a glimpse into how a fictious TV showrunner would do anything for better ratings. The 1976 film dramatized flawed characters who were willing to go as far as a real murder on the air to reverse a ratings slump. In the case of Roseanne, Twitter killed the TV star.

Ms. Barr has always been a cutting-edge comedian and she parlayed her real-life sense of humor into a million-dollar career. No one ever disputed her talent for making us laugh, but we have also seen her outrageously darker and deeply partisan side via interviews and Twitter. Maybe her political and social commentaries wouldn't matter in a utopian First Amendment universe, but today the entire world watches when a celebrity blasts out pure racism on Twitter, and there will be consequences.

I don't believe Roseanne intended to come off as a racist in her tweet. I think her inner chaos is driven by a desire to be loved and to hear the words, "YOU'RE FUNNY!" The reality is it's all too easy to get into trouble if we make ourselves the judge of what is humorous or funny. Sometimes our best judgement falls painfully flat.

ABC made a deal with the devil and lost. They knew going in that Roseanne used Twitter as a platform for toxic opinions, snarky put-downs and conspiracy theories, but they also saw the wisdom of creating a show that would work in this highly polarized place America has become.

When ABC got the news of Barr's racist tweet, they acted swiftly by cancelling the show and firing its namesake star. Without Roseanne, there can't be a show called *Roseanne*. There was a severe fallout. About 200 of the show's supporting actors and crew lost their jobs. Many people felt the pain of Roseanne's words, but ABC eventually saved jobs and face with a spin-off of the series.

What might have happened if ABC decided to defend their star and continue the show? Well, that path would have probably created some pretty intense problems. If they tried to stonewall the tweet, there would have been major backlash with the ABC Board of Directors demanding action from their leadership team. In the early hours of this crisis, some cast members were already attempting to distance themselves and seeking advice on how to get out of their contracts. Wanda Sykes, an African-American and the show's executive producer, quickly resigned via Twitter. That started a fire.

ABC calculated the bottom line impact of a sponsor boycott of the network, essentially a loss of millions in revenue. ABC is owned by the Walt Disney Company, and they do everything possible to keep their family-oriented image free from controversy. I remember once when having my picture taken with Donald Duck and Goofy at a convention. I was asked to move my alcoholic drink out of the frame to, I guess, protect the image of the Goofy brand? This certainly did nothing to improve my reputation, but maybe Goofy has a drinking problem? Who knows?

In a remarkable coincidence, Valerie Jarrett, the target of Ms. Barr's insensitive tweet, was scheduled that same day to be part of an MSNBC town hall type program titled *Everyday Racism in America*. How do serendipitous things like this happen? Ms. Jarrett had an instant national platform for her response, and she asked us to see the event as a "teaching moment." The real question is, can one teach an old dog new tricks? Bark! Bark!

The morning after she was fired, Roseanne made a bad thing worse. After previously apologizing and claiming she was leaving Twitter, she fell off the wagon and got right back on the tweet-monster, facing her demons and enemies alike. She attacked her co-stars Michael Fishman and Sara Gilbert with "You throw me under the bus. nice!" She blamed her racism on Ambien. What? Barr went on to whine, "They brought the show back, so they could inevitably cancel the show when she said something they didn't like" and inferred she was fired because of her support of President Donald F. Goofball. Let's file the fodder in the folder called paranoia. It was her lack of judgment that caused the outrage in the first place? So how can you go from top TV star one day to banishment by an entire industry the next day? Twitter.

Russians clearly used social media to mess with our elections. Those who doubt America was attacked by a well-organized and funded effort to sow discourse and division are more than naïve, they are unpatriotic and stupid. Did I make that point earlier in this book? Doesn't matter. I intend to keep saying it until the Goofballs admit it.

Some of the big lies people repeat aren't so bad when spoken. Things like, "The check is in the mail," "I did not have sexual relations with that woman," or "I'll be ready in five minutes," are fleeting and innocuous when said. Once a bad thought is committed in writing on the internet, however, it becomes impossible to erase.

Even if you think you have deleted all "those" pictures from your laptop, a forensic computer investigator can find them, download them, print them or, worse, upload them to the internet. Let me share something here. A computer keeps many, many things, you know, just like your brain does.

When you "delete" things they don't go away, they just become hidden. A person with only modest computer skills can easily find and resurrect them. Technology is not a sacred place designed to protect your privacy. Remember that the Pentagon designed the internet to be able to survive a nuclear war, or so they said.

Dr. Robert Lustig made a good point in his book, *The Hacking of the American Mind*. He suggested you should stop all social media activity for one week. This will give you a stark understanding of the power social media outlets hold over you and the personal damage they have created in American lives. Abandoning social media will produce the same kind of withdrawal anxiety you would experience stopping all coffee, booze or any other powerfully addictive drug. You will not be able to cope with being away from the "fun" and you will find pleasure only after you get back to it. We are so weak, aren't we?

Someday we will understand just how deeply social media platforms have invaded our personal information and lives. They lure us into activity that gives no reward other than those narcissistic "likes," and all the while they are mining our data and profiting from us. Somewhere in the cloud are folders bearing your name, one for each platform you use. They contain all your likes, dislikes, texts and posts, and by probing all that data a computer algorithm can analyze who you are, where you've been, what you buy, how you search and possibly the details of your extramarital affair. WHAT? Imagine if someone was listening in on each of your telephone calls. They would get far less than what you give Facebook, Twitter, Instagram, WhatsApp and on and on. Shut off those damn permissions!

You know they sell your data for money, right? That is their business. They let you use their powerfully fast servers for exploitation, but not out of good will to the community. They are "for profit" companies, and we're their slave worker. They will keep sucking our souls into folders for sale, again and again.

Yes, they vigorously tap dance on Capitol Hill saying they will give their users the power to control their data. For a day, their patronizing speech will increase their stock prices, but it's only a "we really care" mask worn when adults are in the room questioning their motives. Every time you use a social media site, you are being monitored and traced. You are being watched. They can and will snag your data. Their business model is SELLING YOU!

I remember a time when my oldest daughter was spending too many late-night hours on the computer. She swore to me she left the web at 11 o'clock every night. I pulled the browser history from her computer and printed it. Those ten pages of hits to Buffy the Vampire Slayer web sites at 3 AM really angered her. She screamed, "That's an invasion of my privacy." I laughed and returned, "Hey, don't yell at me, yell at Microsoft. They are watching your every move."

That was more than twenty years ago, when Napster was big, and the internet was the wild, wild west. Today, my daughter would agree with me. She should have been smarter and deleted her browser history every night, but she still would have been too sleep deprived to attend school the next day.

By design, computers store data. The real demons are the people who invade our privacy and exploit our data. The internet is technology that moves information from you to another guy or guys. A computer, a network, a website and certainly a "cloud" are not good places to store your personal information. For those who don't know, a cloud is a server owned by someone other than you. It can be a repository for your personal documents, photos and data, if you allow it. If you store data there, no matter what the fine print says, your stuff is under the control of someone else and can be compromised.

I wrote a rather provocative article about the internet 25 years ago. I said it would have only two viable purposes: (1) finding things, and (2), selling things. I stand by my prediction. The internet can't cure cancer but offers a treasure trove of information about the curse. It can't make you happy, but it'll sell you anything. Mark Cuban bought a jet plane online.

In one of the best books of 2018, *Messing with the Enemy: Surviving in a Social Media World of Hackers, Terrorists, Russians, and Fake News*, Clint Watts summed things up nicely with this sentence, "Online, the pursuit of comfort and confirmation create an alternative reality."

Social Media is a con job. It's skims your information and then sells you things. Every time you use a computer for the most innocent task, like finding a movie's start time or the location of a restaurant, you are being tracked. Turn off all those permissions but know they will continue to trick and track you. Some bad players in that game use non-platform apps that quietly reverse your opt-out. If you want to know the weather where you are, you gotta tell them where that is, right?

No one reads the End User License Agreement (EULA) of every, if any, site they visit, but when you click OK just to use or upgrade a program you are often giving the social media guys a way back into your life. If you are looking for an ATM location, for example, the app asks you for your zip code. Now they know where you are. When you click the ALLOW button, they are back into your life.

Being tracked is creepy to most people, but others enjoy the thrill of all their friends knowing where they are at any given instant. Not to rain on your parade, Miss Popular, but a serial killer may be lurking.

You get into your car your phone asks, "Hey, we noticed you just visited the Erotic Gift Shop. Tell us your thoughts." You immediately think, "Hey, I only parked in their lot. I was getting ice cream next door." Yeah, sure, but do you really want everyone to know you were buying ice cream?

When you proceed to interact and confirm your attendance and location, you are waving your hands and telling them, "It's okay to spy. Here I am. Right over here."

Is the world a better place because of the internet and social media? As someone who made lots of money in the software – internet sector, I can tell you it's the entire world for the more than six million people who work there. When designing software, the boss' first question is, "How are we going to make money with this?" Of course, we could never have stopped the advance of technology, but that isn't my point.

We have solved crimes, brought families together, created relationships and motivated people to enhance their skills in writing, photo and video editing and web building by connecting people. We have used the data and speed of the internet to quickly save lives and right wrongs. Social media is only a small part of what the internet can do. Over time, we will likely create personal and private family networks to replace the big guys. Maybe I'll create Douglas-Net, just for my family.

As long as people can score Gold online, they will continue to skim you. If God and his enablers spread the word of the Holy Bible on the internet, people will find and fight for that connection. Somewhere in the world, Guns will always be bought and sold on the internet. We just need to find the damn web-Goofballs who make the playground less safe. Social media, YouTube and Google are not the problem. It's us, and our laissez faire attitudes.

Hobby Lobby & Jesus

If you asked a random sample of people in this country, "Is America a Christian nation?" most would reply, "Yes." That answer doesn't sit well with those of the Jewish faith, and it highly frustrates members of the Muslim community. And for those who are agnostic or atheist, the constant God-talk downright pisses them off. Now, before you get your magic underwear in a knot, please recharge your electro-psychometer (e-Meter) over there in "ScienceWorld" and follow the bouncing crucifix. We aren't a church-state, or are we?

A thinking person might ask another, equally important question, "What is the nature of our nation's moral fabric?" Our founders made religious compromises. Many of our original white settlers were fleeing religious persecution or legal challenges. Hunger was another driver, but let's focus on the idea of having a country where one could worship any way they wanted. It was a prime reason America was the best place for people who wanted to pray, their way.

I admire President Theodore Roosevelt for his tenacity and style. Sure, he was a rich New Yorker who wasn't supposed to be President, but he made a damn good leader. He inherited his job after a lunatic shot President William McKinley in Buffalo, New York — the mistake on the lake.

Once Teddy got to the top, his ego-driven personality helped him stand up to the monopolies and trusts run by tycoons like J.P. Morgan, John Rockefeller and Cornelius Vanderbilt. Hey, how can you not love a guy who has a bear named after him? Yes, that is why we call it the Teddy Bear.

Teddy had an interesting take on America and our base faith. He told us this, "The teachings of the Bible are so interwoven and entwined with our whole civic and social life that it would be literally impossible for us to figure to ourselves what that life would be if these teaching were removed."

No one can doubt he spoke those words, but just like the founding fathers built in some checks and balances in our political structures, we also must realize it's a problem if we become "too Christian." Should we become too "Jesus-freaky" it would be at the expense of other religions groups and their common rights. If you are a devout Christian, I must first wonder how the heck did you make it this far in this book? And next, religious objectivity is oxymoronic. Religion demands overzealous subjectivity and the unchallenged removal of most doubt. There's even a nickname for a doubt-holding person, "a doubting-Thomas." I would have gone with "Doubting Dave," but I wasn't asked.

Let's veer off into American healthcare. It has never been a right, only a privilege. Why? Jesus was always focused on healthcare. Most of what convinced people he had "God-like" power was his ability to heal people who were sick. Isn't that what a doctor does? I believe they take an oath in order to help us.

In my Sunday school classes, I learned that Jesus didn't pick out the rich to be healed. He concentrated on the poor and disadvantaged. My thought process changed dramatically when I realized some of the most devout believers were deceitful human beings who didn't seem to care about the poor.

I asked my parents about these inconsistencies and the selfish behavior, but, like many unquestioning Christians, they didn't have the wherewithal to explain how it all worked to my inquisitive, asshole brain. They would simply echo the talking points, "God works in mysterious ways" or "God has his reasons." This troubled me because it was the very "reasoning" I was questioning. I bristled at the notion when "true believers" claimed I would never have the intellectual capacity to understand such a powerful deity as God. Really? Why would he be so cryptic? How smart do I have to be to fully understand God?

I never thought of it as a conspiracy. After all, *God loves his children, this I know, for the Bible tells me so.* It just seemed strange that as I reached my teenage years, my government, you know, the one that says, "In God We Trust," was bombing and burning innocent children in Vietnam. I kept asking, "Does God support us when we act this way?" Christians were told we had to fight communism. Wow, so we had to deal with both the devil and communism?

The sins of our fathers were justified by a need to kill people over there in order to stay alive over here. The imperative to kill was based on the premise the United States would be in serious trouble should Asia become a united communist group. I don't remember that assertion in the Holy Bible. I don't remember the Vietnamese army coming to attack us. Did the scriptures endorse the Vietnam war because we were Americans? That seems a bit far-fetched.

I have always wondered why the most devout Christians were also the most forceful about sending their sons and daughters across the sea to kill or be killed. The person who would harm someone going into an abortion clinic to "protect a life," was the same person voting to bomb a city in another nation. I could never reckon the disparity between patriotism and the purity of Christianity. God didn't tell us to kill people, or did he? I guess I should ask a Canaanite, but I can't find their office in the Yellow Pages. Do they exist?

Gangs and street punks puzzle me. They carry out dastardly, demonic deeds, yet they are still in league with the church. You know, they cross themselves when they realize they didn't get killed in a drive-by shooting. And what about those devoutly Catholic Mafia bosses so busy cutting up bodies on the weekend? Does the local church know these "wise guys" are part of organized crime, or do they look the other way because of that large donation to the church school?

The complexities of modern life say secular laws will govern where religion leaves off. What if we flipped that premise? Let's imagine we had started our country from scratch, without consulting the Bible, Quran, Torah or any religiously ordained book to establish the rule of law, how would we proceed?

We might say people are all-important in this new country and no one person should ever decide anything for another person, including who lives and who dies. Okay, that's a good start. That would leave us with the dilemma of needing a council, so no one person's viewpoint and opinion could prevail without the endorsement of the tribe. You know, something like voting. Then, we might consider a representative committee, a governing body to meet and decide things.

We would need a vote from everyone to make us all feel good. By the way, I can't understand why everyone doesn't vote in America. You have the right; use it!

Inevitably, populations grow, and things become more complex, leading to a need for sub-committees of deciders, like judges and courts, to handle specific grievances. Here is where we get into the undertow of religious sanctification and moral code. Some in power might justify the more outrageous decrees they proclaim by saying it's a "blessing" from a divine force.

Compare that to a kid asking why they must do something, and the parent says, "Because I said so." In that case, the parent has positioned themselves as all-powerful. In the ancient world, when an out-of-control leader tried to explain why someone had to sacrifice their virgin daughter so the crops would grow tall that year, he might have explained, "Because God said so." Once God became involved, the leader's words took on more credibility. Then leaders stretched the usage to justify whatever they wanted. You know, like, "I should be the father of all the new babies."

I bet you're wondering when we will get to Hobby Lobby. Well your wait is over, as we now turn our attention to the case of *Hobby Lobby Stores, Inc. v. Sebelius.* This was a federal case in which the store owner said he, and he alone, should decide which specific part of healthcare his company would provide to its employees. Now doesn't that sound somewhat like the old, "Because I said so," line? It went all the way to the Supreme Court.

Let's back up again and look at how we got here. In the 1920s, some hospitals offered services to individuals on a prepaid basis. I remember this concept often came into play when a couple was planning to have a baby. They deposited payments into an account leading up to the baby's birth. It was like a layaway plan for hospital care. In the 1930s, those moves eventually led to companies like Blue Cross selling health insurance to people. In 1929, teachers in Dallas sponsored the first employee-based hospitalization plan. Congress debated whether a law should be enacted that would require all businesses and corporations to provide health insurance for their employees. After some powerful lobbying efforts, the Goofballs made a "gentleman's agreement," stating that government would stay out of employer-employee relations and all the companies agreed they would come up with insurance for their employees.

We ended up with a shared responsibility scheme in which you, the employee, split a percentage of the cost with your employer. The specific details varied widely depending on the company, just as retirement and pension plans were specific to each business providing them. Some big firms attracted and kept the best workers because of their appealing insurance plans. Unions played a pivotal role in the deal its workers got, and companies often tailored their plans to specific kinds of citizens. Military families could depend on USAA, Government workers had GEICO and farm owners had

Farmers. Each state enacted their own insurance laws to make things more complicated. If the economy was stable, all these plans performed well and kept America happy, healthy and working.

The cost of medicine soared due to the need for better technology and higher education rates for those in the trade. The employers became closer with the insurance corporations and conspired with them to lower costs. I use the term "conspire" because time has proven they were in cahoots.

Doctors, as they still do now, held a position of authority over the drugs we took and the treatments we got. Good doctors kept an eye on what insurance companies would pay and let us know if they saw a large expense on the horizon. The claim by the employer and insurance company of a win-win always left out the third party, you. Just as there are unscrupulous people in business and law, so there are in medicine. We've learned this all too well these past recent years. The malpractice law suits and lies exposed have shown that the healthcare system has been, and still is, broken.

Any attempt by government to get more involved in the regulation of insurance companies and healthcare systems has always been met with strong opposition. First, people don't trust the government and politicians who continually traffic in a dire message of fear. They preach that any change is bad, and we shouldn't upset the apple cart. The apple cart is the stock prices of hospitals, big pharmaceuticals and insurance companies. Do we know which Congressional representatives' own stock in those entities? **Why isn't there a website to expose their investments?**

Some of our citizens hold a deep suspicion of doctors and hospitals. If you can throw a stone, you'll hit someone who has been affected by a bad hospital experience or medical calamity. Sadly, the lives of many people have been ruined by healthcare. It's worse than we think it is. Hey, where else are you going to go if you need medical care, Dairy Queen?

In the push and pull design of the Patient Protection and Affordable Care Act (ACA) passed in 2010, there were many paragraphs guaranteeing certain treatments for women that were not approved by insurance companies in the past. The progressive idea of insurance companies paying for treatment of a "pre-existing condition" was a major step forward with the ACA law. The mandate of insurance coverage was a way to pay for all the cost increases. In reality, the ACA was never powerful enough to thwart the price increases of Big Pharma and now the courts are suspicious of the law's intent. Why?

It was clear that female reproductive care was generally over-priced and mishandled by insurance companies. This law attempted to insert some checks, balances and RIGHTS, but the right-to-lifers and conservative anti-government voices revolted. It's funny how the far-right is so hellbent on "choice" when it comes to education, but not a woman's body. Let's give that decision to a bunch of old white guys in Congress. Really?

Now we turn again to the Hobby Lobby case, decided recently by the Supreme Court in a narrow 5-4 vote. They said that individual owners of companies could change the mandate of the ACA. The ruling basically gave the corporation the power to decide which treatments were provided in each person's insurance plan. In the case of Hobby Lobby, the religious viewpoint of the company's owner was deemed more important than a person's right to doctor recommended treatment. So, there you have it. God trumps government and corporations beat employees. What kind of country is America?

The man who played God in the 10th Circuit court was none other than Neil Gorsuch, who later was rewarded by the conservative right with a lifetime appointment to the Supreme Court. With this decision, the United States' high court reaffirmed their conscious or subconscious desire to put corporations and religious beliefs above the basic human rights of all.

By ordaining Hobby Lobby's desire to decide which healthcare options would be open to women, like birth-control pills, we have given the holier than thou corporate lords the opportunity to violate the First Amendment by forcing policy based on their personal religious dogma. In a sense, the Supreme Court ruling said if a company pays you, then they get to make decisions based on whatever their religion says, not on your behalf or beliefs. Did our founders intend morality to be defined by the whims of a corporation?

It's not logical, but one could say, well, if you don't like the rule then do work somewhere else. I would add, if you don't like that policy then don't shop there. Any company can now use a moral or religious contention to determine how they will treat employees and customers. It won't be long before you can use the "religion card" to not sell cakes to gay couples or Guns to Democrats. What?

The results of the letter of the law and the spirit of the judgement quickly came back on the US Supreme Court. At nine weeks into her pregnancy, a woman in Peoria, Arizona got the terrible news that her doctor couldn't detect a fetal heartbeat. The pregnancy surely would have ended in a miscarriage, so the doctor prescribed a drug called Misoprostol, an FDA approved medication, to end her failed pregnancy.

When the woman went to the Walgreens pharmacy to pick up her medicine, the on-duty pharmacist asked if she was pregnant. I'm not sure why that would be important to him, but okay, he's a pharmacist and a medical professional. The lady said she was. The pharmacist refused to give her the Misoprostol saying that because of his "ethical beliefs," he "personally" wouldn't fill the prescription. You see, it's already happening. How shallow must the Supreme Court be to not grasp this would mushroom into even more rights being violated?

If you are a devout Christian, you might applaud the pharmacist, but if you are a woman you are probably disturbed by someone working a nine-to-five shift at one of the drug store monopolies deciding to fill in for God. I'm certain that same pharmacist used his little stapler to seal the bag filled with Oxycontin pain killers for another customer. It's possible that drug took a perfectly normal person down to the bottom of despair and addiction, eventually causing their death. Where were his "ethical beliefs" when helping to get a person hooked on a highly addictive drug? You know, people with existing heartbeats.

If Walgreens is so deeply sincere about the health and the welfare of their customers, why are they still selling cigarettes? Smoking kills as many as six million people worldwide every year, and we make them right here in the good, old US of A.

Are Jesus, Hobby Lobby and Neil Gorsuch, all on the same side? Remember, we don't elect Supreme Court judges, they are appointed for life. I guess they, not God, get to determine what life means. I can say Hobby Lobby is a nice store and I'm convinced they have fine people working there on both sides of this issue, but, sorry, you won't find me shopping there.

Human Rights & Wrongs

The late comedian Sam Kinison had a routine about world hunger. For those who don't remember him, Sam was one of the most sarcastic wits of the 1980s, sporting mangy hair and "protective" wardrobe coverings such as raincoats. He was a former Pentecostal preacher and his fervor surfaced in huge punchlines powered by his patented scream. The anger didn't always fit the content, but some people believe it made him funny. In his routine about people starving in third-world countries he quipped, "…THERE WOULDN'T BE WORLD HUNGER IF YOU PEOPLE WOULD JUST MOVE TO WHERE THE FOOD IS!"

And that, seriously, is why people become refugees. Violence and persecution in their home countries is another reason why a whole family may move from one place to a distant next.

The social contagion that has infected the Goofballs in Washington is demonizing mass migrations. They don't understand that people are moving because they are trying to attain, dare I say it, food and safety. Those assholes in power have no clue about how to seek a creative solution to a simple problem. They paint all migrants with the same brush, saying these poor people are coming to take our jobs, take our food, take our women and to bring their crime. It's asinine to think that a person who would travel 800 miles on foot to escape murder and rape would join a gang to rape and murder in the United States. They could have done that in their home country.

Every generation of political wannabees in America has attempted to put down people who came to North America. The people who migrated to the James River plantation in the 1600s were, in fact, "invaders." I should know. That's how my family came to the Americas. They were basically farmers from Scotland looking for a better life. Being a farmer was a good idea and, keeping with Sam Kinison's advice, we wanted to live where the food was.

After trial, error and brute force, my ancestors moved native Americans off their land to begin their own settlement. Because so many people died in the colonization of America, the pioneers of our land asked for more boats and more people. The more who came to establish this country, the further west the native Americans had to be moved. We white Europeans had no religious understanding that depopulating was wrong. In fact, we justified our acts because the brown people did not worship our God. We could just blow them away and pray to God afterward. We called them savages and they either had to do what we said or be killed. Doesn't this sound a bit like radical jihadist bullshit?

Even when we were the minority in this new country, we demanded the "Indians" do what we told them. We gave them beads and trinkets for valuable pieces of property. Oh, yeah, let the buyer beware. The next batch of arriving Europeans were treated like second-class citizens because others made it here first.

We needed laborers to help with all the land-taking and home-building in "our" America, so we found some cheap labor. They came from Africa and we called them "slaves," because it was a term used in the Bible. As if they were horses, we auctioned Africans to the highest bidders.

At this point, we had three classes of people, the Natives who we thought we were treating well, the white people from Europe who were "naturally" in power and the African slave, who we considered less than human.

Native Americans refused to be made slaves, so we took their food, pushed them west, or killed them. The slaves were on the lowest rung, but we had to protect our investment in them. We had absolutely no moral standing to keep them, but the Bible provided an easy excuse for us to maintain "legal" ownership of these prisoners. Even the slave exporters in England ended the practice long before we got the moral message in America.

We had "fine people" in the first wave from England and Scotland. Scots who stayed in Ireland before coming to America were dubbed Scots-Irish or Scotch-Irish. Then we had Germans who migrated to Pennsylvania for religious freedom. Some of them were Mennonites, Amish and Hutterites, part of the Anabaptist movement of the Reformation. Of course, we also had Puritans, who came to Massachusetts and established communities restricted to members of their faith. Those crazy Puritans never saw the irony that they had escaped intolerance, only to apply draconian religious constraints here in America.

After the 1820s, we had loads of people escaping the clamp-down of Catholics in the Old World, which created the rush of the Irish. The potato famine drove a green immigration wave that totaled more than 40% of all immigrants at one point. During this period signs on businesses read, "WE DON'T SERVE IRISH." I guess the Anglo-Saxons in America thought Ireland wasn't sending their best.

By 1850, the Catholic church was the largest religious group in the country. You might want to check out the brilliant 2002 Martin Scorsese film, *Gangs of New York*, to learn more about the many conflicts between the early settlers of America. Amazingly accurate.

After being degraded, discriminated against and thumped by white Protestant police officers in New York and elsewhere, it's easy to understand why so many Irish ancestors eventually became cops. Payback was a bitch.

Americans have always excelled at assimilation. It's something we do quite well. While we absorb cultures better than most countries, we do kick up the dust when the Goofballs claim that new people are "taking our jobs." When things get bad somewhere else, the locals look to America as a place where something good could happen, and for most immigrants that's generally true.

Right after the turn of the century, the early 1900s saw a wave of Asian immigrants settle on our west coast. Immigrants filled the demands for cheap labor in gold mines, factories and building the Transcontinental Railroad. Irish men wanting a better life manually dug rail routes from the east to the west. To motivate them, the bosses provided Irish whiskey on their breaks, but the working conditions were horrible.

The influx of migrants caused a change in immigration laws and the establishment of entry ports. To get a fascinating look at how it all worked back then, visit Ellis Island in New York harbor. There was a screening process at that port and those who wanted to enter had to pass intelligence and medical tests. We didn't want any migrant carrying a disease that could threaten our general population. When a second boat took those who passed the screening to Manhattan, someone had to be waiting for them on the dock or they had to show proof of employment.

Many would say that we've not done a good job preventing illegal immigration, and I agree, but now that immigrants are here, we must stop labeling them as illegal. Have a look at things through their eyes. They left their home country, came to ours and set up shop. They had been here so long (more than ten years), they rightfully assumed that our government didn't care about their presence, which was true unless they committed a crime.

America has always been on the side of human rights but, just like the situation on the Titanic, women and children were sometimes pushed aside so rich people could get first choice of the lifeboats. We created loopholes so we could guiltlessly look away from suffering people. America is not the place for you if you have any pent-up anger about rich people getting things you don't have. If you want to be rich, however, you couldn't find a better place to give it a shot.

We demonized the Irish, looked down on the Poles, locked up Japanese-Americans and shunned Germans during World War II. The Wisconsin town of Berlin changed the pronunciation of the name because of the war. We justify our bad behavior by citing war, fear, terrorism and politics. We are inconsistent when it comes to human rights, especially the rights of people who live here. Thus, one hundred years ago "Black Lives Matter" would have been "Irish Lives Matter."

Go ahead and point your anti-immigration blame finger at those who were in power between 1920 and now, but that would be doing a disservice to all those who came to America and made it better. We aren't dumb. When we figured out Hitler's brain pool was filled with talented scientists, we immediately (and secretly — Google: Operation Paperclip) moved them here with full, legal citizenship. We should continue this now. Why send a gifted computer scientist back to India? There are places here where one can find good Indian food.

When we need to harvest tomatoes in Alabama, we look the other way and hire undocumented workers at low wages to pick the crop. When some southern states created zero-tolerance laws against the practice, migrant workers left. The first group to complain were the farmers, because they had trouble harvesting their million-dollar crops. Now we find ourselves at the precipice of a major decision, how do we maintain our success? Do we have to figure out a way to keep undocumented workers working? At present, our economy is doing so well we are running out of farm and construction workers. How did that happen?

Some time ago, I met a government operative in Bermuda, and I asked him whether their beautiful Caribbean island had any unemployment problems. He was very quick to say, "No, we have none. When unemployment gets to a certain number, we just pull all the worker visas and they have to leave." An island of 2 by 22 miles can control who lives and works there. We have lots of ground in the United States and the use of worker visas doesn't seem to be controllable. We failed to maintain a balanced system between full "landing status" and the penetration of large numbers of "undocumented workers." DACA was a good start, but major reform is imperative.

One simple solution to these immigration problems would be bending with the flow. We have always wrestled with periodic issues of too many immigrants. By 1912, there were more than 1.2 million. By 2013, according to the Brookings Institute, over 40 million foreign-born residents were living in America, representing 13% of the population.

Some experts say there are 10 to 13 million undocumented US residents. Conservatives and Republicans weaponize this "social contagion" and hold no interest in amnesty. Instead, they use the word "amnesty" to repel liberals and block viable solutions to illegal immigration. They feel we are a land of laws and "these people" broke them. What are we going to do, lock them all up? Is that what America is about?

Remember these so-called experts looked the other way when we killed the native caretakes of our land. Under today's definition, my ancestors would have been considered "illegal immigrants." These modern-day land owners forgot what God taught them about loving their neighbor. Undocumented immigrants are our friends and neighbors. They are everywhere and, short of bankrupting the nation, we aren't going to remove them. Plus, one could make a legal argument that immigrants from Mexico are "Native Americans." Time to use those DNA tests.

A simple solution would be to give them all a pathway to citizenship, so they can easily assimilate into the land they already call home. Amazingly enough, this was one of the proposals Ronald Reagan put forth when he was President. Most conservatives don't, or choose not to, remember this.

Our self-serving Goofballs worry that if we legalize the 10+ million undocumented, or as they call them "illegal immigrants," other family members will soon arrive, and the cycle will begin anew. That's probably correct. Why even Melanija Knavs (Google: Melania Trump) brought her parents into the country after she gained citizenship. A real solution will not be easy.

Another aspect of immigration is unemployment. More immigrant workers mean fewer "white Americans" will be able to find jobs. Immigration reform is best done during great economic times when unemployment is low. We also have learned that "white Americans" don't want low level employment (crappy tasks), so exactly which jobs are we protecting?

Legalizing those who are already working in the USA has a statistical implication. Right now, many undocumented workers are being paid cash under the table with no income tax dollars collected. The foolish Goofballs in power are leaving outrageously large piles of tax revenues on the table. And undocumented people use our medical system and many times do not pay for the services. This wouldn't happen if they had legal status.

The immigrants living here for more than ten years have assimilated and become good members of society. Why not make them part of our great country? There is no way we can afford to deport all those folks. In fact, a large majority of them would find another way back in, creating a migratory crisis beyond belief. These people, especially DACA recipients, aren't going to leave.

Go down to the corner bar and ask Kevin O'Reilly if he and his family would like to be forcefully removed and sent back to Ireland. Ask brick layer Joe Punewski if he would consider going back to Poland to make America great again. When you see your gardener, Jose Garcia, try demanding that he pack his bags and head back to Mexico. Next time you buy that homemade hummus from Farez Khoury at the Turkish restaurant, ask her if she would like a "paddy wagon" ride to begin her return journey to Lebanon. What do you think she would say? By 2045, white Americans will be the minority. Deal with it.

We are a country of immigrants and we need to figure out how to hold onto our frail morality and massage our legal grounding in the world. And here's a final truth about the conservative Republicans. They don't want immigrants in America because, once they become citizens, they won't be voting Republican. Why would they?

American Symbolic Graffiti

I urge anyone coming into this country to travel the land on one of our many federal highways. In addition to glorious beauty, you will see some sad or perhaps disgusting things. Hey, I never said we were perfect.

Before starting your road trip, let's talk about the miles and miles of our highway system. You will see many signs with the name Eisenhower. That's because the 34th President of the US, Dwight D. Eisenhower, promoted and pushed through a major infrastructure initiative called the Federal-Aid Highway Act of 1956. It authorized the construction of a 41,000-mile network of interstate highways that now crisscross the nation. By the way, it's time for us to do more infrastructure work. Some of those highways are crumbling, and we rely on them to bring food to our tables. Are you listening Goofballs?

The Interstate Route signs are red, white and blue. The word Interstate is in the shield shape at the top of the marker and the number of the "US Route" is seen in a field of blue at the bottom. These numbers have a format, as do the mile markets on the side of the roads.

The routes with odd numbers run north-south and the routes with even numbers run east-west. The north-south routes have the lowest numbers in the west, while the east-west routes have the lowest numbers in the south.

A later effort was the construction of perimeter routes or giant "by-passes" to alleviate traffic jams in major cities. These beltways around a city carry a three-digit number related to the major interconnecting highway. To prevent duplication within a state, prefixes are numbered incrementally. For example, if I-80 runs through three cities in a state, routes around those cities are I-280, I-480 and I-680. In earlier days, these roads were a fast way around city logjams. These days, many trucks use the by-passes, so they are not necessarily the quickest way to get to the other side of a city.

Atlanta is a good example of a city in a perpetual gridlock. Its two major roads, I85 and I75, join like worms' mating through downtown. They call the enjoined highway, "the Connector." The highway around the city is called "the Perimeter" and takes the name I-285. That by-pass has a length of 63.98 miles, but the current vehicular volume prevents a travel time of one hour.

As you travel across America, you will get the flavor of who we are. Let's start with signs and memorials. Often along an America road you will see large crosses, sometimes in threes. It's a way for a landowner to demonstrate a loyalty to Jesus Christ. I have often said that a cross is a symbol of that man's worst day on the Earth. Why do we celebrate death and pain?

I wonder what would happen if some farmer put up a roadside black and white ISIS flag declaring that there is "One God and Only One God?" I'll wager it wouldn't take the locals no more than a few hours before they burned the thing down.

Some families place a cross on the side of the road to mark the spot where a relative or friend was killed. It's a memorial to death. I used to think the concept was good in that it reminds people about the dangers of driving, but more recently I feel it's a distraction.

I remember a time about ten years ago when two guys spent the afternoon drinking at a lakeside bar. After an uncountable number of beers and shots, the boys decided to go to another pub. They drove the road at 90 miles per hour, skidded out of their lane and hit a large oak tree in someone's front yard. Things didn't turn out so well. The car split in half, the two men were killed, and the large tree was destroyed. It wasn't long before their family put up a nine-foot cross where the tree once stood.

The people who owned the property were Christians and approved of a memorial in their front yard. In a few more days, however, flowers and smaller crosses grew so quickly in number that clearing the dead tree from their yard became difficult. A few years later, the property owners convinced the family of the deceased to place only a single small cross at the site. Not to be rude, but that memorial always reminded me of the two fools who spent the day drinking. It's fortunate they didn't destroy more families. Today, all the crosses are gone. People shouldn't drive when they are drunk. It's immoral and we don't need crosses to make the point.

When I was a kid, people threw trash out their car windows thinking someone else would remove the garbage. That was embarrassing. Thankfully we now have fines for littering and we certainly see less trash on our roadways these days. Nonetheless, we still have Goofballs who throw trash out of their car windows. If you see men in shockingly orange outfits walking a road and picking up trash, they are likely prisoners from a nearby prison who have the job of picking up after lazy, ignorant people. What a country!

Often you will see large chunks of truck tires on an American road. One would think the damn things must be exploding all over the land, but those are retreads that loosened and flew away. Retreading is a refurbishing process of bonding a new tread to an old tire, making somewhat of a "new" tire. Truckers can mount a refurbished tire anywhere on their vehicle, except on a wheel that steers. It's a Department of Transportation rule that is often checked at those weigh stations you see along our highways. The distraction of large pieces of rubber on the road have caused more than one accident. I'm not sure why they just don't use new, safer tires. Oh yeah, almost forgot, Gold.

In a way, the large black pieces of rubber retreads celebrate the death of a reborn tire. Why are we obsessed with death when trying to drive from place A to place B? Let's get rid of all the billboards, crosses and memorials so we can focus on the beautiful scenery celebrating life.

I should mention the joys of long-distance driving when we must deal with hecklers, honeypots and hackers, who have enough money to erect a huge political sign between two cherry pickers in their parking lot. You know, a bold statement declaring their love of the Goofball in the White House. Who gives a shit?

We have turned our American highway system into a maniacal wall of symbolic graffiti. As you drive from Florida to New York, you will see some people displaying giant Confederate flags. Those jerks are in some confederate mental retardation phase and I wish they would save us all from their racist-driven need to celebrate that dark part of our history. If you want to be clear and honest, why not wave a large flag that says, "BRING BACK SLAVERY!" Sorry, is it too soon?

The "Star and Bars" those folks want to wave is anti-American. They may argue it's their right, and I can't make them take it down, but I would like to challenge their little pea brains. Don't you realize that symbol makes 7,144,530 people or, 12.1%, or more of the US population, feel very uncomfortable? Why would you spend that much money to make people feel awful in their own country? What if someone put up a flag saying, ALL WHITE PEOPLE GO BACK TO EUROPE! How would you feel?

Finally, a word to all the men using the rest stops along our great interstate highway system. Please stop pissing on the toilet seats in the restroom! I also hear that women do the same thing. I'm not sure how they do that, but they do. If you don't have the ability to leave a clean toilet seat after use, you probably shouldn't be allowed to drive a car.

Charter vs. Public

If you take away nothing else from this book, I hope it's the message that thinking is very important. Learning is a good first step. Knowledge leads to thinking, and facts and science help people ride the curve to better understanding. One of the greatest lynchpins of American society is our effort to provide good education for our children. We are far from the one-room school house where our ancestors "learned them some" Readin', Writin' and Rith-ma-tic.

Sadly, American education today is directly connected to an anti-science, anti-factual and anti-climate change mentality. It creeps into our souls. We must have an intervention with these crazy people. Science isn't going away so grasp it, people.

We should lead our young boys and girls into more objective ways of thinking. They don't need to know the story of Noah and the ark without their thinking minds exploring the scientific possibility of whether this tale could have happened and, if it did, on what scale? Is there any evidence? Our country needs an environment of critical thinking, and that starts with contrary views and perspectives. The Bible offers a rich field for young, scientific minds to explore, explaining or disproving every miracle presented there. Such investigation and research would never be allowed in our public education system, due to a fear of reprisal for bringing dissent into the classroom. You know, like saying the Earth rotates around the sun, not the other way around.

People aren't products. An assembly-line mentality cannot create smarts. Most of the great achievements in our country were based on strong learning principles and thought processes encouraged during the early development periods of a person's life.

We sometimes discuss rather famous "college dropout" billionaires whose grand idea propelled themselves and their companies into the Forbes 100 list. However, no single person makes a giant company. By their very nature, companies need many smart people working together to render the dropout's vision. Let's break this down into a simple analysis of what is happening in the United States.

First, you don't pick your parents, but the parents you get will greatly influence the way you proceed in life. Where you grow up is vitally important. Most students don't learn well in chaotic, bullet-ridden environments.

I came from a home of newspaper-more-than-book readers, but they read every day. I became a reader of books because I had good teachers who encouraged me. Once I got into the stories, I didn't need to be nudged to read books. I never was a good reader because of my ADD and was placed in the third reading group, but I was able to harness the strange ADD attribute of "hyper-focusing," and then I read a lot.

My kids are readers to varying degrees. One reads 30 books a year, while the others might get to two or three annually. Some of my kids don't read my books; so noted. If your job requires reading, you probably read less than most during your leisure time. Watching TV is not reading, but if your channel surfing is pursued intelligently you can learn a lot. Don't kill the medium because of the shit. Find the good stuff and avoid the bad. Trust me, the TV show *American Ninja Warrior* will lower your IQ.

My brother had a difficult time reading until a bright, observant teacher discovered his dyslexia, otherwise he might have suffered through life. A lack of confidence in a child can lead to serious life consequences. Each kid is different, or should I say, specific.

We must find a way to improve education in America. Let's talk about charter schools. What are they and why do we have them? A charter school is a publicly funded, independent learning institution established by teachers, parents or community groups under the terms of a contract with a local or national authority. It's comparable to a community getting together to award a cable company the right to serve their town or to permit a power company to build solar panel farms on public land.

But why charter schools? According to National Public Radio, there are almost 7,000 of them in 43 American states with 3.1 million enrolled students. To be clear, these are publicly-funded, privately-run schools. Through them we job out the task of educating our kids and, for the most part, on paper, charter schools appear to be better than public schools. So now you might be asking, why didn't we just make our public schools better?

In some jurisdictions, only the state can commission a charter school. In most places, however, communities establish them to avoid the control of the local school board. Some of these schools implement new teaching methods and they become, in a sense, laboratories for educators and students. Without the strict and sometimes rash guidelines of a school board dictating the details of education, charter schools offer a way to jump start a better school system. Charter schools can be compared to the privatization of prisons; someone is making money with the venture. The decisions in both institutions are made with profit in mind, not always what would be good for the students or prisoners.

Many reformers like the fact that charter schools don't have to hire union teachers. That makes them free of onerous tenure systems that some argue keep bad teachers on the job. Once again, workers' rights are less important.

By and large, start-up money for a charter school comes from the federal government. The school must accept any kid, and this is where it gets a little controversial. The community can apply, for lack of a better term, an "educational gerrymandering zone" to tilt school enrollment toward certain socio-economic clusters. By carefully mapping a zone from which applications are accepted, the charter school could become all white or all Hispanic.

A company managing a charter school operates under a five-year contract. Results are reviewed at the end of its term. If the company has not done a good job with respect to graduation rates and grade improvements, it can be terminated, and a new private firm brought on board. If the charter project is a total failure, the school can be closed. By comparison, it's practically impossible to change a bad public-school board because they are elected officials and a public school cannot be closed for academic underperformance.

Some charter schools have sports programs and, in fact, some of their teams have been divisional and state champs. In many ways, a charter school is like a "regular" school and their presence can create competition with traditional public schools. We know that competition typically spawns improvement to the competitors, but the jury is still out on whether charter schools outperform public schools. After all, we are dealing with many different students, communities and cultures.

I once lived in an area outside of New York City that did not provide special needs teachers or facilities. The local school did well in terms of high grades and academic achievements. Was it because they prevented challenged students from entering their system? This isn't to say they weren't doing a good job teaching the kids who attended, but when judging against other schools you must consider the disadvantages and advantages of the communities involved.

There are ways to determine academic success, like absolute test scores, test scores judged against similar schools (socio-economic clusters) and academic improvement of students over time. There are a limited number of seats in each charter school and many communities use lotteries to determine who will be accepted. That might sound fair on the surface, but those who don't get in might feel left behind. A parent might hear, "Oh, I didn't get in. I have to go to public school." Maybe that kid might think she is a loser.

We want to improve education, but our actions say we must break it to fix it. Some charter schools which culled their student body from disadvantaged or "English second language" communities didn't do well. No matter how much expertise or creative experimentation is applied, some students simply don't move forward. So, let's go back to this question. Why don't the Goofballs in Washington invest more money on education and repair the schools already there? There might be a better argument for mixing and adding diversity to bring out our best.

In some schools, teachers must buy their own supplies, ceilings are leaking, and rats live and breed in the cafeteria. We must address these problems now or they will cause the eventual destruction of our nation. A kid without an education will not get a good job, and the additional stress and anger in schools can lead to bad things happening on our streets.

The current Goofball running the Department of Education has another solution. She wraps her horseshit propaganda sandwich with the word "choice" and the meat of her idea is called "vouchers." According to this government myth, parents who are looking for broader "school choice" in education can pull their kids out of their public school, and then use a subsidy to pay for a private or charter school. Alternatively, they can use the subsidy to home school their kids. Sounds like "socialism" to me.

These government sanctioned "gift certificates" wear a giant mask of racism. Sure, I get it, you don't want your kids in those dirty public schools with all those well-dressed, white kid bullies. You need a handout. Or are you escaping to the church school to get away from kids with darker skin than your offspring? Hey, just saying.

Sure, anyone can get a voucher, but why do we keep putting band aids on education? We need to stand up to the Goofballs in Congress and get them to see the future.

We should mention that the concept of "vouchers" began when the Supreme Court ordered integration of schools in America. On May 17, 1954, Chief Justice Earl Warren issued the unanimous decision in Brown v. Board of Education, which stated that racial segregation in public schools violated the Equal Protection Clause of the 14th Amendment. The state government of Virginia told local schools they would be closed if they continued with integration. After the closing of many schools, the Virginia legislature developed "vouchers" and gave them to white Americans to pay for private schools. So, you see, vouchers came about as a way of segregating and dividing the nation. The term is another dog whistle for White Nationalists, Neo-Nazis and the failing KKK.

Call me a liberal, but I'm infuriated when my tax dollars are used by white middle class families to extract their children from public schools to keep them away from African-Americans and Hispanics. It's a plot to weaken the public-school system and eliminate diversity in education.

In Nancy MacLean's book, *Democracy in Chains: The Deep History of the Radical Right's Stealth Plan for America*, she mentions Oliver Hill, one of the NAACP attorneys who filed suit for the student strikers of Prince Edward, Virginia protesting the closing of integrated schools. Hill proclaimed, "No one in a democratic society has a right to have his private prejudices financed at public expense." That's the real problem with vouchers. MacLean's book outlines the fact that some of these initiatives are being bankrolled by people like Charles Koch, who has been working for decades to eliminate any public funding of education. What a strange agenda from someone who owes his whole success to education. Well that, and lucky sperm.

If we don't improve education we will end up like the Romans, sick on our own vomit. The reason "fake news" is so pervasive in our social media is because we have slowly deemphasized critical thought. We have divided our nation by emphasizing the far ends of the political spectrum. We ignore the middle ground of the regular Joe's who truly do make America great. Even reasonably educated people have been sucked into believing we need bigger bombs more than we need well-paid, qualified teachers.

Some people in the bible belt think normal, secular education is a threat to their kids. We waste too much time debating with educators about whether parents should have veto power over curriculum. Let's face it. We aren't the best qualified individuals to determine what teachers teach, and this diversion is dragging us down. Just a reminder here, unless you have a master's degree in education, you don't have the wherewithal to be editing textbooks.

A dear friend of mine who has passed on wrote text books. He was the head of the Peabody Awards at the University of Georgia. He released a new text book for the Journalism and Communications school about every two years. He worked hard on getting every fact correct and creating a course to accompany the text. I asked if he made a lot of money on those expensive text books. He laughed, and said, "Not that much."

Most professors, researchers and scientists would never mislead students, if for no other reason than a concern for their reputation. The world is not 6,000 years old and Jesus did not change water into wine. Can you scientifically reproduce that miracle?

Recently, a short work dealing with homosexuality was offered at the book fair of a private school. It provided a fair and balanced explanation to kids, but it was quickly moved to the back of the room. Placing a blindfold over our children doesn't protect them. Sooner or later they will discover for themselves and they might be inappropriately shocked about withheld knowledge. Stop trying to protect children from facts.

How can we possibly sleep well at night knowing we have voted against education? Why do we shit on science in the name of the almighty dollar? When will we wake up to the fact that other countries think we are stupid? We aren't stupid, but we waste our money on dumb things. It's time to elect smarter people!

Just Shoot Me, Enough Talk

This country — this big, boisterous, brawling, intemperate, restless, striving, daring, beautiful, bountiful, brave, good and magnificent country — needs us to help it thrive.

John S. McCain III, July 2017

Writing a book is pain in the ass. It's not the writing that's difficult, it's the words. You must use the right words and arrange them in a compelling way to make your point. It's all about stringing together phrases in a melodical way to keep the reader's mind engaged and excited. If you are successful, your readers will ride those thoughts and emotional waves to a landing on a beach of contentment, understanding, and sometimes even anger.

I always ask myself, "Why are you writing this?" I admit that I'm a fool for a good title or a snappy premise. I spent too many years in the marketing business not to fall in love with the process of sailing into a mind, even if I have no idea what is in the boat as I begin. I hardly ever work from outlines, even though I would tell any writer to first organize and build a framework. You see, I'm a real "do as I say not as I do" kind of person. Sorry, Mr. Vincent J. LaBarbera — my professor in the Point Park University Journalism Department, circa 1969.

So, why *Gold, God, Guns & Goofballs*? Well, I wanted to write a book about America with love, tolerance and truth. I'm sure my work doesn't always land in my readers' minds as I intend, but I truly do love my country. I hope that no matter who received your vote or who you follow, you have a sincere respect for the ideal of America. Her principles must never be lost, even if there are times when her citizens think like total idiots.

There is no question that our baby nation began with little more than a pot to pee in, and we had to put forth much effort to get where we are today. Now, the greatest country in the world runs on Gold.

George Washington, our first president, made $25,000 per year. Today that would be close to one million dollars; not bad for a guy with a terrible dental problem. Washington didn't need the money, but it made sense to pay the president so he would not be susceptible to bribes. Most of the first dozen or so presidents had lots of money before they took office, so it was never intended to be a money position, rather a service to the nation.

Today, members of Congress make handsome salaries with excellent healthcare insurance, but it's the money they make outside of their government work that should concern us. Gold is the driver of all major decisions. If you hear a Congressperson say, "You know, I could make much more in the private sector," they're boldface lying. They all make mounds of money on insider trading and business tips provided to them because of their Congressional seat. It's all been disclosed. They may give lip service to cleaning up the place, but remember they determine the ethic laws of their chamber. The fox is running the hen house.

In the pursuit of former President Nixon, investigative authors Bob Woodward and Carl Bernstein got an essential piece of advice, "follow the money." In any corruption case, the trail of money leads to the guilty. Much of what happens in America is based on what is good for the rich. If that also helps the economy, wonderful, but beware of the preposterous "trickle down" myth often perpetrated on the middle class. Rarely does it work. Most of the time, not much Gold flows down to the little guys.

People pray to God for millions of possible reasons. No one, or nothing short of a deity, could possibly keep track of all those personal wishes and supplications. We go through life hearing the phrase, "I pray to God that…" Even the most mundane requests must be heard and weighed by the big guy in charge. The pleas telegraphed special delivery to the heavens above range from "make the next ball I throw a strike," to "save my father during heart surgery," to "please end this war." Sometimes we get an answer, mostly we don't.

God has been way too involved in how America works. Jesus also gets in the way. Muhammad's policies and dictates do the same thing. Religion only hardens the resolve of the "other" tribe, and there is always another side except when it comes to God. Christians, Jews, Mormons, Catholics and all the rest worship the same God. Why then all the drama? If there is only one God, and he's the one God of Abraham everyone claims we should look to, then why do we create a fortress of hate under his name?

Why did I say that Jesus gets in the way? Did I mean that? I would suggest that once his followers and the Catholic church codified Jesus as the son of God, and even went so far to declare him part of the Trinity, the men of the church elevated a "real man" who walked the Earth to a level of infallibility. Most evidence indicates Jesus was just a gifted preacher.

If someone on the Earth is declared perfect, how then can they be judged? Religious men and women paved the way for saints and popes to claim a kingdom here on Earth. If all they wrote about him is true, Jesus was a good guy, but the powerful people in the church made him a martyr. It's what an everyday Islamic terrorist can become, as ordained by Muhammad's teachings. Sorry, but it's true. Jesus died for our sins, while a devout Islamist dies because of the sins of the infidel. Crazy stuff.

Thomas Jefferson was a deep thinker and instrumental in the disestablishment of religion in his state of Virginia. Before he did this, the Anglican Church received tax dollars. You know, "vouchers." Thomas Jefferson sent a profound message to his new nation. He said that any attempt to merge church and state would lead to problems. We should never forget his words.

It's against the law to kill another person, not because of "God's word" but because it's depraved and immoral. When God kills people, we don't call him a murderer or abortionist. We don't need to believe in God, or gods, to live a moral life. People who believe there is only one path to morality fail to understand the historical and intellectual aspects of principles.

America needs God. God doesn't need America. Think about it. We know there are places in the world where young girls are kidnapped, raped and made to marry men they don't even know. Why do we ignore this? Don't we have a duty to protect them? God likes to take vacations. Where was he when a totally Catholic nation of Mexico murdered 29,000 people in 2017? I guess God's message to the devout Catholics down there is to get out and move north to save your kids, *if* you don't lose them at the border.

In early drafts of this book, the word "Guns" wasn't in the title. While writing, I was hit hard by the latest spate of school shootings and the extremely political rhetoric of the National Rifle Association after they were challenged by a bunch of kids. Quite frankly, the most recent speech of NRA leader Wayne LaPierre sounded suspiciously like 1939 Adolf Hitler rants in Germany. To equate a desire for reasonable Gun control to a leftist insurrection is un-American. The NRA should be made to disclose how much money they get from Russia.

The CNN town hall meeting, where students of Marjory Steadman Douglas High School confronted their representatives live on TV, was my wakeup call. During the question and answer session, school shooting survivor Cameron Kasky repeatedly asked Senator Marco Rubio, one of my Senators from Florida, if he would stop accepting money from the NRA. After a stream of uncomfortable, political double-speak, Rubio admitted he would continue to take money from the NRA and anyone else who supported his agenda.

Life is never stark black and white. Michael Smerconish said that sometimes we must think and live in the gray to find the true, objective answers. If you asked Rubio if he would take money from the KKK, he would surely say, "No!" But let's say that a racist fringe group bought into his agenda and decided to give him money under the cloak and cover of a Super PAC. Where would Rubio's red line lie? With so much dark money and stained Gold in politics today, I'm not sure any candidate knows if their contributions come from Russia or the mob.

There are too many Guns out there and too many people in our country who truly believe they need weapons to protect themselves from the government. I, too, believe all citizens should be protected from an overzealous government and selfish politicians who give corporations and certain religious groups more power than they deserve, but I'm not sure a big Gun is an effective way to achieve that.

A lot of confused people in America wake up every day believing bullshit. That isn't to say they don't work hard to earn every penny they make, but they lack information. They need to be able to separate truth from lies.

We don't determine who gets the Guns. We aren't sure if we have paramilitary groups ready to storm the White House or a White Castle. Presidents come and go, but my generation had a deep hope and drive to make America a more free and compassionate place.

Yeah, call me a liberal but I don't want to take your fucking Guns away. STOP SAYING I DO. And you must stand up for *my* First Amendment right with *your* Guns, even if I totally disagree with you. If you can't do that, then we have a problem.

I will always say what I think, and I will always call out bullshit. It's a blatant lie that we can't check every Gun purchase at a store, a gun show or a backyard. We are a technologically advanced society and it's time to establish a national database of mentally disturbed people and proven violent offenders who shouldn't own Guns.

And finally, let's bring the Goofballs center stage. I have recently been rereading the writings of Hunter S. Thompson. I mentioned him earlier in this book, and his "gonzo journalism" should be taught in every college. Hunter took no prisoners and he called people astonishingly lethal names. I admit I have stolen a few of those for this book. I've always believed name calling isn't bad and it's a safe bet that our founding fathers used rich locutions to stab their enemies. **Impotent language cannot penetrate a mind or heart.**

"Goofball," meaning a naïve, silly, or stupid person, has always been one of my favorite sleights. That term rings the bell in these days of self-ordained experts and scum-sucking, bottom-feeder politicians. It can be used as a dismissive slap on the back, "Oh, that guy, he's a Goofball," but when I use the term I am referencing a person so utterly stupid that he can't comprehend just how brainless he is. When I employ the term Goofball in the context of Congress, the Executive Branch or the Judiciary, I am talking about a supreme class of Goofballers.

You might ask, "Surely you don't think everyone in Congress is a Goofball?" I do. They are. Once upon a time, I had a resplendent, rose-colored, optimistic mind. I won a speech writing contest in high school with a work titled *What Democracy Means to Me*. It was one of those "amber waves of grain" flagsucking works, cleverly feeding back all the *America the Beautiful* propaganda pumped into my head by teachers, preachers and parents. Let's not forget that I was named after President Eisenhower.

Eventually I grew up and went off to college. Then, something happened. If the truth be told, and it should be, President Richard M. Nixon triggered a profound change in my thinking. He was a certified Class A liar who should have been sent to jail — a murderous, treasonous, son of a bitch who violated the Logan Act by asking the Vietcong to delay a peace treaty until he became president. It's against the law for any negotiation by "unauthorized" persons to take place with foreign governments having a dispute with the United States. How many US soldiers lost their lives while Nixon used the continuing war to get elected?

The more I learn, the more I realize that not all the Presidents were good guys. Most of them were purely down and out, egomaniacal Goofballs. How could they not be? Every day, newspapers, TV shows and people from around the globe echo the belief that the US President is the most powerful person in the world. Sooner or later, they start to believe it.

We send normal, thoughtful people to Washington, but soon after they spend time with the low-achievers and dirtbags of Congress they sell their souls to the devil. In most of the industrial cities and towns in this country, the government did little or nothing to keep the American workers healthy and wealthy.

You see, the Goofballs at the top of the power pile looked out more for the factory owners and less for the workers. They suppressed incomes, keeping the minimum wage way behind the cost of living. When it mattered most, they took checks from their donors and let those big bosses poison the water and air.

Nothing is the way it was, and some will say my indictment of those in power is naïve. Judging America by the 2016 Presidential election, however, I would like to believe you will agree that we can no longer trust the good guys or the bad guys.

The one side hates immigrants and will do anything to keep them from gaining citizenship. The other side wants to appear like they support labor, immigrants and fair pay, but they lack the conviction to act because they fear losing their jobs in Congress. If they were serious about reform, it would have happened by now.

The current head Goofball, who will sit in that house painted white for four or (shudder) eight years, thinks that he alone can fix everything. He's just another grifter politician who looks at surveys, kowtows to interest groups and donors and doesn't give a flying fuck about some poor guy in Cedar Rapids with five kids. White House Goofballs are always richer when they leave office than they were going in. And just what is a "flying fuck?"

The top Goofball in America is enabled by clown-evangelicals who would suck his dick to get abortion outlawed. Okay, that might be a bit of an exaggeration, or not, but they have decided their goal is so significant that they will look the other way while other sins are committed. Where did we look when Saudi Arabia killed a journalist?

We saw what happened to a kid from Cincinnati who was slowly murdered while incarcerated in North Korea. After he came home to die, the head Goofball genuflected at the groin of a despot for a freaking photo op. Have you no decency, Goofball-in-Chief? You cannot ignore your role in the motivations of a zealous pipe bomber and a Neo-Nazi's attack in a place of worship in Pittsburgh. When people die, your jokes aren't so funny. Come to think of it, they're never funny.

Let's face reality. Our current Goofball is not a decent man. Many presidents have lied and schemed, their transgressions are etched into history, but the current resident is a mega-liar and, at best, a race baiter.

Now I would like to present an unvarnished look at all the Presidents in my lifetime, so far. I'll be brief and direct.

I was born in 1949 and I don't remember much of anything about Harry Truman, but my first recollection of a top guy was Dwight David Eisenhower. From his war experience, my father always referred to him as "his General." When I was a toddler, I thought that "Ike" was my father's personal general. There wasn't a picture of him in my house, but never a negative word was said about him.

Eisenhower warned us about the military-industrial complex and Kennedy did nothing to stop it. Kennedy, Johnson and Nixon kept American soldiers in harms' way longer than they should have. They lied about what was happening in Vietnam as 58,220 Americans lost their lives. I survived that war because of the luck of the draw. My draft number was 251.

President Kennedy was loved by a lot of people in America. He was an inspiring speaker but did not always make the right call. Let me mention two mega misjudgments, Bay of Pigs and Marilyn Monroe. Vietnam could have been curtailed by Kennedy early on, but he never got the chance. He solved the Cuban missile crisis and we can only imagine what America would have become if JFK wasn't assassinated. He was, sadly, a Goofball womanizer.

Lyndon Johnson was a crude master politician manipulating the system for good and evil. For all his positive moves on civil and voting rights, Lyndon lied to us about a lot of things. He masterminded the Gulf of Tonkin Resolution, which says that the President can take *all necessary measures* to repel any armed attack against the forces of the US and to prevent further aggression. He essentially transferred the power of war from the Congress to himself, and it was all based on a lie.

We have already covered Nixon in detail. He was so busy dealing with Watergate that not much happened in his shorted second term, unless you consider his drunken monologues with portraits of former presidents. I wish we had a tape of those!

Gerald Ford's most memorable move was his pardon of Richard Nixon. In a sense, Ford wasn't relevant as a president, but Chevy Chase gave us lots of laughs at his expense and that was definitely worth something.

Poor Jimmy Carter was a nice guy, but he didn't understand how government worked. During his administration, banks and lawyers walked all over him. Jimmy was jet fuel for the lobby industry. He got things done, but only those things the special interest groups wanted, and they weren't always good for America. Oh yeah, Iran kicked his butt.

Ronald Reagan was a traitor to every union worker in America, but they liked him because he was an actor. When Ronald Reagan was President of the Screen Actors Guild, he was an informant for the FBI and a key player in the McCarthy "witch hunt" of "communists" in the movie business. By the way, here's an important lesson about TV stars. They are shells of real people who spend more time on make-up and appearance and less on fully understanding the results of their policies. Reagan's diabolical administration traded Guns and armament for Gold, which he used to fund a revolution in Nicaragua, then he and his administration lied about it. Google the names of the convicted in the Iran-Contra Affair. Reagan was either daft or complicit, but I'm afraid we will never learn which. The guy who protected President Reagan from embarrassment was Oliver North, no honor among thieves.

George H.W. Bush was nothing but a CIA front for globalization through patronage and power. He was a made-man from an old-line power family, just like Kennedy, and he sold America down the oil well drain. Not only did George H.W. pardon people involved in the Iran-Contra affair, he invaded Iraq. Some will say he failed by not continuing the war and liberating the whole country. Others will assert that George H.W.'s short war became the justification for the second Iraq War — the long conflict of George W. and Dick Cheney. On a positive note, the late George H.W. pushed through the Americans with Disabilities Act of 1990, which prohibits discrimination and provides a path to mobility for those with disabilities.

Daddy Bush's biggest failure was the economy, and most of America blamed him. That is why Bill Clinton knocked him off and gave us the smartest-dumb president in history. William Jefferson Clinton got impeached for not keeping his dick in his pants, and then lying about it. I used to like him for making the country financially stable and getting rid of tons of debt, but I should have been move objective. Clinton's shenanigans have become his legacy.

Then there's the lovable, loony George W. Bush, the chosen golden son born to be President. Fifteen years ago, I called W stupid, but today see him as a lightweight bumpkin. He was a naïve, inept, misinformed guy who was trying to do the right things. You know, a Goofball.

Oh George, how we love you now, but let's get serious. He spent more than $2.5 trillion on wars without ends and made the Middle East worse than it was before he got involved. George blocked stem-cell research, which for more than seven years delayed the treatments and possible cures to help people with debilitating diseases. By the way, he did that to keep the evangelicals happy, but I wonder if he ever apologized to Michael J. Fox.

Barack Obama promised hope and change and got us beyond the idea that only a white man could be president. He was constantly challenged by systemic racism and pure-white power politics. The evil witch of the south, Newt Gingrich, poisoned the well with his faux intellectual bullshit and invented new age obstructionism. Obama rates a junior Goofball badge. I have never doubted his intent and honesty, but there were times when I felt he was ludicrous. The scene in the Michael Moore movie *Fahrenheit 11/9* of President Obama in Flint, Michigan after the water crisis became known was disturbing. Why did Obama side with the Republican Governor who was part of the conspiracy and coverup of this disaster?

Arguing with the "hawks" in Congress drains tremendous energy from any president. Obama attempted to use logic and smartly framed claims, but some saw him as lecturing. No matter what he said, to many Americans he was just a black guy talking. They didn't like him; they didn't hear him.

Obama never stooped so low as to constantly blame the previous guy for the pain people were feeling, but there were times when Barack should have been more firmly committed. You don't evolve on gay marriage rights. You either believe in equal rights, or you don't. We must also remind ourselves that Obama could not divert enough funds from the military-industrial complex into the social programs he wanted to deliver. He simply ran into obstacles and out of time.

Liberals said he should have been less intellectual and more "street" and, well, I'll say it, more Black! Maybe he was trying too hard to be liked? The Goofballs in Congress were 80% to blame for Obama's ineffectiveness.

There comes a time for the head Goofball to say exactly what he or she truly believes. We should hear a candidate's promises and imagine what would happen if they delivered them. This brings us to Donald J. Trump.

Most of this book was written during Trump's second year in office and, ultimately, history will have the final say on him. I will never forgive him for the way he treated John McCain in both life and in death, pure douche-baggery!

I don't mean to promote paranoia, but you would be wise to observe and research several important aspects of the United States of America: politics, business, the media, and the courts. We know politics might make a person crazy, but we must keep our eyes on our Goofballs. They are stealing our money. Businesses in America exist to generate cash flow. They pray to God for profit, but that doesn't mean all their actions are "God-like." They will lie and fire anyone who gets in their way. Spend some time learning what a "whistleblower" does and the protections afforded to such a person. We need to make sure people will tell us when a company or CEO is doing something bad.

The media works hard to get ratings, but that goal often gets in the way of truth. Today's news outlets position themselves to super serve a segment, rather than providing good journalism for all. Fox News and MSNBC have overplayed their hands to the far right and far left, but they get ratings. That's all that counts to them and this must change. Sponsor boycotts are a good start.

The courts and judges must be watched to make sure they aren't missing or corrupting their purpose. They are not supposed to make laws but to interpret and apply existing laws in their decisions. The fact we know the political slant of nominees to the Supreme Court is unseemly and a profane reality in the United States. Why can't they be unbiased? The last two justices placed on the court are pure ideologs. It's terrible. After more than thirty Supreme Court appointments in my life, I now firmly believe the court is biased. Why would I feel this? Watch the video of the Brett Kavanaugh Senate confirmation hearing.

When someone talks about how great the stock market is doing, I must remind them that the stock market was there before this president and the stock market will be there after this president. The only person who didn't have the stock market before him was Alexander Hamilton; he invented it. The market will go up and down and we must never believe that any single Goofball has the power to control all the investors in the world. The president may issue a tax cut, but to what end if only the rich get the cash and the price of everything goes up? Did you get an extra ten grand? That is what most experts claim the average American would need just to dent their debt. If you didn't get a ten-thousand-dollar tax rebate, you're running behind.

Keep your eyes open, people. Assuming the Goofball in office does all that he promised, what happens next? This is what we must worry about, you know, the old slogan, "Idle hands…" We can only hope this Goofball is like Eisenhower, and when he gets bored, he will go out and play more golf.

Money is good. Get as much Gold as possible and I guarantee you'll have an easier time in our crazy world.

Here's another thing to keep in mind. This country will not get any better or any worse because you prayed or didn't pray. I appreciate your thoughts, but please don't pray for me. Save that effort for important things like fewer wars, less poverty, no more school shootings and abundant food for starving people everywhere.

Maybe God will hear you and "Make America Great Again," or maybe he will strike down those who lie to you each day. The truth is, when God is on your side, he's your God, but when he's on the other side, he's Lucifer. Who are we to judge?

TO THOSE WHO LOVE THE SECOND AMENDMENT, would you please lock up your fucking Guns! You don't need to make things worse. Instead, sue those shithole companies selling defective firearms and shutter the businesses that promote the insanity of 3-D printable Guns. Stop sending your money to the NRA and give it to your local community center or Big Brothers or Big Sisters. Take in a kid and help him when his parents treat him badly. Make sure you monitor the social media use of your children. Find out if your kid is being bullied and inform your education officials about the bad children in your schools.

Real cops are faced with fear every day and innocent people get hurt. Both citizens and police officers can easily become victims of split-second decisions. Why don't we shoot people with tranquilizers? We don't kill an escaped zebra with a big Gun; we subdue it.

Even a good guy with a Gun can do stupid things. To everyone who has a weapon (READ: Gun Owners), please keep your Guns ready, we might need you to help fight the Russians let into our county by the Goofballs in Washington.

To all those self-serving assholes in government, stop your posturing and non-answering. When someone from our "free press" asks you a question, sit up straight and give us an honest answer. We pay you a lot of money to work in Congress or sit on a court bench or watch TV in the White House. The more you lie, the more you hurt this country. Lying is un-American.

Go ahead and shoot me, but my words will never die. You can try to stop me from telling the truth but remember that one day you will pass away. When you meet your maker, what will you say to God? Will you say, "Well, you know, I had to tell a few white lies, and yes, I engaged in some 'boy talk' but I kept the fans happy."

Will God sit back and laugh? No, I trust that God will lean down right into your face and ask, "Hey Goofball, did you help your fellow man and woman?" And I would suggest, that at that very moment, you not lie.

Thank You Very Much

I would first like to thank all those teachers who worked with me and gave me the encouragement to learn as much about writing as I could, while I was totally distracted by shiny things and working in radio.

Next, I thank my life partner and favorite critic, Roxy Myzal, for her help with editing and confronting me on some of my loose logic.

Then there's Kenny Lee Karpinski, who has been editing my words and listening to my jokes for more than fifty years. We were classmates in college, and later co-workers in the software business. He is ruthless in editing my bad syntax and convoluted sentence construction. He also has served as a prime motivator on many of my writing projects.

Once you write a book, you must have a cover. As I have with all my previous books, I turned to Aimee Lim for her wonderful design talents.

Some of my early readers, like Mike Powell have helped me propel these words into final form. And thanks to Judith Economos, who kicked my butt and demanded I be a better writer.

And finally, I want to thank America for being herself. While I cling to a belief in my country's resilience and eventual landing on the right side of liberty and justice for all, I know she's in rehabilitation. We all know the divide and we, like early mankind, seem to be waiting for a messiah to arrive. More likely, we will solve our divide not by following a person but knowing the good in all our hearts. We must progress. We will progress. Go forward brave heart!

Books that influenced this work

Messing with the Enemy: Surviving in a Social Media World of Hackers, Terrorists, Russians, and Fake News by Clint Watts (2018) HarperCollins Publishers

War on Peace: The End of Diplomacy and the Decline of American Influence by Ronan Farrow (2018) W. W. Norton & Company

Guns, Germs, and Steel: The Fates of Human Societies by Jared Diamond (2017) W. W. Norton & Company

The Great Derangement: A Terrifying True Story of War, Politics, and Religion at the Twilight of the American Empire by Matt Taibbi (2008) Random House, LLC

Kingdom of Fear: Loathsome Secrets of a Star-Crossed Child in the Final Days of the American Century by Hunter S. Thompson (2011) Simon & Schuster

Amusing Ourselves to Death: Public Discourse in the Age of Show Business by Neil Postman (2005) Penguin Books

The Hacking of the American Mind: The Science Behind the Corporate Takeover of Our Bodies and Brains by Robert H. Lustig (2017) Avery

Elements of Taste: Understanding What We Like and Why by Benjamin Errett (2017) TarcherPerigee

The Backlash: Right-Wing Radicals, High-Def Hucksters, and Paranoid Politics in the Age of Obama by Will Bunch (2010) HarperCollins Publishers

Democracy in Chains: The Deep History of the Radical Right's Stealth Plan for America by Nancy MacLean (2017) Penguin Books

The Corrosion of Conservatism: Why I Left the Right by Max Boot (2018) Liveright

About the Author

Dwight C. Douglas was born in Pittsburgh, Pennsylvania and studied Journalism and Communication at Point Park University. He worked on the PBS TV show *Mister Rogers Neighborhood* as a film-telecine technician, and later at ABC radio as they were developing their FM properties.

Douglas moved to Atlanta where he joined the largest radio consulting firm in the world, Burkhart-Abrams & Associates. Later he became president and worked with media companies around the world. During that 25-year period, he was instrumental in recruiting and coaching high-profile radio morning show personalities, including Howard Stern.

He moved to New York in 2000 and became the vice president of marketing for a worldwide software company. In that same time, he produced a comedy web site. Throughout his career, he has written numerous screenplays and magazine articles. He is the author of the books *If God Could Talk, If God Could Cry* and *Donald Trump: Repeal, Replace, Impeach.*

In 2017, Dwight Douglas retired from his marketing job to write fulltime. He splits his time between the Adirondacks in upstate New York and Florida's Gold Coast; depending on the air temperature.

Other books by Dwight C. Douglas

If God Could Talk: The Diary of a TV Journalist

A Cable television talk show host is approached by a friend who offers a guest for his show who has never been on TV before. The Diary of a TV Journalist is the story about the host of the show and his executive producer vetting the guest and attempting to determine... If God Could Talk. Available at Amazon.com, GoodReads.com, Barnesandnoble.com

Donald Trump: Repeal, Replace, Impeach

These diatribes of a delusional blogger offer a day by day overview of the 45th President's first two-hundred days in office. Follow Donald Trump through the tough times on his way to impeachment. Available at Amazon.com, GoodReads.com, Barnesandnoble.com

If God Could Cry: The True Meaning of Mercy

The famous cable TV talk show host, Jonas Bronck, leaves New York on a quest to find truth. He finds himself in the middle of terror and personal torment for the sake of journalism. He asks, If God Could Cry, would he be crying for us or with us?

9 781794 175600